THE BEST OF BOTH WORLDS

THE BEST OF BOTH WORLDS

How Mothers Can Find Full-Time Satisfaction
in Part-Time Work

BETH BRYKMAN

 Prometheus Books

59 John Glenn Drive
Amherst, New York 14228

Published 2016 by Prometheus Books

Cover image © Africa Studio/Shutterstock
Cover design by Liz Mills
Cover design © Prometheus Books

Inquiries should be addressed to
Prometheus Books
59 John Glenn Drive
Amherst, New York 14228
VOICE: 716–691–0133
FAX: 716–691–0137
WWW.PROMETHEUSBOOKS.COM

20 19 18 17 16   5 4 3 2 1

Library of Congress Cataloging-in-Publication Data

Names: Brykman, Beth, author.
Title: The best of both worlds : how mothers can find full-time satisfaction in part-time
    work / by Beth Brykman.
Description: Amherst, New York : Prometheus Books, 2016. | Includes bibliographical
    references and index.
Identifiers: LCCN 2016020431 (print) | LCCN 2016031785 (ebook) |
    ISBN 9781633882478 (pbk.) | ISBN 9781633882485 (ebook)
Subjects: LCSH: Working mothers. | Part-time employment. | Work and family. |
    Job satisfaction.
Classification: LCC HQ759.48 .B778 2016 (print) | LCC HQ759.48 (ebook) |
    DDC 306.3/6—dc23
LC record available at https://lccn.loc.gov/2016020431

Printed in the United States of America

Dedicated to my daughters, Kelsey and Ashley,
hoping that they find that elusive sense of balance
in their professional and personal lives.

CONTENTS

CHAPTER 4: NO NETWORKS? NO PROFESSIONAL CONTACTS?
AM I HOPELESS?   111

CHAPTER 5: STARTING YOUR OWN BUSINESS   143

PREFACE

"The ideal worker image is problematic for all employed mothers because it is based on heterosexual men who are not expected to be the primary caretakers of children. That's why women are changing it. It doesn't work. . . ."[1]

How can mothers bridge the gap between the worlds of "mom" and "career woman" to find work-life balance? How can full-time employed moms prevent stalling out professionally while raising a family? How can stay-at-home mothers redefine and redirect their careers while caring for their children? By working part-time. Stay-at-home, full-time employed, and part-time working mothers see part-time employment as the ultimate situation.[2]

Why? Because part-timers earn income, hold a professional identity, and still have enough time to be at home, raise their children, and participate in their children's schools. These mothers are intimately involved in both the worlds of mom and career woman.

Inspiring and informational, this book will explain why women want part-time work, how they obtain it, and how they keep it. Each chapter is rich with examples of what women across the country with a variety of careers did to gain their dream of part-time positions.

In researching this book, I used the same qualitative research techniques that Fortune 100 corporations use to develop multimillion-dollar products. I formally interviewed over 100 women individually, using an open-ended questionnaire. To avoid regional bias on the topic, I interviewed approximately a quarter of the women from the Northeast, a quarter from the South, a quarter from the middle of the country, and the rest from the West. (See appendix for further research details.) Some women were well-off, while others were clearly struggling to make ends meet. Most had children between the ages of a few months old to eighteen years old and still living at home.

I also interviewed human resource managers from several different companies. This helped me understand what companies need, want, and how one can approach them for part-time employment.

The book is written in conversational style for ease and pleasure of reading. All the names in the book are fictitious since many of the people interviewed want to remain anonymous. But all the vocations, stories, and feelings are real.

I hope you find this book as useful in landing your perfect part-time job as I found it enjoyable to research and write.

Introduction

WHY NOW?

"The older managers think that if the shoe doesn't fit, you should wear it and walk funny. The baby-busters say throw it away and get a new shoe."
—Margaret Regan, a Towes Perin consultant[1]

W hile this book makes it perfectly understandable why more and more women are seeking part-time employment, it may not be as clear why employers are hiring part-timers. What's different now? What is making part-time employment more acceptable among corporations than ten or twenty years ago? What is giving women the ability to work part-time?

It's simply this: women comprise approximately 50 percent of the workforce. Even with the recent downturn in the economy, America can't afford to lose *half* its workforce. America needs working mothers. When many mothers pursue part-time work, they begin changing the face of society.

WORK-LIFE ISSUES

These work-life issues date back to the 1960s when women edged into the workforce. Initial studies were done on women's careers and the relationship of work and family. Corporations began dabbling in family-work balance issues in the 1980s and 1990s. Lewis H. Young, former editor in chief of *Business Week*, chaired the board of directors for Catalyst, a national organization formed to further the advancement of women in professional settings.[2] Work-Family Directions was founded to provide childcare support services for IBM.[3] And in the late 1980s, corporations supported the formation of the Family and Work Institute and the Boston College Center for Work and Family.[4]

Kathleen Christensen of the Alfred P. Sloan Foundation said it best about women in the '80s:

> There was this dissonance, this mismatch between these people, these women; trying to fit themselves into a structure and it didn't work. And in some cases, they just changed themselves to fit; and other cases, they dropped out, and they dropped out with great cost, in many cases, to themselves.[5]

Neither staying in the workforce nor leaving employment was wrong, but neither one seemed really right either, causing internal conflicts that still exist today.

Then, in the '90s, flextime arose. Part-time employment was discussed. But alongside those terms words like "mommy track" were used. To be a "valid" employee, you worked full-time. Even now, many mothers claim that they are working part-time until the kids reach high school age when they can work full-time and get a "real job."

All of these feelings put together in conjunction with globalization, technology, and increased workloads/hours have driven more and more women to require part-time hours. When this trend began, employers generally ignored it. But they can't any longer for three basic reasons.

WHY THE ATTITUDE SHIFT

One, there are more and more, better-educated women in professional roles. More women and better-educated women are entering the workforce. In 1970, women comprised approximately 41 percent of the US labor pool.[6] In 2013, that number was 49 percent.[7] Today, women earn 57 percent of bachelor's degrees, 59 percent of master's degrees, and over half of the PhDs.[8] America cannot afford to lose its women to the home front. It relies on them as an integral part of today's well-educated workforce.

Two, corporations are cultivating a reputation for attracting new employees.[9] According to the Work-Life Evolution Study from the Boston College Center for Work and Family, organizations that are in industries where competition is stiff for top talent are rewiring their workforce management practices.[10]

Three, there's the necessity of corporations to retain the top talent they have already trained. IBM has internally surveyed employees since 1986, using the results to provide links to how work-life issues affect attracting and retaining employees. IBM found that workers who have a better work-life balance are more committed than those who don't.[11] The new generation of workers (those under thirty-four) are demanding control and flexibility. This generation will give up a lot to get it. They won't stay if they don't like what's happening.[12]

These three components put together with work-life issues that mothers experience today have caused many women to "drop out." Women, typically the primary caregiver, drop out of the workforce due to inflexible, long work hours, causing the brain drain that is occurring in America. This exiting of the workforce is resulting in higher employee turnover and shortages of workers causing corporations to incur high training expenditures over and over. It's these very expenditures that have caused the shifts in attitudes.

Kelsey, a librarian, and Cheryl, a marketing director, have experienced these attitude changes firsthand. "When I first got my master's degree, I had talked about just staying part-time with the director of the library. I was told in no uncertain terms, this was 1992, there is no such thing as a part-time academic librarian. This was the director of our library. She simply would not tolerant part-time professional librarians. Part-time paraprofessionals were just fine, but not professional librarians," says Kelsey, referring to her boss in the university system. "There were some issues over that. There were younger librarians who started families and wanted to try part-time work or job sharing. And she would not tolerant it, so they moved to different libraries within the system since the university has many, many libraries. There's a general university librarian, but the large libraries had their own directors. And they are pretty much autonomous. For this particular librarian, that was her philosophy: she did not believe you could be a part-time professional. She sang a different tune a number of years later."

Cheryl has also seen an attitude shift in her company. When she started her part-time position, there was only one other part-time worker there. Cheryl says, "I pulled her aside, asking her, 'I'm curious what your experience is here. How's it been going?' She felt really strongly that by going part-time you were really pulling yourself off of any track. Since then, there are probably five or ten who work a part-time schedule. They have tried to implement a more flexible policy. This company was fifteen years old then and had tons of people in their twenties. Now they have people in their late twenties and thirties. People are pregnant and having babies. That wasn't the case originally. Now the company has to cope."

INDUSTRY REACTIONS

The brain drain is particularly acute in legal and accounting firms, causing these industries to react to it first. Deloitte, a leading accounting firm, has set up career paths and part-time jobs for women with children to hold onto these highly trained employees. Deloitte US is committed to creating a culture of flexibility. Deloitte's annual document titled "The Initiative for Retention and Advancement for Women" states, "Simply put, the workforce is changing. We cannot sustain our growth without attracting, developing, and retaining talented women to serve our clients and grow our business."[13] This initiative has evolved over the last twenty years and is still proving successful today.

Twenty-four percent of Deloitte's partners, principals, and directors are women, up from 7 percent twenty years ago.[14] The corporation recognizes that if it wants to retain women in large numbers rather than having them opt out altogether, it must make remaining in the workforce easier. This corporation is dedicated to creating an environment where more varied roles can emerge.[15]

Here is their "work-life" statement from the Web:

Recognizing each one of us has unique work-life needs that can change over time, we offer a variety of programs and options for our people to take a break, maintain a healthy lifestyle, and provide flexibility around how, where, and when work gets done. Some examples include virtual work practices, Mass Career Customization, internal mobility, global work assignments, sabbaticals, generous paid time-off, family leave, and health & wellness programs.[16]

And the program works. For ten consecutive years, the Deloitte US firms outranked the leading US accounting firms in the number of women partners, principals, and directors. Their Women's Initiative program was featured in 130 major publications and television programs. Fifty-seven of their clients invited them to help initiate and/or execute women initiative programs for them.[17]

When asked why the corporation is doing this, the reply was,

Because today's workforce doesn't look anything like the traditional one. A mere 17 percent of U.S. family structures are "traditional"— defined in economic terms as a husband in the workforce and a wife who is not—down from 63 percent in past generations. So we are realigning—in fact, redefining—workplace norms and practices in light of today's nontraditional workforce realities.[18]

McKinsey & Company, a large consulting firm, is now talking to women who left to start families. They are recruiting these women, asking them to return to the workplace. McKinsey is also offering a "phase back" program to help mothers adjust after maternity leave.[19]

Bain & Company, Boston Consulting Group, and Goldman Sachs are offering part-time options and/or have programs such as "returnship" programs or paid short-term jobs for those who haven't worked for several years.[20]

Law firms are also feeling the effects on a widespread basis. According to Maggie Jackson, "Balancing Acts" columnist for the *Boston Globe*, "Work-life issues aren't just for women, and yet women have driven progress in this area because until recently, they've been most in need of employer support in their efforts to juggle family and career. At the top, inflexibility spells brain drain: While women have made up 40 to 50 percent of law school graduates for two decades, they comprise just 17 percent of partners at major law firms."[21]

Only 4 percent of lawyers work part-time compared to about 14 percent of professionals in engineering, medicine, or architecture according to the Association for Legal Career Professionals.[22] No wonder law firms are looking to change how they do business.

The international law firm of Heller Ehrman LLP launched the Opt-In Project to determine ways that businesses, specifically law firms, could retain female talent by achieving better work-life balance. They tapped into more than 900 representatives of various US industries. Suggestions coming out of this report include:[23]

- Rethinking the concept of billable hours.
- Eliminating the "up or out" legal system approach to partnership in favor of a tiered approach.
- Offering a variety of employment options including flexible and part-time schedules.

Patricia K. Gillette, the head of the Opt-In Project, says, "The younger generation will be a driving force of this new trend. They will insist on a different structure. The current associates in law firms are dropping out in droves because they refuse to bill a certain number of hours. When firms realize that this model is ridiculous, they will have to recognize that they are losing talented, good people because of the inflexibility of law firms."[24]

While the fields of law and accounting are leading the change, they are not the only industries feeling the effects. The medical field is another industry starting to make changes based on the demands of employees, specifically new doctors. According to a 2006 survey by physician staffing firm Merritt, Hawkins & Associates, the availability of free time was causing 63 percent of medical residents "a significant level of concern." This is up a full 15 percent from 2001, only five years later.[25]

These quality-of-life issues have been mounting over the years. Today, new doctors striving to lead a more balanced lifestyle have put a strain on the healthcare system. To accommodate these physicians and ease the burden on the healthcare system, American medicine is moving toward a team-based approach, utilizing multiple doctors, nurse practitioners, and physician assistants, opening the door for part-timers.[26]

Many corporations outside these fields are also realizing that changes must be made. *Industrial Distribution*, a distribution industry magazine, surveyed more than 500 distribution owners and managers from companies of all sizes for their 61st Annual Survey of Distributor Operations. More than half of their respondents said they can't find enough qualified candidates to fill job openings. Bill Purser, president of Applied Industrial Technologies, says that industry will have to accommodate changing employment forces. He feels that it is industry's turn to adjust to employees' new views on work-life balance.[27]

And it's not just huge corporations feeling the talent pinch. Susan works for Baltimore County in Maryland and has a great story. She was pregnant with twins and had to go on bed rest. "I was intending to resign, which my boss knew," she says. "She told me, 'Don't resign until the time you absolutely need to resign' so I could get my medical benefits. She supported me in that. I resigned December 1, 1994. They were born on December 22. Then I went back to the job in March 1996. I only worked four hours every two weeks at first; very, very part-time. My boss was brilliant at this: when she gets people she likes, even if they resign to be a stay-at-home mom, she keeps them in the pool one way or another.

"About every year, she'd say, 'Susan, I've got about twelve hours per week I'd like you to take. Would you be willing to take it?' And I'd say, 'No, but I'll do four hours every week from four hours every other week.' Then I did that for another year. Then she said, 'Would you be willing to do eight hours per week?' So I said, 'Okay, I'll do eight hours per week.' So then she begged me to do twenty hours a week. I said, 'No, but I'll do twelve hours per week.' Then I went up to sixteen hours per week when my kids were in second grade. My boss said, 'Listen, you're really missing out on getting paid vacation days, accumulating medical. Would you consider going up to twenty hours a week?' I said, 'No, no, no.' But then I said yes when they were in third grade. When they were in third grade, I went to twenty hours. Then after that, we were remodeling our house and then we had to refinance. We were scared out of our gourds. She said, 'I have some temporary hours that would give you forty hours a week for about six months. Would you take it?' I said, 'Yes.' So I worked forty hours a week for about six months; then I dropped to thirty-two. I was at thirty-two for a long time. Then I became a supervisor and went up to thirty-six, and I've been at that for about three years."

As you can see by Susan's story, skilled, innovative, and industrious workers will have the most options. They can start their own firms or move on to other employers who *will* fulfill their wants. To attract and retain such talented workers, employers must accommodate their needs.[28] And they are reacting favorably. Based on a survey completed by Hewitt Associates, a human resources consulting company, 36 percent of employers are giving employees a chance to work part-time.[29] While in the 1990s, flexible work arrangements were considered a short-term option to ease a working mother's transition into motherhood, it's now a strategy for long-term retention.[30]

According to a Catalyst study on flexible work arrangements, "working mothers consider the flexible work arrangements to be a career-long tool to help create life strategies and achieve life goals."[31] Having life strategies with a selection of choices helps to create meaningful careers alongside healthy families.

CORPORATE BENEFITS

While as parents, we see part-time work being beneficial to the family, part-time employees bring benefits to corporations. Certain businesses such as financial institutions or retailers may service their customers twenty-four hours a day. In order to do this, some companies hire part-timers to fill hours full-time workers don't want, or to improve customer service at peak periods that may only occur three or four hours a day. Growing firms use part-timers when they need help twenty or thirty hours a week for specific jobs. Their businesses may not justify full-timers in every position. For some corporations, part-time employees are not an afterthought, but an integral part of their overall workforce and success. Companies gearing up after the economic downturn may rehire slowly, using part-time employment as a ramp-up strategy.

Let's look at Digital Federal Credit Union (DCU), a not-for-profit financial service provider with members in all fifty states. To extend its service hours in branches and its call center, DCU designed part-time positions. These positions cover Thursday and Friday evenings until 7:00 p.m. and Saturdays from 8:45 a.m. to 3:30 p.m. There's also a part-time schedule to cover the lunchtime hours from 11:30 a.m. to 3:30 p.m. DCU recruits people specifically for these positions to solve a business problem, adding staff during periods of high demand. Offering prorated benefits to those who work twenty hours or more adds to the attractiveness of the job for those seeking this type of work.[32]

DCU has 105 out of 547 employees working part-time. Lisa Bordinat, senior vice president and director for Aon Consulting's Talent Solutions Group, says, "It's really a business decision that allows organizations to be more nimble from a staffing perspective."[33] It allows firms to incur costs when demand for products or services is high.

According to the vice president of Human Resources at a health services company in North Carolina, "Our scheduling is unique with 24-hour residential service. A worker might get called to do extra hours, to go to a different home, so it's not the same desk or job share. It's not the office setting with the same hours and same department and same coworkers. Someone can work more hours in the same setting or pick up another client. They can work five hours per week with two clients then three clients to get more hours. It's helpful with the flexibility of scheduling having part-timers." Since the company's clients may just need someone a few hours per week, part-timers come in very handy.

For a global biopharmaceutical service organization, part-timers fill a different need. According to the senior director of Human Resources, part-time workers many times fill an immediate gap where there is a need for a half person. "From an affordability perspective, you can fill that need, get the folks in and keep your business running.

"The philosophy is that we are a growing organization, there's so much opportunity for flexibility. It's a means to attract people that today are part-time status, but depending on their needs over time could eventually grow into full-time roles. So we have a flexible philosophy on the types of people we want to bring in.

"It really talks about the shift in the market population worldwide, particularly in the United States where families aren't procreating at the same pace. You have to look at alternative hiring and alternative staffing methods. You're going to look at the older worker. You're going to look at the part-time worker. You're going to look at ways to meet your needs. You're going to train unskilled labor in areas that you can't find workers.

"As a director of Human Resources, I'm going, 'How do I find a flexible workforce?' I think it's really important. For me, the value and pros of the part-time worker is you're going to be able to fill the gaps."

Not only do part-timers help solve issues for these firms, but they also bring a strong work ethic into them. The women I interviewed mentioned over and over again how focused they are in their jobs, how dedicated they are, and how they waste no time. They're there to get in and get the work done, not to socialize.

"When you're a part-timer, you hit the ground running. You have things to do so you can't sit around drinking coffee. You learn to move through tasks quickly. You have less time to smell the roses," claims Gabi, a technical project officer for the Environmental Protection Agency (EPA).

Catie, an associate director of College Admissions agrees. "When you're a part-time employer, you get more bang for the buck. I don't work Wednesdays, but if there's something I need to do, I'll come in and do it. I don't get paid extra for it. Part-time people say, 'I'm only two days a week or three days a week,' yet will do what needs to get done, especially if they're a salaried employee."

Kelly concurs. "I'll work an extra day, rearrange the schedule with my partner. I try to accommodate so no one feels shafted that I'm part-time," she says regarding her job-sharing position in purchasing. "If someone feels they're not getting a benefit, they won't go for it."

"Being part-time, I've always done more than everyone else because people think part-timers don't actually work," says Kim about her technical computer work. "I was a role model for other women getting part-time positions. I didn't want to be a black mark in the system. I wanted people to say, 'Hey, this woman is in a part-time position and doing a great job, getting everything done, being a real asset to the workplace.' When you do that, prove yourself, then they'll work with you.

"I realized that it was incredibly efficient: I went to work, did my stuff, got home. I realized how much I could get done in a day of part-time, almost as much as full-time. I've talked to other part-timers, too, and you can get almost as much done as full-time people. There's been occasion for meetings or projects where I work extra hours. I can see a huge slide in the work from Monday to Friday, also from eight a.m. to four p.m. As you hit Thursday and Friday, people are just sort of starting to dog it. Past three o'clock in the afternoon, there's not a whole lot going on. And you can feel the energy level in the workplace; I don't know if other people feel it or if it's because I work part-time."

Kim agrees with Kelly about being accommodating to her employer. "With part-time, I always made it clear to the people I was working with that if they ever needed something extra from me, if anything ever came up, I was available. I was always available for them to call me at home, or e-mail. It's not like I'm on vacation and I'm not there."

MEANINGFUL EMPLOYMENT/INCOME PART-TIME

When I tell people the topic of this book, they ask, "Aren't most part-time jobs just at retail?" Absolutely not. You've just read about what's happening in the legal, accounting, and medical industries. As you go through this book, you'll read about software engineers, social workers, bankers, purchasing agents, lobbyists, food stylists, human resource directors, librarians, and office managers to name a few part-time positions. Some examples from my interviews include:

- A part-time English tutor earning more than she did as a full-time teacher
- A direct sales executive making over $100,000 per year working approximately twenty hours per week
- A senior marketing manager promoted to marketing director while working twenty-four to thirty hours per week
- A lawyer bringing in more money working part-time than minimum full-time hours

Connie is one of my best examples. She has worked between ten and thirty hours per week for over seventeen years at a scrapbooking company. She's now among its top people and one of the executive directors in the company. With her title, she still works thirty hours or less per week. Her success has led to magazine articles being written about her. Because of this publicity, she has been approached by not one, not two, not three, but four other companies for employment. Full-time workers would love to be as successful as Connie.

Chapter 1

WHY WORK PART-TIME?

"It made me feel good about using my skills, earning some money and still caring for my daughters."

—Dianne

Two days working in the office and one day at home, leaving two weekdays for errands, appointments, and being with the kids. Good, right? What about working five mornings from 8:00 a.m. to 1:00 p.m.? Not bad. Or how about working four days a week, getting every Friday off? Pretty nice. This is the world of part-timers. And no one wants to enter that world more than mothers.

What drives women to move into part-time employment? Is it to relieve stress in the family? Is it for a paycheck? Is it for peace of mind when considering a prospective job in the future? Or is it simply the emotional draw that mothers have of wanting to be with their children? It's all of these reasons. Mothers see part-time employment as a way to obtain a sense of balance in their lives by bridging the gap between the worlds of "mom" and "career woman." According to the Pew Research Center, 47 percent of mothers prefer part-time jobs over staying home or working full-time in 2012, up from 44 percent in 1997.[1]

With all the recent talk of leaning in and breadwinner moms, most mothers still work two jobs instead of one. According to Sylvia Ann Hewlett, director of the Gender/Policy Program at Columbia University's School of International and Public Affairs, "Even when women are highly qualified and highly paid, they routinely pick up the lion's share of domestic responsibilities—typically 75 percent of the housework and child care."[2] No wonder these women are struggling for balance.

And stay-at-home mothers have traded their professional identities for one that holds little social status in most people's eyes. In our society the lowest form of work, in terms of status and finances, is day-to-day childcare. Even domestic cleaning work pays more.[3] So a stay-at-home mom feels much less empowered than when she was employed, often losing a strong sense of self.

Most women feel they fall short of their own self-imposed standards to do well simultaneously in the professional world and on the home front, bringing us to the issue of balance. Balance is full of compromises. For Michele Bolton, author of *The Third Shift*, balance lies with having part-time flexible employment, a lack of willingness to relocate, only a few children, and limited involvement with school and community activities.[4] She advises others to ease up on themselves, realizing that nobody's perfect. While the women I interviewed may not agree with Bolton on exactly how to attain balance, they do agree with her on letting something "give," not trying to attain it all, all at once.

PART-TIME WORK MOTIVATIONS

Women become part-time employees for a combination of three major reasons: children, professional identity/personal fulfillment, and income. Being able to spend time with their kids while pursuing either a career or obtaining self-satisfaction was, hopefully, going to bring balance into the lives of these women. While income is obviously part of the total picture in part-time employment, surprisingly, it is a secondary or tertiary reason to work outside the home for the majority of women interviewed. Women say primarily that they "want to grow as a human being and give back to [their] community" or "desire to be back in a professional environment" or "want to use [their] education."

The tugs of family life and income bring full-time workers into part-time employment. For stay-at-home mothers, self-satisfaction combined with income bring them back into the workforce on a part-time basis. Surveys dating back as far as the early 1990s show that up to 80 percent of mothers, employed or not, consistently want to work part-time.[5]

Ingrid, an air force captain at the time, says regarding her son, "I had very strong motherly instincts and couldn't fathom leaving him with someone else for five days a week. I felt like I needed to be with him to raise him. At the same time, we needed the income."

"Sure, I wanted the money, but I wanted value in my own world," adds Julie, a garden center salesperson.

"I wanted to do both things and do both well. I wanted to keep my foot in my professional life that I had for so long before my children came along and not to miss anything with the kids," agrees Noel, a lobbyist.

"My intent was to stay home full-time, but then after several months, intellectually I needed more," says Doreen, who then became a human resources consultant.

These women voice what Sylvia Ann Hewlett learned while researching her book *Off-Ramps and On-Ramps*. In order to find balance in their personal and work lives a third of highly qualified women work part-time during their careers.[6]

Best of Both Worlds

For a majority of women who trade full-time employment for part-time, their primary reason for working less hours is to have more time with their children. Secondarily, either they want to continue with their careers, holding onto their personal identities, or they need the income. Not surprisingly, 40 percent feel the best aspect of being a part-timer is having the "best of both worlds." These women have integrated raising their children, being intellectually stimulated, having adult interaction, and having control of what is happening in their homes.

Three things have increased pressure on work-life balance since the 1980s and early 1990s: technology, globalization, and increased workloads.

- Technology has blurred work versus home boundaries. It's a double-edged sword that cuts both ways. On the positive side, mothers can work from home when a child is sick or telecommute one day a week. On the negative side, we can work from anywhere, anytime, invading our personal lives and turning our homes into "satellite offices."

- Globalization is another trend putting pressure on work-life balance issues. Now we work in a 24/7 environment, e-mailing each other across the globe at all hours, every day of the week. And since many holidays vary by country, we even get work sent to us on Thanksgiving or the Fourth of July. This is one more contributor to the excessive work hours, adding to our already heavy workloads.

- Organizations have been attempting to "do more with less" for the last three decades. When profits are squeezed and stock prices drop, downsizing occurs. Many times three jobs are folded into two or, even worse, two jobs folded into one, causing excessive work and stress. Add globalization and technology on top of that and employees have enough work to labor around the clock making work-life balance issues even worse.

The desire for women to succeed professionally and raise a family in conjunction with increased technology, globalization, and "doing more with less" has driven women to pursue part-time work. Kim claims switching from full-time to part-time employment was simply the "guilt of not spending time with my own children. I would go two whole days with just getting my children out of bed, dropping them off at daycare, and then getting home in time to put them back to bed. Other people were raising my children."

Many others feel like Kim, that they are being selfish in fulfilling their own professional wants at the cost of their children's emotional well-being. Mother after mother reiterates, "I wanted to make sure that I could spend adequate time with my children" or "I felt that I wasn't giving my family enough time."

Margo, formerly an English teacher, says, "This decision was based on how I wanted to feel as a mom. I was a very high-energy teacher, and I never wanted to feel as though I spent so much of my energy on other people's kids, that I came home and I didn't have enough for my own. I had always wanted to have a ton of kids, so from the very beginning I thought about teaching as a great career to have kids. I'd be on their schedule, everything would be great. And once I started teaching, I realized how much energy it required every day to do it well. And that's when I realized that I can't do this and be the kind of mom I wanted to be."

So she started working as an SAT/academic/college tutor. "I knew that I had a skill that could make a lot of money, even more money than teaching with no homework and no grading. It enabled me to do swim class, music class, and all the fun classes I wanted to do with my daughter.

"When I was working every weekend and holding many weekday classes, I more than doubled my teaching salary. That's when I sent out postcards and worked with the math tutor at the local high school."

Jane, who had worked in nonprofit management, also wanted time for her family. "The big thing was quitting full-time work. I said, 'Oh my God, I have one life to live and this job is eating me up. I have no time or energy for my family or myself. I can't do this anymore.' So I quit. I never intended to work part-time. I just woke up one morning and I knew I couldn't keep working full-time. I woke up—it was 5:30 a.m.—I couldn't sleep once again. I was writing in my journal, and just found myself realizing as I was writing that I actually could quit my job. The YWCA would not fall down. I would not go to pieces. I played around with the idea for a little while, gave them a whole lot of notice, and it worked. I told myself I could have the summer off.

"I knew we could not make it financially without me working at all; plus I would lose my mind if I wasn't working. But I didn't want to jump back into full-time work." Leveraging her past experience, Jane now consults for nonprofits. She facilitates groups, leads board retreats, and trains others on nonprofit programs at locations such as local universities.

It is all about balance.

Balance—having time for ball games and school parties, being home after school for the kids while also bringing in a paycheck, and using the education/training/skills that women have worked so hard to obtain—that's what makes part-time employment the "best of both worlds." Working part-time keeps women from getting in a rut by challenging them, keeping them up-to-date, giving them a sense of being out in the world, and expanding their knowledge base. Then, because it affords them enough time to manage home life, it helps them maintain a balance that is elusive for full-time employees.

"What I like about it is that I can have an impact, I can make it challenging, but I can be there for my family with the flexibility," says Missy, a law firm researcher.

Jane adds, "It leaves me time and energy to come home and be present for my children and husband. They get off the bus, and they have my complete attention, time, energy, and emotional space when they need it."

"When people ask me about it, I always say, 'It's the best of both worlds,'" claims Tessa, a Michigan teacher who job shares. "My sister dropped out of the workforce. She had been a paralegal and then dropped out. She was a house mom for ten years; then she tried to go back. She had a hard time so she didn't know what to do. She wound up being a teacher's aide for a while. She wanted the same schedule as her kids, having the summer off with them. Now she's a substitute teacher. I was always glad I did it the way I did it. I still have lots of time with my kids. When I was working afternoons and the kids were little, they slept in the afternoons. I was never out of my profession; it kept me in the loop. I really recommend it, especially for teachers. The job share is really nice for kids and teachers because we both get to teach the things that we love the most. If you do have a difficult class, you get a fresh teacher, not one who's tired and impatient midday."

As a part-time purchasing agent for aircraft engine parts, Kelly agrees. "It's the best thing for a woman who wants to do it all, still keep a career and raise her babies. I wouldn't have been a good stay-at-home mom. It's good for [my children], and it's good for me."

And for Cheryl, working part-time gives her the balance she needs for herself as contributor to the family income. After Cheryl and her husband purchased their new home, she had stopped working, but something was missing. "It was not like I could be out of the labor force and then be hanging out at the country club and hiring a nanny at the same time," she says. "So . . . living in a place like my town where there are a lot of people who don't [need to] work and [who] spend a ton of money, I felt like getting back to work gave me back some financial independence. I was staying home, but I spent very little money on myself, and I felt I wasn't contributing much. It's okay to stay home. There's such a difference between being a stay-at-home mom and a stay-at-home mom with a lot of financial resources. We were down in income. I don't know how much of that was self-imposed versus reality, but it's what I felt. The community of stay-at-home moms I was in was not in that position."

Additionally, two women cite that they can earn income to pay for hobbies without encroaching on the family's finances needed on a day-to-day basis. And as a bonus, they actually have *time* to enjoy these hobbies *because* they aren't working a forty-hour workweek.

Flexibility

Balance includes the *flexibility* of being able to work the hours women desire. For some women, this means working the exact same hours every week so they know their schedule and can work the rest of the family around it. For other women, it means total flexibility with no set hours at all. This enables them to react to family issues on a weekly basis without cancelling meetings or irritating customers. A quarter of the women interviewed feel that flexibility is the best part of working part-time.

Sanity and balance, not only for herself but also for her husband, was Lorrie's reason for moving into part-time work. Her husband worked the night shift at the airport, and she worked during the day. "I would have to scramble at five in the afternoon from work and get back home so he could get in the car and get to the airport by six. It was a major hassle all the way around because the job I had at my level wasn't one where you could punch a clock at five. There was lots of stress. We really talked about 'How do we do this?'

"Both of us agreed we didn't want to put our children in a daycare situation; we didn't want to get an au pair. We wanted to be the best caregivers we could be. The option was if I could go part-time, work a couple of days from home, a couple of days in the office, then it would work out. That slight change made a huge difference in our balance.

"Then he changed his job because he was running on empty. He was able to move into a weekend position. We both work thirty hours each. We won't be wealthy in monetary ways; we made that choice. Our priority is our health and the happiness of our children. We need to make money to provide for them, but they come first. That's not always accepted in an employment setting."

Job Itself

Whether women were moving from full-time to part-time employment or from staying home to part-time employment, the single best part of working part-time is the job itself. No matter what type of job, whether tutor, doctor, sales representative, engineer, lawyer, interior designer, nanny, banker, artist, lobbyist, secretary, computer programmer, or food stylist, women like being employed. These women enjoy being out in the world, continuing with their careers, being intellectually challenged, contributing to society, and using their training/skills/education. Providing a valuable service, making an impact, feeling a sense of accomplishment, connecting with wonderful people, these are reasons half the women cite the work itself as the best aspect of part-time work.

Over half of the women who left the workforce and stayed home for some time returned to the workforce primarily to regain an identity, interact more with adults, meet a challenge, and gain intellectual stimulation. They have spent time with their children. They have gone to the parks, read stories, and colored with their kids. Now they want something for themselves. Simply stated, they like working outside the home.

"I had an intense desire to work, to get back in the saddle," says Lisa, an attorney.

"I needed my own time, my own space, my own interests for my own mental health. That will benefit my children to have a happy mommy," adds Kim.

"When you're the mom and have children that young, you're around them all the time and immersed in their world," says Heather. "With my husband working his busy schedule, I didn't have a lot of adult interaction. I felt like I had lost a piece of myself. Even though I had become a mom and I was very happy with that role as a wife, I had worked all those years very hard, so part of my identity was missing." Heather returned to work as a registered nurse case manager in a Mississippi acute care hospital facility, reestablishing herself in a field where she had worked prior to stepping out of the labor force. She adds, "It wasn't money; it was purely an intrinsic motivation: something I felt within me that I needed to do."

"It was my desire at the time," claims Leanne. "I felt like I was losing a sense of myself. I wanted to do something other than just be a mom."

Secondarily, Leanne wanted to bring in another income stream. "My husband made plenty of money on a day-to-day basis, but I felt like there was a lot of pressure and stress on him being the sole breadwinner with our current plan, which was that I was just going to be home. I thought, 'This is something I can do.' I didn't want to really do something full-time because I wasn't willing to give up being home with the kids, but I also wanted to do something where I could contribute something financially, help out that way." So Leanne became a successful consultant for Arbonne skin products in eastern Ohio, working twenty hours per week.

By the time Missy's children had all entered first grade, she was ready for a challenge. "I had walked the dog; I'd gone to the mall; I'd been out to lunch, and needed something else to do—there was only so much of that I could do. I don't know how to say it more eloquently: it was time to go back to work. But it was still very important for me to be home for my kids. That was my primary goal." Missy became a reading specialist at her children's school in Kansas City so that she could work while her children were in class.

"I was going out of my mind at home," says Beth. "I'm not built to be a stay-at-home mom, but I'm not really built to work full-time and have kids either. So I needed something in between." She found part-time work in database development and analysis in the Atlanta area.

"You do tend to identify yourself by what you do. And when people say, 'What do you do?' it is nice to say that you are doing something more than being a homemaker," claims Monica. She started with volunteer work for the Maple Chamber Chorus and eventually moved into a thirty-to-thirty-five-hour-per-week paid position as the executive director.

Once Jane started her consulting for nonprofits she was relieved that she had figured out how to balance her intellectual life with her family life. "Partly financially relieved, partly 'Okay, now I know where I'm going and what I'm supposed to be doing and, phew, I don't have to figure it out anymore' relieved. It's pretty clear I was not wired to be a stay-at-home mom with a baby, so I had no doubts about that. I knew if it was just the two of us at home all day long I would get to understand where the term 'shaken baby syndrome came from.'"

Ellen, an attorney, liked both the challenging work *and* the interaction with her colleagues. "There are two things. One, camaraderie. I'm working in an environment with three attorneys, two staff [members], and one part-timer. We get along well, like a family. It's a very close-knit situation. I really like that. They like me and care about me. Two, my boss is wonderful and attracts great clients. He could bring in more mundane jobs, but in my case, I have interesting and cutting-edge cases. They are always mentally challenging and keep those neurons firing. It demands that I be technically able."

Many other women agree with Ellen, citing teamwork, personal interaction, and connections with professional organizations as being the key to happiness in their jobs and careers. They mentioned interacting with colleagues, whether on the phone or in person rather than working in isolation, as being one of the best aspects of their jobs. In fact, some women structure their jobs specifically to include interaction with others.

For Leanne, it was "definitely the people who came into my life. I've met incredible people. I like to be surrounded by motivated, positive people every day. I love that every day I'm always learning."

Michele, a mental health worker who worked for the community and now runs her own private practice, says, "When working at the hospital, I loved working with colleagues, working with interdisciplinary teams on cases. It was very satisfying. With my private practice, I strive to have as much contact with colleagues as possible or it would be isolating work. I'm excited to learn and grow to become a better therapist. I like to challenge myself."

Carolyn, a salesperson, also agrees that working with people makes the job enjoyable. "It's the interaction with customers. The fun of taking a situation where customers present their problems, and instead of the knee-jerk answer of, 'This is what you need to do,' I walk them through the solution, whether it takes five minutes or an hour and a half. That's what I enjoy. It's challenging, like a game. It's being honest. I could have sold them anything, but I give full disclosure."

Several women have opportunities and experiences that they would not have gained in a full-time position. This has boosted confidence for some and made the job even more rewarding for others.

Stacy takes her children to work with her. As a director of a child care center, she says, "I love going to work and doing what I do. I also love that my children socialize with other children while I work. I have one of the most supportive employers ever. My personal growth is fantastic. I am getting my cake and eating it, too."

Sandy's job share as a lawyer afforded her the ability to work much closer with another woman than she ordinarily would have. "I had a great time in the job share, the camaraderie, working with someone as closely as I was. I was learning a lot and felt like I had somebody on my team. It was nice."

Income or Benefits

It isn't surprising that women work part-time for income. What is interesting, however, is that *only a third* of the women mentioned it as the primary motivating factor.

"Financially, it was not an option with kids. I had to work for money," declares Paula, an emergency room doctor.

Stacy, initially a daycare provider, concurs, "Financially at the time, we couldn't wing it on my husband's salary."

"My husband was transitioning into a different field, so his income was going to drop," adds Angie, who went back to work as a therapy counselor.

Sherry's divorce pushed her into obtaining a flexible part-time accounting job to create a steady stream of income.

Unlike the others above who earned the income to fund the family's needs, Edith wanted her own money. "I wanted to have my own cash flow. I was used to having my own money. I hated at Christmas or Valentine's Day or birthdays having to buy gifts with our joint bank account where [my husband] was the only one putting money into it. It didn't feel good, a Christmas present from yourself. I felt guilty buying an expensive Christmas present for him because it wasn't my money; it was our money." She began painting murals for others as well as babysitting.

Linda initially went back to work as a nutritionist for intellectual stimulation. But when her mortgage payment increased, she was able to easily ramp up, earning extra income. The money, which was a "nice bonus," suddenly became a necessity. "I stayed home for six to seven years, working just four hours every other week. During that time, I was on full 'mommy' everything. I really did feel that I wasn't getting the kind of emotional reward I got when I hung out with working women. The first few years after having kids, your brain is kind of squeezed. You don't go back to work and you're talking baby talk, which is great at the time. I also spent lots of time volunteering for infertility, bed rest, and twin support, which is also very, very good. But then I felt, 'I've got to get my brain back in shape.'

"The kicker was our mortgage payment doubled. And I realized, 'I don't have the opportunity anymore to be a stay-at-home mom; I've got to go out there and work.' That was a huge motivator for me to go above twenty hours per week and get benefits.

"We now need my paycheck. If we hadn't remodeled our house, I wouldn't have to work at all. So what happened is what happens with many things that are a pain. I thought that it was horrible to go back over twenty hours a week. But the struggles and opportunities that were presenting themselves to me just catapulted me way out of what I thought

I'd ever be doing. I'd always thought I'd be a stay-at-home mom, but now I'm a supervisor."

Several stay-at-home mothers mentioned returning to work to specifically cover tuition costs for private schools or college. Catie returned to work as an assistant director of Admissions at a local college in Connecticut to do just that, to obtain college tuition benefits for her two children.

When women are looking for benefits, they usually want healthcare benefits. Several women explained that their husbands provide a good income, but for various reasons, they don't receive benefits. So these women started seeking out jobs where they would receive a good benefits package.

Suzy explains, "We were covered. My husband went into private law practice. We had obtained health insurance through the Florida Bar Association. It was okay until we had to use it; then it was really expensive. My daughter had a seizure a year and a half ago. That's when we had to use the insurance. We got this huge bill from the emergency room."

When Suzy and her husband realized that the healthcare plan wasn't working, they decided to obtain coverage under an umbrella of somebody else. She found work that provides her with the healthcare coverage she needs at Fresh Market, a specialty food store chain. "I went to work to earn a little bit of money and pay for health insurance that's less than our previous plan. We are covered so much better. Now I don't have to worry about having to go to the doctor. That's the last thing you need to be thinking about when you need to make a split-second decision whether you're going to the emergency room or not. If I had that old insurance, I hate to say it, it would cross my mind. It would scare me to death even more. Now it's not even a concern. Break an arm, it's okay, I'm safe. I don't have to worry about putting us into financial problems.

"It's insane for me to ever think about paying for benefits out of my own pocket. I'll always have a job for benefits. I honestly believe that, because it's so much cheaper to get it through a company."

AND THE REWARDS ARE . . .

So is the payoff what everyone expects? Is part-time work as good as it appears? Does it resolve work-life balance issues? As with all things, it's not perfect, but *two-thirds*, I repeat, *two-thirds* of the women interviewed "love it" or claim it is better than full-time employment. That's amazing. I can't imagine getting two-thirds of full-time employees claiming that they "love" their jobs. Part-time employment is truly a wonderful blend of home and work for women.

The majority of women describe themselves as being "110 percent satisfied, thrilled." And many state, "There's no comparison to full-time." It is portrayed simply as being the "best of both worlds" by many mothers.

Why do they feel so great about their current positions? Primarily, it is because the majority of them acted out of choice. This means they feel refreshed instead of tired on an ongoing basis. They maintain a sense of self-esteem from their jobs, and they have time for their children and husbands.

Of the third of women who don't view part-time employment as better than full-time, half feel it is at least equivalent to full-time work.

110 Percent Satisfaction

Many women who are very satisfied with part-time work set their own hours and run their own show. Carol, a real estate agent from Oregon, is a good example. She says, "Emotionally, it's high. Intellectually, it's high. It's as challenging as you want it to be. I'm happier than when I was doing full-time work because I know that everything I do is a direct result of my own actions instead of relying on other people's actions."

As a therapist running a private practice, Bonnie states, "I'm much more satisfied with the schedule I have now because I have ultimate control. When I was in the salaried positions, I was much more bound to other people's schedules. It was much more stressful, trying to get the kids off to school, myself off to work. I'm fortunate not to have to do that anymore. It's a luxury to make my schedule that way. I like it. I have friends who don't have a choice."

But you don't have to be managing your own business to be extremely satisfied. Carolyn is in sales at a birdseed store. To the question, "How satisfied are you?" she replies, "Very, more satisfied than full-time. When it comes down to it, I love the self-satisfaction that I get from the job. It's not rocket science, but I get a good feeling unlike all the years I worked full-time. I was the support person for three high-wheeling-and-dealing stock brokers who had huge egos. I was going home every day exhausted, upset, angry, and frustrated and waking up exhausted, frustrated, and angry. Now when I walk out of the store, I lock the door and that's the end of it. I know that I've done a good job."

Kara, a dental hygienist, claims, "Love it, much better than full-time. In my situation, I do the majority of everything at home: raising children, taking care of home maintenance, paying bills. I'm allowed to stay in my career and do the mom thing and the house thing—wear all the hats that I wear."

"It leaves time for the other part of me," says Leticia. "It leaves time for a real life. My husband never went out into the community. As a full partnership, I'm the one giving back. He makes the money so I can give back to the community. Part-time work allows for that." She has worked several different part-time jobs ranging from a sales support job to a cor-relation coordinator for a textbook publishing company.

For others, the ability to avoid being overworked while running the household makes part-time employment truly enjoyable.

"I love working three days a week. When I was working full-time, I knew I was getting burned out. There were so many times when I was working five days a week that I was, 'Uh, I just wish I had a day or two off during this week [so I'm] not always . . . working so hard.' I definitely say that I'm happier now than when I was full-time," claims Linda, an optometrist.

Janette, initially a part-time human resources consultant and then a decorator, says, "I loved it compared to full-time. Part-time gave me more energy for my family. It was the first time that I could decide on a Friday, not on a Saturday, whether to take my kids to an art museum. I felt more fulfilled as a mom."

"Very satisfied. I'm considering going more part-time down to three days a week from four. I have a supportive spouse who covers for me. He's encouraged me to make the decision that I'm happiest with. Our family income is not totally dependent on my income so that takes the burden off to free me up to do more, to get involved with sports or lessons my children have. Ultimately, it's a family decision. But when the age is appropriate, I'll go down to three days, always continuing to work because that's an integral part of my personality," says Noel.

"I love it. It's hard though, as I'm back up to twenty-four hours a week from ten hours. My husband has his own business, and I added the hours to earn more money," expresses Faye, a nurse from Chicago.

Equal to Full-Time

For some women, like Gabi, the part-time job has its ups and downs much the same as a full-time job would. As a technical project officer for the EPA, Gabi says, "I like it. I have been doing this for thirty years, so there are real highlight days and then days that I want to go sit by the pool and eat bonbons all day. No two days are the same. I have the ability to self-direct. This is a good, challenging part-time job. I get to go out to the schools and do 'meet and greets' with the college students at various universities."

Less Satisfying

Part-time work satisfaction was lower than full-time for a few women. Interestingly, women's answers concerning the worst aspects of working part-time were fragmented. The least favorable aspects of reduced hours are much more splintered, personal, and less easily categorized, with some women having no complaints at all. Their reasons related to the amount of money they bring in, the low level of work versus their skill level, or the fact that the job still doesn't leave enough time for their families.

The least desirable factor is—you guessed it—an aspect of the job. Yet this was only mentioned by a third of the women. A full 10 percent of the interviewees could not come up with anything that they did not like about part-time employment. Nothing. That shows the satisfaction that women have with reduced hours.

For most, the answers came slowly because they had recognized the trade-offs part-time employment requires prior to making the commitment, and have made their choices. They are happy with their decisions and don't dwell on the trade-offs any longer. In fact, the trade-offs are so worth it to them that the downsides are not in the forefront of their thoughts.

"It really boils down to, if you're looking for a part-time job, you're probably going to be giving up some control, some job satisfaction," claims Sandy. "You're making a choice not to get the best opportunity and the most challenging work. Life is all trade-offs. You must be willing to pay that price, if you're going to do it, or you shouldn't do it. Because if you do it without being prepared to pay the price and then try to undo it, you will have shot your wad, and you'll be punished for it, whatever company you're working for."

"There's the myth, we can do it all," agrees Judy. "We can't do it all at the same time. You must make choices. Is it your ego getting in the way? For me it was."

"It's important to talk to people who have done it and who are doing it," claims Paula. "Women need to reach out. It can be isolating. You can feel like you're not fulfilling your dream. It's good to get reassurance that it's okay to do part-time work."

As with any job, whether full-time or not, there is usually some aspect that you don't like. And for one-third of the women interviewed, it was an aspect of the job itself that was mentioned as the "worst thing about working part-time," *not anything regarding the downfalls of part-time versus full-time work.*

Another aspect of a part-time job that may frustrate women is lack of advancement. A few women interviewed are frustrated by their lack of title or promotion. Losing a big title to move into part-time work is hard.

Staying in place while those you train continue to advance is difficult. Being a solid performer, given excellent reviews, and not receiving a promotion after twelve years is de-motivating. Despite this, the women that mentioned it remain working part-time because balancing their home lives is worth the trade-off to them.

Joan feels she missed opportunities from a career perspective. "Although, on one hand, I want to be a mother first, you compromise your professionalism when you're part-time, even if you have big responsibilities at your job. Your first priority is not your job, and everyone knows that, so it colors everything. I don't like that. I don't know if there's anything you can do about that. It is what it is. You're not taken seriously, not a player. I like to be a player. I like to be in on the decisions. You can't do that if you're only there three or five hours a day. It's frustrating. Over the years, people who I trained are now presidents of banks all across Oklahoma City. I see it in the papers. I find that frustrating. It's a choice I made, yet it's still frustrating to me. Like you want your cake and eat it, too. It's not reasonable. You just deal with it."

Despite being employed part-time, approximately 20 percent of the women still feel that they aren't doing both the job of "mother" and the job of "career woman" well. They feel like they "can't get everything done that they need to get done" and that "something always slides," causing them to compromise on both sides. While a full 80 percent are thrilled with the blend of work and family, a minority still can't find that sense of balance.

"Not feeling like I can give 100 percent to anything," says Karen, an artist and yoga teacher. "Home, teaching, the art—I feel like everyone gets gipped. But when I'm doing what I'm doing, I'm very present. But once I'm done, I've got to scoot."

Laura agrees. "I've always been the room mom for [my son's] class. I feel like when you're part-time employed you are part-time everything. People expect that I have plenty of time because I only work part-time. Whereas with full-time employed moms, you really can't expect anything from them because they're at work all day. Sometimes I think I'm being pulled in so many directions because I work part-time. I'm part-time homeroom mom; I'm part-time mom. I don't get 'credit' for working part-time. I struggle with that all the time."

And Rosemary, a political campaign consultant, feels similarly. "With part-time work, you trick yourself into believing you're going to have more time. And so you probably take on more than you would if you were working full-time. In the last year, I was chairman of my children's school board, which in itself could have been a full-time job. If I had been working full-time, I'd never have agreed to that. But working part-time, I had faked myself into believing that, 'Sure, I can do this' or 'I can teach Sunday school' or whatever. You tend to take on more than you really should because of the word *part-time*. You have to be aware that part-time doesn't necessarily mean having more time than you would have had if you were working full-time. You have to caution women looking at part-time positions for it to be rewarding and fulfilling, and for you to have more time you have to be willing to set limits on yourself. You have to be willing to say, 'No.'"

Ten percent of the women interviewed mentioned being the "odd duck" at the office, feeling a lack of team purpose, and having the stigma of the part-timer taped to their foreheads. It causes them to feel "out of the loop" and puts the burden on them for being updated on current issues and sometimes even training.

"I'm definitely the odd man out. I think it's probably jealousy, and that I understand," says Molly, a physical therapist. "They are not all able to work part-time. They have kids the same age I do, and their kids have to go home all by themselves. They're not very friendly, but you can't blame them either."

Effect on Family

For the most part, women are pleasantly surprised and often thrilled with the effect part-time employment has on their families. This is good news because the biggest concern of stay-at-home moms returning to work is the effect it will have on their children. Part-time working mothers see their children becoming more responsible, more courteous, better organized, and even proud of their mother's efforts. Additionally, several interviewees see themselves as positive role models for their kids.

Initially, a few women had to wrestle with conflicts between themselves and their husbands regarding part-time employment. Some spouses didn't want them to return to work at all. For others, sorting out roles of who would do what, when, and how became an issue. But after a few months or so, these issues faded away.

For Karen, the issue surrounded her husband endorsing her going back to work. "My husband was not supportive of my yoga certification; he thought that I was too busy already. I did it anyway, paying for the $200 class. The program cost $200 and ran in a short amount of time [for me] to obtain the national certification. He didn't want me to teach yoga; he wanted me in the home. It was the first time that I said, 'Too bad, I'm doing it.' He said, 'Do the yoga, don't teach the class.' But now, my husband has learned to accept it. My work is a world that he's not part of; it requires different parts of me that he doesn't see. So it's understandable resistance because he's not part of that world. More recently he has been supportive of it, and the momentum is coming around to it."

"If you're in a relationship or a partnership of some sort, you need to discuss how part-time work fits in your life as a couple, as a family," says Leah regarding her work as a reference librarian. "It was difficult for me to go from full-time to part-time without feeling less of a person until I communicated with my husband about that. We worked out the details about the housework, the expectations, the kids. It's really important to know the expectations of your spouse. Generally, men are defined by their work, job, and paycheck. That's how they think, particularly my husband who grew up with a full-time working mother. That was his expectation."

But for Julie, the reaction of her family has been favorable. Her children have been treating her better and more courteously since she started working part-time in the gardening center. "They have treated me so differently. I brought them in the truck showing them, 'This is where Mommy works.'" She showed them the beautiful twenty acres where the trees and shrubs are grown for the nursery where she works.

"Now when they come home from school and I come home from work, they say, 'How was your day, Mom? Did you sell any trees today? Did you sell any bushes?'"

Julie adds that she used to tell her kids to make their beds. Since she is a type A personality, if they didn't do it right, she'd go back and remake them. "Now I'm saying, 'You guys have to help out. I'm going to show you how to run the washing machine. I'm showing you how to work the dryer.' I don't know if I would have done that if I didn't go back to work. It's really pushed them to having to plan their schedule. I tell them, they can't tell me, 'Oh, Mom, I need this for a project, it's due tomorrow.' You've got to tell me a week in advance. Because now I've got to try and get it on my way home from work or get it on my day off. You can't do that to me the night before. So it's caused the whole family to be organized. Everybody's got to do their part. Now they pick the dishes off the table. Last night I was dog tired. They said, 'Okay, we'll load the dishwasher, Mommy.' I don't think they would have done that if I hadn't started making them."

One of Nancy's biggest surprises with her part-time jewelry business is also the effect it has had on her children. "I'm amazed at what this has taught my children. I have a fourteen-year-old who owns his own business. He actually purchased several thousand dollars' worth of equipment. He has college kids that work for him. He owns a DJ business. He files his own taxes and keeps his own books. I know that he watched me do it. He knew he could do it. My oldest son has landed incredible things in his short lifetime. They both have an 'I can do this' attitude."

And for Sylvia, being a role model for her children is the biggest impact on her family. "To demonstrate to your children that it is important to work and make a contribution and to volunteer and give something to your community. While I do bring in income, it's not the primary factor for doing it. It allows you to be a role model for your kids, especially your girls that you can be self-sufficient. For me, it's security. I know that if something happens to my husband, I could kick it into full gear and we'd be fine financially. It's almost like a little insurance policy."

FINDING BALANCE

I can't summarize how the majority of women feel about part-time employment any better than Cheryl, a marketing director from the New York suburbs. "I love it. I love the essence of where I feel I am right now, a grasp on a very elusive thing, which is balance. I spend enough time at work and enough time at home that I enjoy both and I don't dislike either. I'm not at home so much that I'm 'What am I doing here? I'm not contributing.' But I'm not at work so much so that I'm feeling like I don't get to see my children, that I never get anything done, and I'm all harried. I can still do PTO stuff, go to things at my kids' school, and go to all their practices."

As with all things, part-time work is not perfect, but as I said in the beginning of this chapter, *two-thirds* of the women interviewed "love it" or claim it is better than full-time employment. Since so many women like it, let's see if part-time employment is for you and how you can find that part-time job.

Chapter 2

MAKING THE LEAP

"Don't let irrational fears or thoughts hold you back from pursuing a new path."
—Bradley G. Richardson, *Career Comeback*[1]

So you've decided to go for it. You're thinking that part-time work is worth pursuing. Based on others' experience, it's probably a good decision. About half the women interviewed felt happy or excited about their decision to work part-time *prior* to obtaining the job. After starting the job, *70 percent* described their emotions regarding the job as gratifying, empowering, and fulfilling. The work-life balance is as satisfying, if not more so, than anticipated.

But where do you start? Who do you contact? How do you make the leap to get the job you really want? That's what the remainder of this book is all about, finding the right part-time job for you.

The first step is to evaluate what you're looking for in a job, what your objectives are. For part-time work, these objectives may be very different than they are for full-time employment. Next you need to assess your skill sets, some of which are obvious, others are not. Then see what's out there. By valuing yourself and taking the time to size up the various possibilities, you'll end up with work that's right for you.

How long will this take? This was a fast process, under three months, for about a third of the women I interviewed. It was even a quicker decision for those who were pregnant or had an infant at the time. The exploration, preparation, interviewing, and decision-making process took about three months to a year for roughly 40 percent. The rest took a year to three years to get everything aligned in order to be comfortable with working part-time. The point is that there's no set timetable, no right or wrong way to begin. Giving yourself the time to investigate what's out there and weighing the various trade-offs will ensure that you pick the right option for you.

KNOW YOUR OBJECTIVES

"Being patient and proactive is the way to find the right opportunity for you. You have to have an idea where you want to go and the hours you want to work and generally what you want. It won't fall out of the sky," says Rita, a human resources part-timer.

To be most efficient with your time, you must determine your objectives. From a self-interest standpoint, why are you pursuing employment? To maintain a position that you've worked hard to attain? To pay a portion of the bills? To have a sense of self beyond being "mom"? To obtain health benefits for the family? To keep your skills updated, enabling you to revert back to full-time work down the road? Or to simply just get out of the house and be with adults?

Regarding hours, what hours are you looking for? Can you work only during school hours? Do you want to work evenings and weekends when it's easier to find family members to watch the kids? How flexible are you? How many hours a week do you want to work? Setting parameters around hours is key for part-time employment.

As far as income goes, is there a minimum you must make? How much do you need to earn beyond childcare costs? Are health benefits more important to you than income? Or on the flip side, are health benefits irrelevant to you because you're covered by your husband?

You need to focus on what you really want. The hours? The income? The sense of learning something new? The social interaction? The glamour of getting out of sweats and leaving the house? Pinpointing objectives will help steer you in the right direction.

Outline Your Personal Goals

"Anybody who's going to work part-time must first decide what needs it's going to fill in your life, whether it's monetary or whether it's just to get you out of the house or using your brain. Then find what fits that. Don't just take anything," recommends Sherry, an accountant. "Find something that fits because it's a struggle to balance your life with part-time work, because you're not really at home 100 percent, not really at work 100 percent. It's such a juggling act. I feel it's just not worth it unless you're really filling a need. Whether you really need the income or you really need the intellectual stimulation, make a list and really find out what fits those needs. Make sure that what you're getting out of it is worth what you're giving up to do it."

Susan concurs. "Talk about what you want and how you're going to contribute, what you need to reserve for yourself and your family so that you can be clear about what works best. Moms need to be healthy for the world to be healthy. Each mom has to figure out what keeps her healthy so that she can be the giver that women always are in our families and societies, all over the world. It's important for women to figure out what feeds them in many directions so that they can stay balanced."

"If you're going to work part-time, you have reasons why you're working part-time. Make sure that you fulfill that role. Otherwise you'll begrudge the work because you're not making as much money as you would full-time. Be persistent. Find an area that you really enjoy and then tap into that. Find that role and make it work. You need to have the balance and satisfaction," adds Doreen.

Rosemary took time to determine how she would step out of her chief of staff full-time position for a state governor into the world of part-timers. She thought about what would work best for herself and her family. "I made the decision to not return to the governor's office when I was six months pregnant with my second child. I decided, 'I'll pursue part-time work, and it probably will be the governor's reelection campaign.' Given the work I was in, that's what the next step would be."

She has worked as a political consultant for about five years since that decision. "Campaigns have a shelf life. There's a start date and an end date. In that sense, I've been able to find opportunities frequently. The downside to that is it's an extremely intense business. And I often think that people who can work from home or telecommute or have work that stays consistent from day to day, those people have an advantage over me because the type of work I do starts at a level and over time builds in intensity. For example, in the last three weeks I haven't been home with my children. I was on the road; I was in a headquarters; I was working really late. My husband had to be the mom for a really intense three-week period. So I don't have a lot of balance in this type of part-time work."

Despite that, Rosemary continues with her work. She comes off a campaign, decompresses, reengages with her children, and then goes back in when the right opportunity comes along. And since she stays in contact with her connections, the opportunities keep coming, making this a winning strategy for her. Rosemary asked herself a few questions before deciding how she would pursue part-time work. These questions helped her to develop a position that suited herself and her family

- Questions Rosemary asked herself:
   ° Am I working so that I can keep my skills updated, giving myself the ability to return to my career full-time in the future?
   ° Am I looking to utilize my skills/education/training for self-fulfillment and satisfaction?

For Jesse, a part-time worker for fourteen years, determining her objectives wasn't straightforward. "In my life I needed all the components. First, I was married and working. That wasn't enough, so I had children. Then I was married with children and not working. I still felt that something was lacking. So I needed to work again. I like the triangle of all three: marriage, work, and children. It's part of who I am."

Deciding what was best for Jesse wasn't easy. She had previously held the title of vice president of Sales in a hospital information systems company. She was at a crossroads. Should she go back to her previous area of employment with all the daily stresses of a high-level job? If she didn't, what kind of job did she want? To help her determine the best job for her, she talked it through with a friend who worked in human resources. "I discussed it with a good friend of mine on my morning walks. She helped to clarify for me that I wasn't looking for a high-level part-time job. We worked it through that I was looking for flexibility. Once I put that in perspective, it allowed me to hone in on what I needed. I stopped looking for part-time work from my past career. Now I looked at what are the hours, what is the flexibility?"

- Questions Jesse asked herself:
  ° How much flexibility do I need?
  ° Am I looking for work that is different from my previous career?
  ° What level of responsibility do I desire?

Lorrie, working part-time in human resources and then as an interior designer, realizes that maximizing her earning potential is not her goal. "People need to know themselves. What is your first priority? You always need to be sure of what that priority is. I struggle with 'If we only made a little bit more money, we could do this or we could have a bigger house. But wait a minute, that's not going to make my kids any happier.'"

According to Carolyn, "A need arose quickly within my husband's and my financial situation. I couldn't sit and not be a contributor. He didn't ask me, but I knew I wasn't going to put all the burden on him." Her goal was clearly to earn income.

- Questions Lorrie/Carolyn asked themselves:
  ° Am I working for income?
  ° How much do I need to earn?

Robin, armed with her master's degree and a few years of experience, didn't want to lose everything she had been working to attain as a survey research and statistics analyst. "Being a stay-at-home mom didn't look attractive to me, and the full-time thing didn't look attractive, so part-time was exactly what I wanted, and I was very pleased with it," she says.

- Question Robin asked herself:
  ° How can I hold onto my current career?

Virginia initially entered part-time work as a commercial litigator. "It was pressure and stress because it's all battles. I came home and I was stressed. I had three children under the age of four. That was enough battles for me. As a mom, you're in the resolution phase; you solve problems. But in litigation, they don't want to solve the problems because they're billing hours. It was total frustration and stress.

"Let me go further and share my experience quite a few years ago when the kids were in preschool and I was first returning to litigation law and the firm. I thought I could be home with the kids most of the time, working just Tuesday and Thursday afternoons. I was so positive, confident, and upbeat. Little did I know. My sense of accomplishment plummeted one particular day when I caught myself on the phone demanding immediate settlement. I was due to be home in thirty minutes and knew the sitter would be tapping her toes if I was late. I had no patience or time for the other party's delay tactics. I started asking myself if this was what I wanted to do, monitor these fights. I had enough of that already at home with the three kids. After several months, I gave up. I realized my litigation work with corporations was very much like my toddlers arguing at home with one exception. At work, I had no way of stopping the abysmal behavior of the opposing attorney when what he needed was a time-out." Obviously, Virginia's experience with part-time work was negative, and she quit.

Then more recently, the editor of the city's newspaper coached her child's baseball team and was starting to develop a mom website as part of a Gannett national program. Since she got to know him via the baseball team, she was willing to serve on his start-up committee for the website. The editor made the part-time contract work very appealing to Virginia. "We tested the waters, and then I started writing and realized I could write. I just write the way I speak. I'm connected. My gift is I'm a newspaper junky, and moms call me anyway. They always call me and ask, 'What do I do for this? Who do I call for that? Have you heard about this?' I say, 'You need to call so and so. Yeah, check this out. And no, I didn't hear very good things about it.' That's exactly what the mom website is. So he was looking for a mom who was already connected. I was getting paid for what I was doing already anyway. I can make a lot more money practicing law, but please don't make me."

Now she works part-time and loves it. She writes online and cohosts articles for her local newspaper. The website is a center for discussion and help for mothers in her town. She blogs twice a week and monitors the website forums, earning pay for about twenty hours a week. She loves this work, saying, "The kids love it. It gives them something tangible to be proud of for me, not just the laundry lady, the carpooler, all that. I can't believe they'll pay me to do this because I do this anyway." Her view changed dramatically based on the type of work she was pursuing, the hours she was working, and the flexibility that she had with those hours.

- Questions Virginia asked herself:
  - Am I seeking adult interaction and intellectual stimulation?
  - Do I want to work from home or in an office?

Look at the pros and cons of what works best for you. Know who you are; know your personality. Give yourself time to absorb the difference part-time employment will make in your life. Then organize and prioritize your thoughts. What is *most* important to you? Prioritize what you really, really want and go after it. Ask yourself the following questions to help you determine your needs. By answering these, you will start to outline your job requirements:

- Am I working for income? If so, is there a minimum amount I need to earn?
- Am I working to hold onto my current career?
- Am I working so that I can keep my skills updated, giving myself the ability to return to my career full-time in the future?
- Am I looking at work that is different from my previous career?
- Are benefits a necessity or are they irrelevant to me?

- Am I looking to utilize my skills/education/training for self-fulfill-ment and satisfaction?
- What level of responsibility do I desire?
- Am I seeking adult interaction and intellectual stimulation? Does that need to be in person or can it be over the phone or via the Internet?
- Do I want to work from home or only in an office (see chapter 7)?
- Is job sharing for me (see chapter 3)?

The Hours/Flexibility

Hours and flexibility: it's all about the hours of the week and the flex-ibility with those hours. While you don't have to pinpoint exactly how many hours per week you require, it's good to have a general idea of the number of hours you're willing to work. Knowing when you want to work those hours is also helpful. Considering the type of work you do, some structures regarding hours may be better than others.

For example, Elizabeth chose to work five mornings a week as a marketing consultant for Johnson & Johnson. She arrived at their office each morning at 8:00 a.m. and left at 1:00 p.m. This worked well for her on several levels. First, she was in the office every day. If someone was looking for her to ask her questions or hand her a project in the after-noon, he or she knew that she would be back in the office first thing in the morning. No one would have to wait from Thursday afternoon to Tuesday morning to talk to her. This boosted her self-confidence regarding her level of professionalism and was well accepted by the company. Second, her two daughters had the same schedule Monday through Friday. They knew that mommy was always home in the after-noons. This also helped her to find consistent daycare for her children. Flexibility wasn't an issue for her.

As an attorney, Sandy also chose this schedule. "If you're at all depen-dent upon other people to generate your workload, what happens when you're not there predictably enough? They just don't come by your door anymore. If they physically walk by your empty office when they need work to be done and they think you'll be there and you're not, then you are working yourself out of a job. This is a practical matter. And it's one of those reasons why, as much as I'd love to take Fridays off, or Mondays and Fridays off, I don't. It's egocentric to think that your company is going to keep track of which days you work and which hours you work. It shouldn't be your coworkers' responsibility. So if you are going to limit your day, I think it's better, but not nearly as much fun, to work every day because you're much more likely to have a successful part-time arrangement.

"But if you're not, I'd recommend to post your hours on your door or on your desk so that they're easily recognizable by everyone, so that they don't think that you just didn't show up for work. Because if you modify a full-time job to a part-time job, that's already planted in their minds. You're not really committed anymore, so are you going to show up to work? Even if you're meeting exactly what you promised to do, exactly your hours, it's going to be an assumption in the back of everybody's mind. It's just funny because I've talked to enough women who want to work part-time or tried to work part-time who said, 'Nobody understands me.' It's business.

"We entered my child in a private school this year, and most of the mothers stay home. My child didn't know any of the other kids. So I was really working hard to get him integrated with the other kids and get him comfortable there. I was complaining one day that I had to take time off of work to make a playdate. I had to be gone for the afternoon in order to do that. My husband said to me, 'That's not fair. Those mothers should accommodate you. They should know that you're a working person, so they should plan things that are after your workday or on weekends.' I said, 'The world just doesn't work like that.'

"And the same is true of the employer; you can't expect your employer to accommodate you. You have to design a job to be workable and as easy as possible for them. That's what's going to make it successful for you. Coworkers hate, 'Oh God, which day is it she works?' They hate that. Knowing that you'll be there tomorrow is good."

Cheryl, on the other hand, negotiated working three days a week. She worked with her employer to develop a three-day-week schedule.

She's been there four and a half years with an increase in her responsibilities over time. Initially she worked alone, but now she has three employees working for her as a part-time marketing director.

Clearly, these hours have been successful for both her and the company. But it hasn't happened by chance. Cheryl has made a concerted effort to make her hours clear to everyone. She says, "You have to teach the people you work with what your boundaries are and what's acceptable and what's not. If you do it in a nice way, then they understand. My voicemail says, 'You've reached Cheryl; if you've reached this message on a Wednesday or Friday, I'm not in the office. I'm not checking voicemail, and I will return your call when I return to the office. If this matter is urgent, please contact blah, blah at blah, blah.' It's very clear, if you're leaving a message here, I'm not touching it until I return."

For Missy, it was all about her working while her kids were in school and, more importantly, being home when they were. She held a job as a reading specialist in the schools, keeping the same hours as her children. "It was the right fit in public schools. Since we have Wednesdays off early in public schools, my hours match my children's. I didn't want the job to impact the kids. I still wanted to drive the carpools. That's why it works for me. There are probably jobs more challenging, but one of my important goals is to not impact my family."

Leanne loves her work, partly because it is on her own terms. She picks the hours; she picks the days. As an Arbonne sales consultant, Leanne works at other women's homes as well as her own. "I don't know if I would have been as excited if someone said to me, 'You can work twenty hours a week, but you need to come into this office. I'm going to tell you the twenty hours you're going to work.' I like that I'm working some from my house. I like that I can determine my own hours and that I can make it as big or as little as I want to."

When Kim was seeking a part-time opportunity as an appellate lawyer, she was asked if she wanted to work 50 percent of the time, 75 percent of the time, or full-time. She says, "There was a goal of briefs per month that was based on the caseload. I chose 75 percent based on that. Is it something that I can get done? You have to be careful because 75 percent of the time can end up being full-time. Part-time attorneys who should be working thirty-five hours per week are working a lot more. I hear of women signing up for fifteen to twenty hours per week at a law firm. The cases are more demanding, so they work much more. My position turned out really well. The goals they set are reasonable and doable. I can say that there are times when there is a deadline and I do extra time. But in the end it evens out because there are the times I need to pick up a kid from school or a kid is sick. I have that flexibility. I also have the flexibility to stay at home if I need to work from home."

Several women reported being asked to work more and more hours. Know what hours you are willing to work and stick to them. This happened to Kara, a dental hygienist. "The biggest thing is don't overextend yourself. If you're going to do part-time, make sure your employer knows you want so many hours and you're not willing to take on more. One of the things that happens is they keep wanting more, especially if you're a good employee. They want you there 24/7. You have to learn to say no to that. If you have a set number of hours you're willing to work, stick to it and don't let them talk you into any more."

Some jobs have fluctuating hours and are more intense at certain points in time, like Rosemary's as a political consultant. Several women mentioned this as happening particularly at the beginning of their jobs. This should be kept in mind when pursuing various jobs, particularly if you are setting up your own business.

For Monica, her job as executive director was overwhelming because she wanted to improve the way Maple Chamber Chorus was run immediately. "That first summer, it was like a sixty-hour-per-week job for three months. I was trying to improve every aspect exponentially of the organization. As the years have gone on, I have spaced out things instead of securing venues and writing contracts all in the early summer. My season is all set up by February now. As you work, you learn what to do in advance; you have more things set up. I was trying to reinvent the wheel for everything that fit into the summer."

Margo's job was also overwhelming at the beginning. She was setting up her own business as an English tutor. "It was overwhelming because I was keeping track of where each kid was—one would be in reading comprehension, someone else in sentence completion—keeping track of where every kid was and who owed me money and who had paid for the next ten sessions in advance; it was brand new to me. I had to put systems in place, and my hall at home was a mess. I had SAT books on one chair, college stuff on another. I made business cards and had to photocopy the curriculum as well. I was still teaching a college essay class through the high school, so that was a couple of nights a week that I was out. It was a little overwhelming that first year. I had a dog walker because I never got home in time to walk the dog. Getting organized for a new type of life, new kinds of work took a little bit of adjustment."

No matter what hours you settle on, be sure to build face time into them. Yes, even part-timers need to maintain some sort of visible presence in the organization to receive recognition for their work and to stay up-to-date on their firms' and industries' ever-changing marketplace. You can remain visible by attending key meetings, partaking in organizational activities, and communicating your in-and-out-of-the-office schedule. With employees of organizations scattered around the country, and globe for that matter, simply participating in conference calls from home may give you all the presence you need to remain visible in some companies. Others may demand your physical presence on a regular basis. Learn what's best for your industry of choice and build it into your anticipated working hours.

Obviously, hours and flexibility are an important factor in a part-time position. Consider the following questions to further outline the job you want.

- How many hours a week do you want to work: ten, twenty, thirty?
- Do you want to work half days, partial days, or full days?
- Do you want specifically set hours?
- Do you want total flexibility?
- Are you only available during specific times of the week?
- Can you accommodate a learning curve that entails more hours at the beginning of the job?

- Are you able to work for intense periods of time followed by a lighter load?

Once you've honed in on the hours and flexibility that you desire, it's time to determine if benefits are crucial to you.

Benefits

Do you need benefits? Maybe you're seeking employment *solely* for the benefits. Several women I interviewed did just that, sought employment *only* for the benefits. You *can* be employed part-time and receive benefits. Employers may offer healthcare options including medical and dental, 401(k) plans, and paid vacation time for part-timers.

Generally speaking, to receive benefits you must work an average of twenty hours a week or more in a regularly scheduled, year-round position. Usually the benefits are prorated, based on the number of hours that you work. Many times benefits are set at a fixed rate per person. Human resources may be able to help you with this. There is usually a set amount of time that you must work before you become eligible for benefits, usually sixty to ninety days, but this range varies by company. Employee benefits often increase as the firm size increases. This makes sense as the cost per person covered goes down (to a degree) as the base number of people covered goes up.

That's why corporations such as Costco and Trader Joe's can offer part-time benefits. They are large with thousands of employees. Other national corporations that offer part-time benefits include IKEA, Starbucks, Whole Foods Market, REI, Lowe's, Land's End, and Nike. Corporations that are retailers may also give merchandise discounts.

I found browsing the Web that many government positions also offer benefits to part-timers. Municipal governments such as Boise, Idaho, and Los Angeles provide benefits to those working under forty hours per week at the time of writing this book.[2] I also interviewed several women, who worked for local municipalities, who were happy with their medical coverage. Sections of the US government also extend benefits to part-time employees. The US Office of Personnel Management is one example of this.

Colleges and universities are another area to explore for benefits. The University of Illinois, Nashville State Community College, and the University of Texas all extend benefits to part-time employees. Some even offer tuition discounts for your children, depending on your job.[3]

You may remember that I discussed Suzy's situation earlier in the book. While her family had health insurance coverage through the local bar association, it was horrendously expensive when they had to use it. So Suzy and her husband decided that the best thing to do was to get under someone else's umbrella by having her obtain part-time employment that offered benefits. She says, "I went online starting to look for jobs with part-time benefits. I kept looking for places where I could work opposite my husband's schedule. The only thing I could find was retail, which I swore I would never go back into. But we didn't want to put our kids in daycare. We had to be able to flip-flop each other. He'd come home and I'd go to work. At first, I thought I'd go wait tables to make the money, the difference in the insurance. But then I found the Fresh Market, an upscale grocery store. I had been a deli manager for several years. I know the business. I didn't know that Fresh Market was good. I knew they had a part-time benefits plan. I thought, 'Okay, I'll check it out and see what it is. I'll get the job, and if it's no good I'll keep looking.' They have it on their website. I filled out an application online. They didn't call me for a week, and I thought, 'Why not?' So I called them. He said, 'Oh, you put too much money on here.' I said, 'How about I just come in and we talk?' He said, 'Sure.' I accepted such low pay. I make no money. I told him, 'You need me as much as I need you. I will be that employee for you; I'll always be here. You know I need the thirty hours per week.'"

When Suzy was looking, she didn't realize that Starbucks offered part-time benefits starting at twenty hours per week. Her current position requires thirty hours of work per week. Since she didn't want to go back to work, that extra ten hours means a lot to her. "I'm looking for a job at Starbucks right now. It's a really bad time to get a job at Starbucks. The college kids are going back. I heard about Starbucks because my brother's girlfriend's brother worked for them throughout college, and they've been very flexible about moving him from this store to that store wherever he lived. It was convenient. They had benefits. He maintained that he didn't get his benefits from his parents, but through Starbucks."

Income

How much pay should you expect? What's fair and unfair? That's a hard question as all jobs vary regionally and with level of experience. Even people working a forty-hour workweek have a tough time determining if they are being paid equally to their peers.

Initially, you can scan the Internet to give you a ballpark idea of where you stand regarding income. Search for "pay scale ___ (fill in your specialty)" on the Internet. Various sites will appear. Use those which seem most reputable to you. Using www.GlassDoor.com, a salary review and employee review website, may be helpful. Salaries are listed by job type and positions at many companies. The Department of Labor statistics may also be helpful. Income quoted is for full-time work, so you need to prorate salaries according to the number of hours you plan to work. Some sites are more accurate than others, so it's good to double check your facts by then asking others in your field about pay expectations. You can also question professional associations (see next section) in your field for advice on pay scales based on level of experience.

The federal government lists pay scales for federal jobs by grade and step level on the Internet at www.fedjobs.com/pay/pay.html. It also lists pay percentage adjustments by geographic location. This is a useful website for those interested in government work. Make sure that you take the emotion out of your conversation. Remember you're asking for fair compensation for your work as a capable, smart employee.

When Gina began her part-time contract programming work for the University of Iowa, she did her homework to ensure that she received equitable pay. "So when I went into contracting, I went and looked up my peers throughout the University of Iowa system and aligned myself with them. Most state universities' salaries are public and online. Then I added in benefits as I would no longer be receiving benefits. I presented this formula to those that contracted me, and it was accepted. I feel very strongly that I want to make a good wage, but only if it is a fair wage."

Key Learning—Know Your Objectives

- Outline your personal goals by determining the following:
  - Am I working for income? If so, is there a minimum amount I need to earn?
  - Am I working to hold onto my current career?
  - Am I working so that I can keep my skills updated, giving myself the ability to return to my career full-time in the future?
  - Are benefits a necessity or are they irrelevant to me?
  - Am I looking to utilize my skills/education/training for self-fulfillment and satisfaction?
  - Am I seeking adult interaction and intellectual stimulation? Does the work need to be in person or can it be done over the phone and/or via the Internet?
  - Do I want to work from home (see chapter 7)?
- Determine the hours and flexibility that you desire:
  - How many hours a week do you want to work: ten, twenty, thirty?
  - Do you want to work half days, partial days, or full days?
  - Do you want specifically set hours?
  - Do you want total flexibility?
  - Are you only available during specific times of the week?
  - Can you accommodate a learning curve that entails more hours at the beginning of the job?
  - Are you able to work for intense periods of time followed by a lighter load?
- Do you need benefits?
- Determine the amount of income you can realistically expect to earn.

DO YOU KNOW WHAT YOU KNOW? ANALYZING YOUR SKILLS

When reviewing your skills, the obvious ones appear first. What degree did you earn in college? What were your previous jobs? Additionally, everyone has skills that are undocumented. Throughout my research, I talked with women who found jobs totally unrelated to their résumés. I was amazed by the number of women who pursued second and sometimes third careers, often based on knowledge gained from places other than past education or jobs. They used their life experiences to obtain work.

Janette went from human resources into interior design. Dianne went from being a stay-at-home mom who had previously been an insurance adjuster to becoming an English tutor. Ilene moved from family therapist to stay-at-home mom to becoming an integral part of several adoption agencies. And Celeste evolved from a systems engineer and sales manager to a stay-at-home mom to a craft teacher. Here's how they did it.

"I totally renovated and updated a Greek revival farmhouse built in 1844," says Janette. "We started by replacing the roof. We went room by room. Then we made sure the electricity was up to code. The house itself had three bedrooms. Then there was a detached barn that my husband, one carpenter, and I made into a guest quarters from an empty shell. It had a downstairs living area and two tiny bedrooms with a bathroom upstairs so that when the grandkids came down, when the older kids came down, or when the friends came down, they had a place to go. This was our own project. My friends had been telling me for years, 'What are you doing in human resources? Why aren't you in interior design?' This was because I had such a good eye for detail, antiques, and furniture. So what happened was, the house was so lovely, my friends started coming to me and saying, 'Janette, I want to redo this room. Will you come and choose the furniture for me? Will you come and look at fabrics for me?' When everyone saw this house, my name started to get out there. I ended up with twelve to fifteen clients on the coast. I charged them $65 per hour for my services and ran my design firm out of my home for five years."

As a first generation immigrant, Dianne learned English when she started kindergarten. She lives close to her kids' elementary school, a school with 90 percent Spanish-speaking children. Whenever she drove by the school, she considered helping these Spanish-speaking kids the way her teachers had helped her. Dianne says, "So I thought, every time I passed by, 'Maybe they need someone bilingual, as a teacher's aide or as an assistant. I should go in and find out.' So a lot of time passed because my daughter was little. Then when she started kindergarten, I decided to see if they needed my help at the school. I got ready, I got in my car, and I went to the school. I went directly to the office. I asked the secretary if I could speak to the principal, saying that I wanted to talk to her really quick. She said, 'Oh, she has some time right now.' So I went into the principal's office, and I told her, 'I'm a school mom. I volunteer all the time with the kids. I'm bilingual, and I just thought that you might need someone to help the children who don't speak English.' She said, 'You know, as a matter of fact, I do. The job pays $25 per hour. Do you think that would be okay for you?' And I said, 'Sure.' And that's how I got the job."

Ilene wanted to return to her previous field, family therapy, yet was having a difficult time doing so. She decided to try to volunteer to get her foot in the door. When doing so, government agencies asked her what areas she had experience in other than therapy, as they didn't need any therapists, paid or volunteer, at the time. Telling them she just adopted her baby daughter, they put her in contact with a new adoption agency that could use her help. Her part-time career in adoption took off from there. She has worked anywhere from ten to twenty-five hours per week for the last fifteen years for various adoption agencies. "Use what you know. You may not know what you know," claims Ilene. "Having just adopted a baby is what brought me in. It has been key to my career. For people who have felt that I met their needs, my adoption was certainly part of it. They felt like I understood them."

As a stay-at-home mother, Celeste did lots of crafts with her daughter and her daughter's friends when they came over for playdates. "Since we did cooking, we did sewing, and my crafts were more advanced than most; my friends said that I should do it as a business. So I said that I would try it, and I did. It caught on. I didn't wake up and say that I wanted to go back to work; it just evolved on its own," claims Celeste. She has run a craft class that includes cooking, sewing, as well as high-quality crafts on Friday afternoons for over eight years now.

When asked how she felt about her decision to start up this business, she answered, "A little scared. I asked myself, 'Can I do this? Will I be successful? Will I infringe on others' territory?' But there was no other activity like mine in town, and I thought to myself, 'Oh, I've found a niche.'" And in addition to being fun, it's a profitable venture. "This job makes me appreciate working. I love it more than the serious jobs I had in the past. My husband thinks that it's great. He would like for me to get a space somewhere and do it every day. I think that he wants to retire off of me."

Using life skills and experiences, these women developed and obtained jobs they wanted. But many women go the more obvious route, that of using their education. Like them, Sylvia used her education to obtain her part-time position as an attorney. But unlike most women, Sylvia had just graduated from law school, had no experience in her field of education, had an eighteen-month-old child, and was pregnant. So how'd she do it? How did she obtain a part-time job as a lawyer without any legal experience *and* while being pregnant? She knew what she knew.

"A lot of it wasn't being the new kid out of school. I was someone who had been successful in another profession, an account manager for a technology firm. Because of that, when I was going to become a lawyer, I was in a position where I had a network of people I knew through business, family, and friends," says Sylvia. "I had all these potential clients. I wanted to be able to take advantage of that. In terms of the folks I was going to work for, they thought, 'Here's somebody who's walking in and she's going to bring us clients, not a seasoned attorney, yet she's almost a rainmaker.' That's attractive to any law firm. My contacts were appealing. I always knew they'd be interested in talking to me. Someone figured we were both interested, and it fell into place. I didn't interview with a lot of places. I wanted part-time, and they wanted part-time, and I did it. It was almost an entirely male firm. They weren't progressive at that point. They thought this was a good deal. They could tap into me as a resource."

As would be expected, numerous women use knowledge from their past careers to acquire their part-time positions. All of them did not go directly to what they were doing in the past. Several of them thought outside the box and applied their experiences and knowledge to new areas of work.

Having a specialized skill in social service counseling, Christi knew that she could convert a full-time position into a part-time one. By turning a full-time permanent position into a part-time contracting job, she makes more money on a per-hour basis. A hospital was willing to take her on part-time because it was having a difficult time filling the position. Few people in western Tennessee had the appropriate qualifications for the job. With that knowledge in hand, Christi was able to obtain the hours and pay that she desired.

Rosemary's political consulting job was much the same. "It was a natural progression of something I was already doing. I had a relationship with the boss. I had institutional knowledge of the governor's organization, what we had done over time. So a logical progression for me was to go in that direction. But from there, people approached me. I got calls for people looking for a political consultant, to underwrite a campaign plan."

Starting her own jewelry line and business was not intimidating for Nancy. "I had experience out on the road selling in a more commercial environment. That's where I had the edge when I went in a salon or boutique. I knew when I went in how to make it professional. I knew where to invest. I knew what would overwhelm them, what wouldn't. I knew to stick money in the business cards." Her whole background made it work: her experience in jewelry stores for the product, her experience selling office supplies to aid her in cold calling, and her experience owning a flower shop helped her to file taxes and keep records straight. Using her entire background, she developed and grew her own business, which has been successful for over twenty-one years. You'll hear more about Nancy in chapter 5.

Much like Nancy, Jesse used her past experiences to obtain part-time positions. But Jesse used her background as an entry into new areas of work for her. "My sales experience helped to obtain the jobs. It comes into play in two ways: one, when I'm interviewing, and two, when I was applying for a sales support job, my sales background helped for me to understand what they were doing. My nursing background helped with Jazzercise. You know the body so you can help with aches and pains. I could give queuing to the class in safety."

Broaden your perspective to identify the work you want to pursue. Think about what excites you, brings you pride and satisfaction. Everyone does better at tasks they enjoy versus jobs they dislike. If you're having trouble "thinking out of the box," brainstorm with friends and family. Have a get-together with those who know various aspects of your life and discuss your strengths, your skills, your life experiences. The worst that can happen is that you have some fun, and at best you'll gain some invaluable ideas on new paths to explore.

In analyzing your skills, go through your entire background to capitalize on your best assets. Remember to think broadly. A prior sales job exemplifies that you work well with people. That could lead to customer service work. A prior sales career may have given you insights to your customers, leading to marketing positions. A technology job may have made you extremely comfortable with manipulating data, making you a good candidate for companies that need to develop a mobile app or track behavior through social media. Go beyond the job itself and determine *all* the skills you have.

"Get a niche, identify something you are very good at, know what you specialize in, know what your skill set is or what you have to offer as a part-time employee. That's tricky," Robin summarizes. She returned from out of the country and obtained a part-time job by using the yellow pages to hone in on companies that might need her specialized skill set as a survey research and statistics analyst. "A lot of people feel you don't get work done if you don't work a forty-hour workweek. That's not true. Know your skills, what you can do, and know them very well so that you can sell yourself. If you don't know your specialty, it's hard to convince somebody else."

Key Learning—Analyze Your Skills

- What marketable skills can you draw on from your education?
- What job experiences do you have that are valid and useful today? Remember to think outside the box.
- What life experiences can be useful in obtaining a job?
- Write down all the volunteer work you've done. What skills have you gained from that?
- What excites you?

NETWORKING

Either through friends and family, colleagues from previous jobs, or word of mouth, about 60 percent of women interviewed obtained part-time positions by networking. Some went from being full-time employees to part-time workers while others went from being stay-at-home moms to gaining part-time employment. Receiving recommendations from friends can go a long way toward getting an interview. Having a past colleague speak up in your favor can swing a job in your direction. Learning about a position that hasn't been posted yet from a friend of a friend can give you the edge on getting your résumé in near the beginning of the interview process, potentially shutting down any advertising. Whether you're working or not, networking can help you to obtain that part-time position you're seeking.

Networking is important because 70 to 80 percent of job vacancies are not available to the average job seeker.[4] These positions are not advertised and therefore available only through word of mouth or networking. In order to hear about these unadvertised opportunities, talking to as many people as possible about your job search is key. Katherine Hansen, author of *Foot in the Door*, claims, "Study after study shows that networking is the most effective way to get a job."[5] A recent study done by Career Xroads, using forty-nine firms with over a million employees, shows that 29 percent of external hires were made through referrals from employees, employee alumni, and vendors, among others.[6] My interviews revealed a 60 percent rate of hiring success from networking, specifically for part-time work.

Who are your best networking contacts? Where are your odds the greatest in finding that right part-time opportunity for you? Based on my interviews, friends and current or past coworkers help women land more jobs than any other venue.

Hansen defines networking as "establishing relationships so you can enlist support and comfortably ask for ideas, advice, and referrals to those with hiring power."[7] She points out that successful networking is a give-and-take proposition. "It's most effective when the networker and the contact benefit from the relationship. Even if your contact does not benefit immediately from knowing you, he or she should gain something from the relationship eventually."[8] Try to think of how you can help your contact. You can simply ask, "What can I do for you?" Networking is not a one-time event. It's a relationship built over time, much like friendship.

As with anything else, you need to set out a goal for networking. What are you looking for? A reference? A job? An introduction? Make a plan. How many new contacts do you want to make a week? How will you do that?

And as old-fashioned as this sounds, make business cards. Put your name, e-mail address, and phone number on them, just what people need to contact you in the future. Some people add their LinkedIn page or website, too. Carry them with you everywhere. This makes it easy for you to pass along your information to new contacts easily and with little fuss.

Additionally, develop your elevator speech. What if you bump into someone who says he or she knows of a job opening, then asks you what you are looking for on the spot? What value can you add to that position? What makes you unique? Have a one to two minute speech ready to go. You've got the person's attention, use it.

You will see in the following sections that you can make contacts anywhere, anytime: on the soccer field, in the grocery store, on the phone with a friend. Everyone you talk to and see is another potential contact.

Friends and Colleagues

While Carol was attending real estate school, she began networking with an old friend who had been in the business eighteen years. Carol eventually joined her as a partner. "I highly recommend that. When you're connected with someone who already has a business, you're instantly busy," she says.

Some people are reluctant to ask for help, believing that they are an irritant to others. Don't think that way. Most people feel important when they are asked for help and advice. Instead of being bothered, most people are flattered when you consider them an expert and ask for help. Old coworkers remember you as they knew you when you worked with them, not necessarily as you are now.

Weezie worked through friends and colleagues to obtain her positions. She knew teachers in the elementary school where she was substituting and where her children went to school. By knowing these people in the system, she's currently working her third temporary position over the last several years. Working these temporary positions reaps much better pay than the substitute rate because it's at a regular salary level. "I know all the teachers; many of them had my children. They know me as a parent *and* as a teacher, so it's worked out great. These jobs weren't posted; I couldn't apply for them. They were just word of mouth," she says. "The second grade was totally stressed with huge classes. One of these teachers said to the principal, 'We need help.' They came up with PTO money. They said, 'Call up Weezie and see if she'll do it.' So it's worked out perfectly for me. I'm supporting the second grade. I go in from 12:30 p.m. to 2:30 p.m. every day, only for this school year. Next year I'll go back to subbing again unless the principal comes up with something like this again. In fact, I have an appointment to ask him, 'How can you fit me in next year?' Now I don't want to go back to subbing because this is a better schedule and better pay."

Think you can't get a job while on a soccer field? Think again. "I heard about the legal job through a friend on the lacrosse field. She said that it was crazy at work and they were looking for someone to do some research," says Missy. "They had a very big case, and it was overwhelming the firm. I said that summer is coming up. 'I'm not working at school, would you like some help?' She said sure. I went in, met everyone. In my gut, I knew it could turn into something more if I wanted it to. I don't know if I want it to because it is thirty minutes away from home. Do I want it to be a bigger thing? We'll see when I start paying for college."

What about your spouse? When pink slips started flying in late 2008, couples began swapping contacts. David Mezzapelle, founder of JobsOver50.com, recommends sharing lists of contacts. Even if spouses work in different industries, he's found that the tactic results in better networking and more interviews.[9]

Jane obtained connections from her full-time position that enabled her to move into part-time employment. "My last full-time job was director of operations at the YWCA. We did a major renovation of that building. The architect was the architect I work for now. In the middle of the renovation, I went to her and said, 'If you ever have an opening, I would sure like to work for you.' I liked her, and I liked her firm. I liked the way it felt there. I really enjoyed it. I had never known anything about building or construction before I worked at the YWCA, yet I ended up being the person who was responsible on the owner side for this huge $3.5 million renovation of the building. So I worked very closely with her. As a result of that, I just fell in love with the whole process. The architect hired me initially to do construction administration, and then that dried up. But she didn't want to lose me, so kept me on with an administration project here and there." Now Jane continues to work with the same architect in a business manager capacity.

Part of networking is making sure that people know where you are when you leave your full-time position, even if you're becoming a stay-at-home mother. About 10 percent of the interviewees were called by past employers or associates who asked them to come back to work with them on a part-time basis. After staying home for a few years, Cheryl received a call from a former colleague who had moved from one company to another. Having an employee go out on maternity leave, the colleague needed contracting work. "At that point, both my kids were now in preschool and they had been in preschool for three months. It was the first time the youngest one was out of the house and essentially out of my care for any sense of time, even if it was only two days a week. But all of a sudden, I had free time. They were much more self-sufficient on what they could do on playdates and activities. So when this friend called and said, 'Do you want to do some contract work?' I said, 'Full-time?' She said, 'Yes.' I said, 'No thanks.' Then she called back two days later and she said, 'How about part-time?' And I said, 'Three days?' She said, 'Okay.' I said, 'Okay.' I figured at that point, I had not been job hunting, but the phone call came at a time when I didn't feel like I had to be home all the time. The activities that I was doing at home weren't super stimulating all the time. The phone call came at the right time that I would consider it. It was serendipitous. I knew it was a contract position and if it didn't work or I didn't like it, hey, what did I lose? If I did like it, it was an entry back into the workforce in a part-time capacity without having to sell myself in a part-time capacity. I couldn't lose. It was a no-lose situation for me, so why not do it?"

Word of Mouth

Even if your past colleagues have no openings and your friends don't work in your field, you can pass the word along. Talk to old school buddies, neighbors, relatives, and even your professional advisors such as your accountant, dentist, doctor, or lawyer. It's amazing how many women interviewed gained employment via word of mouth. Believe it or not, friends of friends can be very helpful. Experience being equal, people would rather interview someone who has been referred to them than call in a person whose only contact has been a résumé. Don't be shy to spread the word.

Cindy aids ADP in payroll preparation. "I found the job through a friend of my sister's. She also had a child and started to work part-time. She said to my sister that they had part-time work. My sister said,

'Oh, I know someone who wants that.' They have benefits, so I went and applied. Of course communicating with other people when you're looking helps. If you tell them you're interested, 'If you hear anything, please let me know,' it helps."

During Margo's first year of tutoring, all the people in the guidance department from the high school where she had been teaching referred her to parents for college applications. "They felt comfortable making the referrals since I had taught there, and they felt good about my credentials. They knew that I was nice to the students and didn't do anything inappropriate. I kept going by word of mouth. I never advertised for myself. Then it was all word of mouth from parents who thought I'd done well with their kids to other parents."

Victoria found work just by talking to someone who looked like she was having fun at her job. "This woman said she had a balloon delivery business. I said to her, 'That sounds really fun; I'd like doing that.' She said, 'Would you really like to do that?' I said, 'Yes.'" So Victoria accepted an offer as a part-time balloon delivery clown. "I put a clown suit on and took helium balloons that I had in my basement. They'd write these fabulous poems. I would go to hospitals, nursing homes, and parties, any kind of thing you can think of, and deliver them. It was fun! Mostly on weekends, Friday and Saturday nights were the big times. If I was going out on a Saturday night, I put on my outfit and then would put the clown suit over it. I'd deliver the balloons, put the clown suit in the trunk, and off I'd go."

Social Media

Part of networking with friends and colleagues is utilizing social media. Using LinkedIn, Facebook, and Twitter can help you to find the job you want.

LinkedIn is an excellent way to post your résumé or a condensed version of it online. Friends and colleagues can quickly reference this if they are selling you to others. Are you on LinkedIn? Have you updated your LinkedIn page to reflect your current job objectives/goals? Check out LinkedIn pages of others working in your industry. What do you think works? What doesn't? Use this information to aid you in developing the best page possible for yourself. Then share your page while networking. Don't forget to message others on LinkedIn about your search. This website was built for professional networking, so use that to your advantage.

You can view job postings on LinkedIn, too. Enter a key phrase such as "marketing analyst" along with a specific geographic location(s). If you find a promising posting, refer to GlassDoor.com to check out how reputable the company is, how much employees like working there, if other part-time employees exist there, and, if possible, salary ranges for your type of work. Next determine if you know someone through your network who can refer you for the job. If so, contact the aforementioned person. If not, apply online.

This process can be used for any other job-posting website as well (more of those listed under "Cold Calling" in chapter 4). College alumni websites are particularly good for this.

An alternative option is contacting people you don't know directly, but you have a connection with them somehow. This can be through professional associations or through your university alumni association. It can also be done via LinkedIn. Find people who work at companies where you would like to work. Message them regardless of job postings, letting them know you are interested in working at their company. Ask them questions and/or get them to vouch for you with human resources.

Let your friends know you are looking for work via Facebook, too. Send them to your LinkedIn page for more detailed information.

If you are in the fashion industry, an interior designer, or even a gardener, you should use Pinterest or Instagram, too. Job seekers whose vocation has a high visual element should use these social media sites to show off their skills and designs. Rather than tell potential employers what you can do, you can show them on the Web.

Online networking may naturally fall out of the other work that you do. A neighbor may suggest that he introduce you to one of his fellow workers via e-mail or Facebook. Once the introduction is made, you can follow up with a more detailed e-mail outlining your desires, a résumé, or phone call. This is an excellent way to make new contacts and get your name in front of others.

Associations

While passing along your wants and needs throughout your networks, don't forget about professional associations and organizations. Real estate agents, doctors, chemists, marketers, teachers, lawyers, independent business owners, engineers all have professional associations on local, state, and national levels. There is the American Association of University Women, Association for Women in Computing, Association for Women in Communications, Federally Employed Women, National Women's Political Caucus, Women in International Security, and Women's Caucus for the Arts to name a few. Such associations can provide inside industry information, trends, recent changes in the area, and job opportunities. To obtain access to this information, you must usually become a member of the group.

To find the association that's right for you, look to Associations Unlimited. It's a database containing profiles of 23,000 US national associations, 101,000 US regional, state, and local associations. It also includes more than 300,000 US nonprofit organizations, agencies, and service programs. Association Unlimited provides contact information including websites and information on meetings and conferences. Since this information is accessed by subscription only, costing well over $1,000, you'll want to access it free through your local library. It's included in many library reference sections as a reference database.

Other ways to find organizations relating to your profession include accessing the Internet Public Library: associations on the Internet (www. ipl.org/div/aon). This site offers a plethora of information on all kinds of organizations. Did you know the following organizations existed— American Planning Association, Professionals Against Confidence Crime, American Name Association, National Fire Protection Association? Neither did I, until I went to this easy-to-navigate website.

You can also check out Weddle's Guide to Associations (www. weddles.com/associations/index.cfm). This website profiles over 1,800 of the leading professional associations and societies in the United States. It is also quite easy to use and another good source of information.

Using associations works because the members are employees and managers of the organizations where you are looking to get hired. By attending meetings and seeking advice, you're working toward obtaining the leads and referrals that will ultimately land you a job. While most associations charge a fee, they are usually quite reasonable to encourage membership. Christi and Linda found their employment by using such groups.

To develop her business as a consultant in professional counseling, Christi used a statewide group of friends who were addiction specialists. Since she consults in fetal alcohol education, this group is extremely helpful to her. She says, "We called them Fellows, the Fellows Program. I leaned on them since they were across the state, sort of giving me information as to what's going on statewide. I drew on them for a long time because our state was changing in the mental health system. I took advantage of that change. I was teaching some of the changes across the state. I was riding the wave."

Linda is an optometrist who took maternity leave and then started making connections with doctors and associations in her area to find part-time employment. "It's a combination of word of mouth, who you know, and finding out who needs a doctor. There are also organizations, like the American Optometrist Association as well as state optometrist organizations, that put out newsletters. They have listings as well. There are optometry schools postings. My university has a website. They put postings on the school website for jobs for recent graduates, but basically anybody from the university, recent graduate or long-time alumni, can use it for a job search."

Meeting people at continuing education classes or industry shows is an extension of various associations. Consider them as solid, networking contacts as well, especially if you happen to hit it off well with one or two people in particular.

Kate wasn't planning to go back to work, but received a job offer she couldn't refuse during an education class. "I was going to do volunteer stuff with the Red Cross. I was going to see patients until I had a community of therapists that I liked to work with. I was keeping up my license, but I sort of felt 'fake.' Everyone else going to get their license update was working, and I wasn't working, but I wanted to keep up my license. They were working, and I wasn't, so I felt like I really shouldn't be there. I know that wasn't true."

Recounting how she obtained the job, she says, "It was a very funny day. It was a horrible snow storm. People were sliding all over the road getting there. The seminar was on stress and anxiety. Everyone was literally out of their minds: the hotel holding it, the attendees, the presenters. Everyone was in a panic after driving over icy roads to get there. People were literally screaming. I just turned to this person I did not know sitting next to me and said, 'Oh good God, what are we going to learn today?' sort of joking. I liked her and had lunch with her. She mentioned, 'We live close together, and my office is only one town over.' She started telling me what she did. She said, 'My boss is great. We have a lot of moms who work part-time.' On the way out, we set up an interview for me. I immediately responded to these women, neither of whom were mothers themselves." Feeling that these women respected her as a mother and as a psychotherapist, she went to work with them. After working with this group sixteen hours a week for six years, she's still happy.

Key Learning—Networking

- Network with friends and past/present coworkers.
- Don't be afraid to ask for help; people are flattered.
- Create business cards.
- Develop an elevator speech.
- Keep your ears open in places that are not thought of as "networking opportunity" locations like the soccer field.
- Remember networking is a give-and-take proposition; help others whenever you can.
- Ask friends to spread the word about your job search and skills since their friends may have opportunities for you.
- Join one or two associations in your area of expertise.
- Network with others attending continuing education classes or trade shows in your profession.

TAKE YOUR TIME

Give yourself the time to find the right option and to ease yourself into your new work life, if possible. Women specifically mentioned that their emotions needed time to even themselves out, to work through feelings of guilt, to come to terms with what their decisions meant in terms of their lifestyles, to realize the great benefits of working beyond just the paycheck. Usually the first day is chaotic, but things start flowing well after a few weeks.

While Laura felt empowered by her work as a nanny, it took time to get there. "In a way, it was a really difficult time when I was a daycare provider. The mommies were coming in; they were friends of friends. I knew some of them. They were coming in, all in their cute little outfits. They were all going to work. Here I was in my shorts and T-shirts because I was going to be home giving bottles to their little ones. So they were jealous of me because I was home with the kids. I was jealous of them because they were all cute and going to work. We were all finding our own way."

"I want women to know when you work part-time, leaving your babies, it may seem hard at first, seem like you're neglecting your child, but you're really not," adds Missy. "Because you're helping financially with the family, so that's helping the child along the way, and as they get older, they see the importance of work and family, especially in today's society."

"Some days are crazier than others, and I say to myself, 'Why am I doing this?'" says Jesse. "When I look hard at it, I don't have to do it for financial reasons. But I realize that there's a social benefit, I'm doing something for myself."

Kara agrees, "It's truly been a challenge being a part-time working mom, but I think it was good for me somehow. I truly believe that the people I've treated in the dental office have given me a feeling of being needed. Working in the health field will do that for you. It's good to be needed."

And, above all, continue to have faith in yourself throughout the process. "Life is a wave pattern. There are ups and downs," says Peter Kash, author of *Make Your Own Luck*.[10] Give yourself time because you will find success. All these women did, so will you.

Chapter 3

SCALING BACK: MOVING FROM FULL-TIME TO PART-TIME

"More satisfying than full-time work because I didn't feel so overwhelmed."

—Debby

Whether you plan to move to a part-time schedule to spend more time with your children, to continue contributing income to the household while fulfilling motherhood duties, to retain your healthcare/retirement benefits, or to maintain your professional identity while balancing family situations, moving from a full-time to part-time position is a big step. Not one woman I interviewed took this lightly. Most took a lot of forethought and planning before making the change.

"The whole nine months while pregnant, I was weighing it out, making sure we had the insurance, making sure we could afford it," says Molly, a therapist. She's not alone. Twenty-five percent of the women interviewed thought about scaling back from their full-time careers when they were pregnant or right after their babies were born and made the switch at that time. The emotional pull of motherhood drew them in.

PUSH-PULL OF STAY-AT-HOME MOM VS. CAREER WOMAN

"When my first child was born, I was totally unprepared for how I was going to feel the day I had to leave him—after my maternity benefits were expired—totally unprepared for how I was going to feel on the day I walked out and left him with a caregiver," says Noel, a lobbyist. "So I realized that I needed to do something that would allow me to do the things I wanted to do with my children every day."

For all women, deciding to move from a forty-hour-per-week job to hours ranging from fifteen to thirty-five hours per week is difficult. It means less income, but more time with the children. It means less empowerment, less independence, but more nurturing, more special moments together. The trade-offs have to be well thought out.

Jodie had to wrestle with the trade-offs to make her decision to go part-time as a physician in a hospital. She was shocked at how little some part-timers receive in benefits. "If you're a part-timer, you lose vacation, health benefits; it's a big problem. I'm sure all of us feel similarly. There are definitely trade-offs. You may be able to work your way back after being part-time and get promoted or advanced; you may not. As long as you're okay with that; you have to think through that decision for the long-term."

While benefits were the trade-off for Jodie, it was all about the professional ego for Judy. "The biggest struggle was I always thought one parent should stay home. I thought that's the way you were supposed to do it. But when it came time to let go, I had a hard time letting go of the ego that came with being an accomplished attorney. I went to school for all those years. I spent twelve years with this craft, and now all of a sudden I'm supposed to walk away and just be a mom." She initially worked a job share for eight months then opened her own legal firm. When she moved from a forty-hour to a twenty-hour workweek, her greatest concern was how she was going to get back in. It was a needless worry, as she returned to a full-time position after running her own firm for two and a half years.

Even though Rosemary realized that she was risking her career by reducing her hours, she was at the point where a change was a necessity. "At the time, I was relieved as I was very pregnant. I knew that in the line of work I'm in, stepping back would be a risk because in politics, campaigns, and government, one job builds to the next, builds to the next job. If you make the decision to step back from that, you run the risk of not being able to reenter that field one day at the level at which you left it. I probably had some anxiety over that. At the time I made the decision, I was six months pregnant and had another young child who was four, so I felt more relieved than anything."

As a lobbyist, Noel was concerned that her clients might abandon her if they learned about her decision. Leah, on the other hand, was worried how her husband would feel about his wife not being a full-time earner since he had grown up with a working mother. She was also nervous about losing income. Each woman had anxieties and concerns regarding a reduction in working hours.

Despite these worries, each of these women moved into part-time positions. Some did because it alleviated guilt and gave them a balance between work and home life that full-time employment didn't offer. Some broke out of the system because it created a world that they wanted, giving them the employment hours that worked for them and their families. Others liked it because it gave them a peek into the world of stay-at-home motherhood without committing to it fully. Part-time work also gave them the ability to swing back into full-time work easily. Each had her own reasons to pursue part-time employment.

PLAN IT OUT

Start by planning. Beyond a reduction in income, consider medical benefits and retirement accounts, too. Can you swing it? Will it work? Do you need a larger savings base before you cut your hours?

Margo began planning how she would teach high school English for twenty to twenty-five hours a week long before she had her child. "I even wanted to go part-time a year before I did it. I was too scared to do it because my husband and I had just bought our house. We weren't married yet, so I couldn't get his benefits. And I wasn't sure with the taking out of insurance what would be left of my take-home pay. I was nervous and afraid not to contribute because he wasn't making as much then. And you know, as a first-time home owner, it's scary. It's a good thing that I didn't because within a month of moving we needed to mitigate for radon, the basement flooded; everything went wrong in the first six months. It was a good thing that I had a check coming in every month. I also had a slightly more complicated situation, as my husband works on commission. He's in commercial real estate and doesn't get paid a base salary. So with the first year of the mortgage to have something come in on the fifteenth and thirtieth of every month made a huge difference. You don't get tenure or what they call full-time professional teaching status until you've been teaching for four years at my high school. So I had to do the four full years full-time to get full-time tenure. That's when I thought, 'Okay, now I can start thinking about this.' This is still when I thought I could get pregnant easily. I figured I'd plan a pregnancy for a May birth, after a few months of summer with the baby, and go back in September."

Most of us, however, are not as good at long-range planning as Margo was. Most of us are like Kim who wanted to reduce her hours the day her child was born. "The minute my child was born I thought, 'How can I go back to work?' I then worked eight months to transition my job into a part-time job. I remodeled my job over that time and prepared other people to take over some aspects of my job."

Doreen felt similar to Kim. "We were in a crisis. You are at the point where you have this new child. You have no idea what you are doing. Your life is upside down, trying to figure out how to get it back to normal. This isn't what I signed up for; this isn't working.

"I approached my boss and said, 'I can't continue full-time. I'm not asking you to make my job part-time, but I have a suggestion. Could I do this other type of job on a part-time basis? I'm asking to drop from forty to thirty-five hours per week.' He said, 'Put a white paper, a proposal, together and I'll look at it.' I had a day-to-day operational job, and I wasn't kidding myself that I could do that part-time. We had so many projects that never got anywhere because we were in such a huge growth mode." So Doreen developed a proposal outlining a part-time position working on all those projects that weren't getting off the ground. "I said, 'Would you let me do some days at home, some days at the office? I could step out of my role.' I discussed it with my husband in August, approached my boss in September, and moved into the new role in March."

To start the planning process, ask yourself the following questions as well as those in chapter 2 under "Know Your Objectives." This will help you to determine if you want to continue in your current career part-time or if this is the time to redirect your focus on other positions:

- Do you want to work part-time in your current career for continuity purposes until you are able to go back full-time in the future?
- Can your current position be reworked into a part-time one?
- Are you willing to step off the "fast-track" for a while?
- Are you stagnating in your current position and need a change?
- What jobs are natural links to your experience? Are they less demanding than your current position?
  - Look at your current job.
  - Look at jobs related to your current one.
  - Look at skills and experiences that are easily transferred to other positions and industries.
  - Consider the use of a career coach or counselor. Career centers at large universities will usually let locals use the facilities. Outline what you want to accomplish.
  - Bounce ideas off friends and family. They know you best and can be good sounding boards.
- Based on your exploration, what positions suited to you translate to part-time work best?

ASKING FOR REDUCED HOURS WITH CURRENT EMPLOYER

Remember that almost any job *can* become a part-time position *if* the management is behind you *and* you're open and creative in working with your employer. Approximately a quarter of the women interviewed obtained their part-time positions this way. Just look at what Doreen experienced. She knew that her company was in a huge growth mode.

But she also knew that her full-time human resources job was too big to be turned into a part-time position. Since the work was there, she approached management by offering to pick up projects that weren't getting done. These certainly weren't the highest-visible projects in her department. In fact, they were clearly the second- or third-tier ones, but that was okay with Doreen. She got what she wanted: part-time hours in her current company working with people whom she knew. Since everything was familiar, her learning curve was low, enabling her to hit the ground running *and* to occasionally work from home. This ensured her success.

And don't fool yourself into thinking that you're less professional or dedicated because you're working less hours. You're trying to balance two jobs, not one. Paula, a physician, was concerned about that, and it turns out that she was wrong, really wrong.

"It's interesting because initially I was a little bit scared. If I was working part-time, would I be doing my job enough to be fresh and to be on top of it?" Paula recounts. "I actually found that I was doing a better job because I had more time to keep up with my reading and think through how I'd approach things. I was also somewhat more rested. Initially I was scared because I thought in order to be a really good doctor, you have to be working all the time. I quickly learned that actually you're a better doctor when you're *not* working all the time. I think that you're in a better state of mind for the patients; you feel more informed because you have time to read."

How to Ask

Before asking for reduced hours, determine your bargaining position. How long have you been at the company? How much experience do you have? The more experience you have, the more likely management will want to keep you. Make a list of your skills and accomplishments. Don't be afraid to promote your strengths and accomplishments to your employer. Have you gotten good reviews? Again, if you're a solid worker, they'd rather keep you instead of going through the hiring, training process and learning curve of bringing in someone new. All new hires go through a learning curve, no matter what the level. In some cases, it's simply more cost-effective to keep you than bringing in someone new.

Corporations *will* listen to full-timers who want to shift to part-time hours, if the shift is presented in a positive manner that fills a need for the company. "Most of our decisions are based on corporate needs," says the senior director of human resources at a pharmaceutical company. "If an employee comes to us and has a situation that has changed, we'll look at it and consider it. I have a director of HR who works for me and has children ages six and seven. When she had her first, she came back and said, 'You know, I can't work full-time. I want to have family time.' The vice president of HR said, 'I'm going to accommodate this schedule.' He has accommodated it for seven years. We've crafted the position around this individual because she is such a talented individual. We said we can craft a role for her that will serve our needs. We never do it just because an employee asks. It's got to serve a need for the company."

When asking for reduced hours, keep the following in mind:

- Can the work you're requesting be completed in the amount of time you're allotting for it?
- Can you give your manager a problem or issue that's affecting the company that you can solve by working part-time?
- Does the part-time position that you are proposing fill a company need?

Bonnie had solid experience with her employer prior to asking for reduced hours. She recounts, "I said, 'After maternity leave, I'd like to come back at such and such hours.' One of the benefits of working for a nonprofit, where you certainly don't make the big bucks, you do get more flexibility around changing hours and accommodating your life. They were quite accommodating; it was a combination of the job and the agency and that they wanted me to come back. I had a good reputation."

Joan's track record of four years also helped her. "I was straight up with my boss. I said, 'Look, I'm going to be a mother and I want to be at home with my child, but I'd like to continue working. I'd like to come up with some kind of mutually agreeable arrangement.' So I presented the proposal to him, and he said, 'Yes.' He didn't want to lose me, so he was willing to do that.

"But I was the first one in the company who did that. I had women calling me saying, 'How did you do that?' I wasn't sure whether to talk about it or keep it quiet because I didn't want to jeopardize it. I was a trailblazer. I really do believe it would never have happened if he hadn't known who I was, if he hadn't wanted me."

"Being established with an employer and set of clients is important," says Brenda. "You get a reputation over time. My law firm was comfortable creating a schedule that would benefit me, keep me employed, and keep my revenue still coming into the firm because I'm satisfied with my work environment. In a large structure such as a law firm, they realize women move up and over time have families, but can continue to be very productive for the firm and for the clients. I think that there's recognition in that environment that there might not be in others to try and create situations that work best. In a law firm, unlike perhaps another environment, you don't have to be sitting at your desk or accountable to a supervisor to get your work done. You can serve your clients hanging from a chandelier if that helps get the work done and the revenue in the door. It doesn't matter to my law firm, generally, if I work in my car or if I'm working at Starbucks; we just get our work done. We have a job to do, and the law firm can identify at the end of the year whether the revenue is coming in, whether the hours were met, and so on and so forth. They don't necessarily see you do it every day."

Doreen not only had experience within the company, but she also had a very good understanding of her department's issues. She presented her part-time role as a solution to a problem within her department. The solution just so happened to align with her needs. "I had been there three and a quarter years. I was established. I said, 'Listen, I've never brought my personal life to work, but I need to be candid, we're really struggling. I need to make a drastic change. I have to go part-time and would like to do it here. But I understand that you won't make part-time in the role I am in today. Here are all the projects that got started then pushed to the side. You need someone to take those unfinished projects, dust them off, and get them implemented. If you can't accommodate me, I have to look outside this company to go part-time.' My boss said to put a proposal together, 'Tell me the business problem and solution.' I told him in September; we agreed by October, and it was implemented in March.

"I wrote a white paper," Doreen continued. "I was a director and in the know on what was going on, understanding department priorities and needs. I knew how valuable it would be to take these projects and finish them off. They were things like a new-hire orientation program, policy things like who signs what confidentiality agreement, relocation policies."

Understanding business goals can help your case. For example, by working nontraditional hours, a part-time employee can help an East Coast headquarters extend its business hours to accommodate West Coast offices or client needs. You can also suggest a temporary assignment for a position where someone has recently quit or retired and no one has been hired yet. If the job goes well, you might turn it into a permanent part-time position. If not, you've shown your willingness to help the firm out and your ability to work part-time, possibly leading to other options.

This brings us to the next two questions:

- Do you have a good understanding of your department's needs? Can you obtain that by talking with others in your area?
- Do you know what's important and where you can contribute on a part-time basis if you can't go part-time in your current job?

Don't forget to do research on your own company and industry. You may gather information that strengthens your case. Are there any examples you can leverage as precedents? Are there any part-time programs already in place? Can you demonstrate where this has been done successfully either in your own company or in your industry? Has a leading employer in your industry done this successfully? If so, can you get comments from media coverage, social media, or the company's own website that reflect those successes?

Here are some employer benefits that might fit your situation and be useful when making your presentation:[1]

- Ability to work varied hours in response to pressing deadlines or unexpected crises.
- Completing projects that never get tackled.
- Working outside the 9:00 a.m. to 5:00 a.m. timeframe, particularly helpful with queries from different time zones.
- Reduced travel costs/time.
- Reduced absenteeism or turnover.
- Filling voids for those on maternity leave.
- Increased retention and recruitment of talented women.
- Decreased costs in turnover.

When asking for a part-time position, explain why it's important to you without belaboring it. Explain how much you appreciate your experiences so far and why you wish to continue with modified hours from both a personal and professional standpoint. Explain how it will benefit the company. For example, you could say, "With the birth of my third child, my responsibilities have increased at home. I'd like to reduce my working hours from forty hours a week to thirty hours for a year to accommodate my family as well as the company. Would you be willing to discuss possible ways of making such an arrangement?" Ask if your boss would be agreeable in helping you transition to these new working conditions. This shows respect and helps avoid confrontational attitudes.

Have a few options developed and ready to discuss on how this may work. What days would you work? How many hours per day? Would you be working from home? Lay out what you want clearly so there are no misunderstandings. Anticipate potential issues ahead of time so that you can address and, thereby, avoid them as reasons for your superior to say no. For example, what if there is a meeting that you usually attend, but it's outside your new work schedule? How will you handle it? Know ahead of time how much you're willing to negotiate. Consider proposing a trial period of several months to evaluate the new arrangement if necessary.

Be prepared to answer questions regarding objections. Three examples of objections and responses are listed below. Remember to keep it positive and upbeat.

- Objection: We've never done this here before.
  - Response: Let's give it a trial run for three months and then evaluate it.
  - Response: Present positive examples that have worked in your industry if possible. If not, see chapter 2 for ideas.
- Objection: This job can't be done part-time.
  - Response: I think that it can. I have delineated clear responsibilities and believe that the work can be done on a timely basis in the hours I am requesting.
- Objection: My hands are tied. This is not my decision.
  - Response: Offer to take your proposal to the next level. Ask if you can present the idea to those who can make the decision.

If you ask and get "no" for an answer, ask why. Sometimes "no" is a request for more information, and you can explain why it should be "yes." Get to the root of why you were turned down. Then you can determine if a further follow-up is appropriate and what additional information can help. If the answer doesn't help for this job, it might be invaluable for the next one.

If your superior flatly says "no" right up front, you can consider consulting with human resources for part-time work in either another department or for another manager. Let them know that you have approached your boss first to show that you're not attempting an underhanded move.

Take the Time to Develop Your Position

Allow your employer time to set up or develop a position for you. No one I interviewed asked her employer on Friday about a part-time job and started new hours on Monday. Do whatever you can to help your employer through this transition period. It's to your benefit. Most women take anywhere from three to twelve months to transition from their full-time jobs into their new part-time positions. Here's how Stacy and Janette shifted jobs.

"My employer is a mother," says Stacy. "She started her own child-care facilities because she wasn't happy with what was out there when she was looking for her own children. When I came to her, I told her that I didn't want to give her 100 percent as a full-time employee. But I didn't want to quit altogether either. She said, 'Great.' We split the job up. I took myself out of the daily running of the business, and now I am managing three team leaders. This took eight months to set up. I was actually promoted with this part-time position by taking over all the director aspects of my previous job."

"I approached my boss during my pregnancy," claims Janette. "I was working an average of fifty to fifty-five hours per week in a management role. I approached my boss and said, 'I don't want to leave the company,' but I wanted to return in a part-time capacity. He said, 'Of course, Janette, I'd be delighted to have you return on a part-time basis.' He created a four-day-per-week position, an executive recruiter position. We collaborated together to develop the position. My strengths were in recruitment, as I had been a senior recruiter and my company was growing exponentially, partially internationally. I had developed the relationships with many of the executive recruiters and placement agencies. My boss liked the way I was customer-focused. Different departments in the company were my customers. We were bringing European executives over to the United States to make the culture seamless. There were a lot of things I could do to help as I had grown up in the New Jersey area where we were relocating them. I could steer their spouses to schools and relocation real estate agents. A lot of my job was not only recruitment, but also to make them feel welcome."

Even if you're running your own company on a full-time basis, there may be a way to cut back on hours. By exploring your options and being creative, you may find an acceptable substitute to cover some of your work. Hire someone else to run the payroll, bill the clients, or collate the mailings. Think about the routine chores that can be farmed out to someone else. Maybe you only need them ten hours a week. That's what Vicky did.

Vicky and her husband ran a construction company together. She says, "When we sell a project, he takes it over and designs it. Then I coordinate all the relationships between the person we sell the project to and the men in the field installing the work as well as the relationships with the fire marshals and code officials that govern the quality of work that we do. We both owned it until about three years ago when we merged with my husband's brother's company. So we're in more of a management position now than an ownership position."

So her issue of going part-time was crucial to her entire family. "It was really a matter of investigating options out there. How could I move from full-time to part-time? That's when we discovered the outsourcing that you can have with human resources. It was a lot of investigating. It had to become a priority for us to figure out how to make it work. It really did take several months to investigate, a good six to eight months to be really comfortable with the decision we were making. Turning that portion of the company over to an outsourced group, which is what we had to do at that time, you have to trust you're hiring the right company to do the work.

"At that time, we had fifteen employees. Plus the bottom line is when all the reports are filed with the government, it's still our signature on it. So even though we outsourced it, we were still responsible for it. I did a lot of Internet investigation. We also talked with our accountant. He was a great source even though we didn't choose his company to do our payroll. So we went to him and asked him questions. On the Internet we found other organizations that could handle not only payroll, but all the other benefits you offer employees."

Whether you have your own company or are part of a large organization, be sure to formalize your arrangement when setting up your position. Document the expectations and parameters of the job so it is clearly defined on both sides. Define what part-time means for your position and outline clear professional goals. Are you going to work from home some days? Is your employer going to provide you with a laptop or a cell phone? Do you have any special requests such as not working during the kids' vacations or on holidays? Get these points hammered out prior to accepting the job.

Approaching the Issue of Pay

As a lawyer, Sandy had a good idea of what the firm expected of her. Law firms set goals regarding billable hours for each attorney. So Sandy understood what was expected of her, costs that had to be covered, and then prorated her hours to determine what she should be paid.

If you are currently working for the same employer that you're hoping to work for part-time, the issue of income should be straight-forward. If you're going to work 50 percent of your full-time hours, you get 50 percent of your paycheck. Your benefits may also be prorated. If the company is not going to offer you benefits, then you can ask for an increase in income per hour as you will have to cover those costs your-self. If you have a choice in how to set yourself up, hourly versus com-mission versus salary, be sure to set yourself up as favorably as possible.

Allison O'Leah, CEO of Mom Corps, suggests, "Work on an hourly basis. If the hours creep up, you need to say, 'You need to pay me more.' They can either decide to pay you or decide to give you less work. You have more leverage. Get it out of your head that 'hourly' means working at fast food. I have people who make $100 an hour."[2]

Christina had to work through that issue. Her boss wanted to pay her a salary, yet she felt that being paid hourly was to her benefit. Christina explains, "We agreed that we should try something. My boss is very much an entrepreneur, very interested in always growing, growing, growing the business. So he saw it as an opportunity to extend our reach and develop more connections. We agreed to revisit pay after a few months. We went out in a salaried position. We've gone back and forth between salaried and hourly, two times each way, mainly to keep everybody happy.

"At first, expectations were extremely high. He said, 'Oh, you say you're going to work part-time, but you love this.' I really wanted part-time work. You have to work hard to keep yourself working part-time. It's very easy to start doing everything and agreeing to everything. He insisted that I go out at the rate being paid full-timers. We cut it a little bit because then he said, 'You've got these two clients, but you're barely meeting where you need to be hour-wise for a salary.' It wasn't a big surprise. My boss compares apples to apples. I don't want him to do a value versus expenditure analysis.

"When I'm hourly, it's 'Here's what I'm worth; here's what you're paying me.' I meet the firm's minimum billable requirements for full-time people. I don't want that. I would not be happy meeting full-time minimum requirements. I get paid as much as some people full-time. That's why I want to stick with hourly pay. My point is to look at what I'm bringing in, the value to the clients. My clients are worth much more; my time is billed out at a higher rate. If you can avoid unflattering comparisons, do so."

Working through the pay issue with others can also be helpful. Holly and Sandy talked through the budgeting aspect of their legal job share position with another female attorney who was their friend. How much was it going to cost the firm? How could it be beneficial and appealing to the firm, but also work for them? Then later, when Holly went off on her own as a part-time lawyer, she called on the Georgia Bar Association for further help. It has a support team for sole practitioners. She had extensive conversations on obligations, on bookkeeping requirements. She did a lot of reading to ensure that she was charging appropriate rates, covering her costs, and running her business in the best manner possible.

Be Prepared

Make sure this is what you really want. Decide what you would say if management said, "It's full-time or nothing." Would you threaten to quit? What would you do? Be prepared. Know your answer.

Roseanne, manager of investments for a high net worth individual, remembers, "I sat down and told him that I needed to discuss something important with him. I said to myself, 'If he says no, I'll quit.'"

And sometimes bosses do put people on the line. Nadya, a social worker counseling high school students, says, "When I went in and asked my supervisor if she'd consider job sharing, she asked me on the spot if I would quit if she didn't allow me to job share. I had to make a decision right there on what I was going to say. I thought that was pretty risky, but it did work out okay."

Yet don't be afraid to ask. "You have to ask, have to be prepared to say why it benefits them (the employer)," says Kelly. "You don't get what you don't go for. You have to have your ducks in a row."

Noel, who was afraid she'd lose her clients by going part-time, holds a different view today. "A woman who made partner two years ago had a set of twins and a three-year-old. She said if she doesn't get in the shower by 6:15 a.m., her whole day is thrown off. Everything is planned out; every ten minutes of her day is planned out. I would say if you are really good at what you do, ask. You shouldn't be afraid to ask your employer to be accommodating. If you're really good at what you do, most employers will try and find a way to keep you. A lot of women are hesitant because they don't want to rock the boat. We want to please people, we don't want confrontation, but think after a certain amount of time you have the right to ask for something for yourself."

Tips for Success

Once you obtain the reduction in hours, your work isn't over. Being a part-timer puts you in a special category, many times under a microscope. Here are some tips from those who have done it on how to succeed after making the leap:

- Be determined to succeed on a personal level. Have the attitude and willingness to make it work, even if it means commitment beyond that of a full-time worker.
- Remember to remain visible. This will prevent you from being seen as a slacker and enable you to receive recognition for your contributions.

- Chart an anticipated schedule of projects for the next three to six months, if possible.
- Post a sign on your door or desk noting your schedule and hours of availability.
- Set automatic e-mail returns and voicemail messages about your availability so colleagues can anticipate when they will hear from you.
- Communicate any changes in work schedule to supervisors, subordinates, and team members, even if only a day's vacation, to avoid any conflicts and misunderstandings.
- Remember to repay the flexibility your employer gives you. If your employer lets you stay home with a sick child, then you should be willing to work a few extra hours.

Key Learning—Asking for Reduced Hours with Current Employer

- When asking, determine your bargaining position:
  - How valuable is your experience to your company?
  - Have you received good reviews?
- Understand your department's/corporation's current issues and needs.
- Have your part-time request play into those issues and needs.
- Remember, it takes three to twelve months, on average, to set up a part-time position.
- Account for benefits.
- Consider prorating pay to match the prorated hours versus being paid by the hour; ensure your choice works for you and your company.
- Know what you would say if you were told, "It's full-time or nothing."

CHANGING JOBS TO OBTAIN PART-TIME WORK

While the best situation is to reduce your hours with your current employer, that's not always possible. Unfortunately, sometimes you have to change jobs. And that's difficult. Here you are already overburdened with family issues and a full-time job, knowing that reducing your hours would help tremendously, yet you have to spend *additional* hours seeking out another job. It's almost too much to think about. But do forge ahead, as it's worth the effort when you obtain those reduced hours.

In addition to using job search ideas on "Networking" in chapter 2, "Cold Calling" and "Further Education" in chapter 4, and "Starting Your Own Business" in chapter 5, consider going to job fairs in your industry and your geographic area. These are particularly useful if you are currently holding a full-time position. To find upcoming fairs, search online for "job fairs part-time." You'll see virtual job fairs as well as local ones, particularly if you live in or close to a large city. Some are better for part-time jobs than others. While you are there you can glance at the job opportunities as well. At WomenForHire.com, there are listings for upcoming career expos across the country. Another useful site is Women AtWorkNetwork.com. The *Wall Street Journal* also holds virtual job fairs every few months that include a few part-time opportunities.

While most of the women I interviewed found part-time work through networking, Ingrid attended a job fair that led to an excellent part-time opportunity for her. Here's what she did.

"When I got pregnant with Sam, I was a captain in the air force," she says. "I had no choice; I had to come back to work full-time. I remember saying to myself, 'Let's see, have an open mind, and see how it goes.' I will tell you, I grew up with a mom who stayed home. My thoughts from the beginning, being pregnant with a child, I wanted to be home as much as I could, especially in the early years. At the same time, with the economy today, unless your husband makes a ton of money, so few jobs make enough to survive. I remember thinking, 'I should give this a shot working full-time; I could make so much more money, and maybe it's not so bad.' So I went back full-time.

"I brought him to work with me every day, dropped him off with a friend who was home with her baby. She was a stay-at-home mom living on the base. I would go to her house at lunch and nurse him and go back to work, and I would pump at work. It was a great situation, but I was exhausted by the whole process. There would be days when he would be in the car, there would be an accident on the way home, and our drive would be ninety minutes. He'd be crying in the back. It was not ideal. This is not what I wanted.

"I remember crying on the phone to my brother, 'But we can't afford for me not to work.' My brother said, 'Ingrid, I know you. You're probably going to find some high-paying part-time job. Just go look for it.' I know I wanted to leave the air force. I was not going to make an air force career and have a family. I couldn't do it. It wasn't in the cards for me.

"So I started going to job fairs. I went to a technical job fair. I met the HR person for a major accounting firm. She said, 'You're very impressive; we want to bring you in for an interview. We need project managers for IT.' So I went in for an interview. When I interviewed for the accounting firm, I did not even consider part-time work for them. So when I interviewed it was all with the assumption that it was full-time. Only after they offered me the job did I truly realize I just didn't want to work full-time, even though the money would have been nice as much as it was necessary.

"That is why I called and turned it down. I explained, while turning it down, that I felt I just couldn't be a happy, productive employee working full-time with a six-month-old at home. It was then that the hiring manager called me back and said that he would be *happy* to hire me part-time. He literally said, 'You are just as valuable to me part-time as full-time.' That is when I realized *I could do it*—work part-time, make money, and have meaningful work. That's how it all started. Half the time I'm more productive than people who are there forty hours per week. Ever since then, I've worked part-time."

Since then, she has left the accounting firm, started her own consulting business, which she successfully ran for over six years, and now she works for a company specializing in government defense. (More on why she gave up her own business in chapter 5.) She obtained the government defense job by attending an industry association networking event.

Ingrid says, "One day I was at my neighborhood grocery store and I said to myself, 'Why don't I work right there?' Because across the street from the store is a government defense contractor. I've been in defense, I'm a project manager, I know IT. I happened to be at a women's engineering networking event in downtown. There was a table for that corporation right there. I chatted with a woman there. I said, 'You know, I live right down the street. I would love to work for your company.' She said, 'We'll see what we can do.' A long time later, this woman had kept my résumé, she called me up. She said, 'I think I have something for you.' I interviewed three to four months later, and sure enough, they wanted to hire me full-time. I said, 'No, thank you very much. Option A is hire me part-time; option B is nothing at all.' So she got me in touch with her director.

"First of all, I was going into hard-core engineering, where there were few women. There certainly weren't women working part-time there. I felt like I had to show these people the way. 'Look I can do this job for you and you don't need me forty hours per week.' I convinced the guy who wanted to hire me, no problem, but he had to convince his boss. And we did. I started working for them, two and a half years ago, twenty-four hours per week. I made a deal with them. Two days a week at the office, the other eight hours spread throughout the rest of the week from my house. I said, 'Look, it's not like I'm going to be sitting on a couch. I have an office, a fax, a copier, three laptops.' So my boss was, 'Okay,' but we had to convince his boss. I can say with 100 percent confidence that I made a huge believer out of both of them.

"They even posted a part-time position for the first time ever. A couple of years later, they needed a training person and said, 'Oh, we should pick up a part-time mom.' They didn't need forty hours. I've been promoted and moved divisions. After a couple of years in engineering, there wasn't a path for me moving forward there. In order for me to move up within that division, I would really have to work full-time.

"So I started looking around, and I met with the chief information officer over the entire company. I met with her one day and explained my situation. She put me in touch with other women who she thought could help me out. So I started networking with a bunch of people in her department, and sure enough a position came open. I applied for it, I interviewed, and I got it. It was a big promotion. I changed positions. I now work for the corporate office, and I'm a senior specialist for IT project management. I'm still part-time, still twenty-four hours per week.

"It was a full-time position, and I convinced them, 'You don't need that.' Here're a couple of things in my favor. The woman that hired me also works part-time. She's also a mom of three, and she's well aware of the efficiencies of part-time working moms. In my opinion, they're some of the most productive employees you can find because, at least for me, I know I go to the office two days a week. There's this laundry list of things that need to get done. I actually sit there and get them done because I'm only going to be there two days a week and I don't want to have it creep into the time I've set aside for myself. We saw eye to eye. I asked what project she wanted me to manage. I asked what phase it was in. We talked. She said, 'You could totally do this part-time.' There was no clause saying if this doesn't work out, you need to come on full-time."

Ingrid feels, "Anyone can work part-time. You have to convince people that you can do it. I would tell women to look at jobs advertised full-time and tell them they can do it part-time." While this may be a risky strategy, it certainly has worked for Ingrid several times.

Key Learning—Changing Jobs to Obtain Part-Time Work

- Attend job fairs in your industry and geographic area.
- Network with friends and past/present coworkers.
- Keep your ears open in places that are not thought of as "networking opportunity" locations like the soccer field.
- Ask friends to spread the word about your job search and skills since their friends may have opportunities for you.
- Join one or two associations in your area of expertise.
- View virtual job fairs online.
- Be very positive.

JOB SHARING

Job sharing is a good way to reduce your hours. The best way to form a job share is with your current employer. They already know you, they know your skills, and they know your track record. Based on the experience of the nine women who job shared, I have some tips and advice.

The first bit of advice is, "If you want a job share, go after it." I interviewed two women at two different divisions of the same Fortune 100 Corporation. Both broke ground in job sharing in their divisions. Debby took a year and a half to obtain her job share approval. Kelly was assigned with the task of "making it work" twenty-four hours a week and has done so for over six years. Another woman, Chelsea, initiated job sharing in public schools in Wisconsin.

"I thought about it when I was pregnant with my first baby," says Debby, a member of the contract-purchasing department in her division. "I pursued it before I left to have her, but there were no part-time or job shares at my company at that time. There were part-time engineers, but they were in a league of their own.

"We presented it to HR. We put everything together and presented it to a lot of people, had to get the buyoff. At my company, the biggest thing is headcount. With a job share you have two people, that's two heads, but it's one job. We had to work that out. It took a year and a half to get it approved. There was a gentleman in HR who I had contact with who helped me gather the information and put the package together.

"There was a girl who just had a baby who wanted to do the same thing. She and I worked together with him to put all the data together and do the presentation. We had to go up many levels, presented several times."

Figuring out how to offer benefits was the corporation's biggest issue for Debby and her job share. Working through this took well over a year and caused delays for her. Yet with help from human resources and the willpower to move forward with the job share, Debby and her partner got it approved, allowing Debby to work the twenty-four hours a week she desired.

Kelly was also a job share trailblazer in her division. She didn't have the luxury of time to plan it out as Debby did. She was in the midst of adopting a baby. With eight weeks' notice, she had to decide if she should continue working full-time, quit altogether, or go part-time. "After eleven years of waiting for a baby, my gut feel was to quit," she says. "But my second instinct was, 'I don't want to quit.' I didn't want to give up my work, adult conversation. My boss asked me what I wanted to do. I said, 'I don't know. I haven't thought about it. I think the best scenario would be to work part-time.' So we started thinking about a job share, and the HR department got it approved. They said, 'Look, you're the guinea pig. You've got to make it work.' It had been done elsewhere in the company, but not here. She didn't want me to quit. I said, 'I'll make it work.'"

Another trailblazer, Chelsea developed a job share as a teacher for special needs children. "I worked in a progressive school district," she claims. "They didn't have a job share. My partner and I were the first ones. We put a proposal together. Due to the number of students, we proposed two half-time teachers to share the room in the morning and cover all the students. It was still one full-time teacher, with no afternoon class. It worked out great. The students really benefited. We started a trend in the Wisconsin schools. We worked in teams, and all the other people on our team started job sharing in one capacity or another."

Chelsea, Kelly, and Debby point out that many employers are skeptical of part-time work until they try it. Once they try it, they realize that they get people who are energetic and not burned out—a virtual gold mine.

As a job share buyer for aircraft engine parts, Kelly points out the essential elements in a successful job share position. "In my job share, we overlap eight hours together to tell each other what's going on. You have to have chemistry, you have to know you trust each other, believe each other, like to work with each other—almost like a marriage. We have a seamless job share, very trustworthy. We talk daily about business and babies. We became very, very close. As long as you can let your guard down and trust each other, it can work."

Several other women mentioned that touching base with one another and even overlapping by several hours a week is beneficial.

Setting expectations up front and working out most of the details before starting the job share worked to ensure a smooth relationship for several women. The key is developing a job share with someone you trust, whose work ethic and values match yours.

"You have to make sure that the person you job share with has the same work ethic that you do. If not, it would be miserable," agrees Sandy, a job-sharing lawyer. "When you're gone, you know they are going to take care of things and not leave you more work when you get back. It depends on if you design your own work share or if you're looking at a corporate environment that has a work share. It depends on who you're pairing up with. If you're pairing up yourself, there's a lot of politics involved. You have to look at how it's going to be received. To a certain extent, look at the amount of political clout that you have versus the person you're job sharing with. You could be tanking your career, and they might not. If they're the kind of people who aren't going to speak fondly of you in your absence, that could be pretty bad." Not selecting the right partner can be fatal to your success in a job share situation. Unfortunately, that's what happened to Sheila.

Sheila had a full-time job at a large corporation as a manager of community relations in Chicago. "Soon after my daughter was born, a colleague of mine approached me with a job share proposition," says Sheila. "She had adopted a child about the same time that my daughter was born and suggested that we share my current job. This sounded great to me as it was a way to keep my current job and not have to work a forty-hour workweek after my six-month maternity leave ended. In fact, we set it up that we each worked two and a half days a week with the half day as being crossover time. We put together a proposal, presented it to my boss, and then it was forwarded to the vice president of the department. It was approved on a trial basis and would revert back to full-time for me if it didn't work out.

"While it would have been nice if it had worked out, she was actually trying to take over my job and not job share at all. On the days I wasn't there, she was attempting to discredit my work. Since we weren't there together, it took me a while to piece the situation together. So after pushing for a job share position in a company where no such positions existed, now I had to make the case for reverting back to my full-time position. I hadn't explored the ramifications of the job share as fully as I should have. So I went back full-time, negotiating for four days in the office and working from home on Fridays."

But a good partner alone doesn't ensure success. Sandy recommends looking beyond just your partner and to analyze the commitment of your company as well. "Look at the job share policies. They may not be particularly reliable. You've got to ask questions about how people are actually doing job shares, how committed the company really is or are they just paying lip service to it. You can tell by how they respond to the questions." Here are Sandy's and Holly's stories about their job share as attorneys that were undermined by their law firm.

Sandy and Holly gave birth to their children within eight days of each other. While on maternity leave, they hatched the idea of job sharing with their current employer in Atlanta. Holly litigated estates and trusts while Sandy was an estate planner. Sandy wanted to learn about probate litigation. The plan was for Holly to train Sandy as part of the job share.

The first thing that they attacked was how to make the job share work for the firm while also fulfilling their personal requirements. Holly committed to bill fifteen hours per week. That meant actually working twenty to twenty-five hours because when she was billing forty hours per week, she was working sixty to eighty hours per week. So Holly's proposal was for her to work Monday and Tuesday in the office, Wednesday and Thursday from home, and not at all on Fridays.

Sandy planned to be in the office Monday through Friday. While a full-time lawyer is billable 1800 hours per year, Sandy negotiated a billing obligation of 1300 hours per year, working from 9:00 a.m. to 5:00 p.m. five days per week. It gave her the flexibility to come and go as she needed within that 9:00 a.m. to 5:00 p.m. window, depending upon what her children needed. Even though she was working hours that most people consider full-time, it was part-time versus her current full-time job. Because she cut her annual billable hours, Sandy took a cut in pay.

Holly and Sandy worked on the numbers so that put together, the number of hours they were going to bill and their salaries, equaled one very profitable associate. Separately they were doing only part of the job, but together they were profitable. They ran a lot of numbers in conjunction with the chief financial officer and made a formal presentation to the firm. Thirty days later the firm got back to them.

"Lawyers are driven by costs, overhead costs. So we were asking them to consider us as one attorney for overhead purposes," claims Sandy. "It was ridiculous. They put us on a floor that only had administrative people; that had not been renovated like the rest of the floors had been. It was not like a regular lawyer floor. They put two desks in one conference room, which we shared. It would have been much more difficult if we had been in the office at the same time as one another. We were not in the office together over long periods of time. I was there every day. Holly would come in for a couple of hours here, a couple of hours there. She worked from home at night a lot. It would have been difficult to be in the same room and on the phone as much as we tend to be. Discrete projects worked out fine."

Holly goes on to explain. "My caseload was no different that it had been, so Sandy was taking over some of my cases. She was generating her own, too. We were supposedly one body working forty hours a week, sharing time between the two of us. Her twenty-five billable hours and my fifteen billable hours translated to one full-time lawyer. We had more work than we could handle. I couldn't get any support from anybody else in the firm, staff-wise or associate-wise, because we were considered the part-timers and always unimportant. I finally said that I'd had enough." Holly left that firm after attempting part-time work for eight months.

"They didn't know how to support women part-time in that firm. They're nationally ranked and a big firm; it's very sad. I've done a lot of research about part-time work in the legal field, and there are a lot of law firms who have creative structuring. The most interesting thing is when I went around and said good-bye to everybody, men who had children were so supportive. A lot of men had wives at home; a lot didn't. Every single female who had children was hostile and antagonistic toward me."

Sandy explains what happened to her when Holly departed. "At that point, I was working reduced hours with reduced pay. One of the part-ners made it a point to get me moved to a floor where the rest of the attor-neys were because she said my career was taking a nosedive. I probably worked reduced hours another six months. Then I got busier and busier. I got things settled at home. I'm still at the same firm."

Sandy worked her hours back up to sixty hours per week within a few months, but the compensation took well over two years to catch back up to where it had been prior to the part-time work. She feels, "The firm was clearly punishing me." While you would think her pay would go back up commensurate with her increased hours, as she says, "It didn't work like that.

"I think whether it was this law firm or other law firms in general that have nice policies that are posted up on bulletin boards and in e-mails, the application of the policy is pretty tough. There's a lot of stigmatism that comes from trying to pursue that role. It wouldn't surprise me now if someone didn't say something to me like, 'Oh, I'm surprised to see you. I thought you were working part-time.' I was there every day; I was working forty hours per week. Part of it was they squirreled us away on a different floor, and they didn't see us. They pretended we were never there. It was tough. There was a lot of stigmatism about mommy tracking. Holly actually brought her baby in from time to time, and that was not well received. The firm assumed that I had my baby in all the time, which was not true. Frankly, if she brought her baby in and we were getting work done, it didn't bother me. I don't know why they cared. There was a lot to live down. It was a bummer; it was too bad.

"If you really want to know truthfully, I think that there are very few industries that are tolerant of permitting this type of lifestyle. I think you can't have it all. You can get angry about it, you can get frustrated about it, but it doesn't change the fact that you've got to work in the workplace. The workplace is what the workplace is. When you make the choice to work part-time, you are earmarking yourself, whether you mean to or not. The work world I work in punishes women for working part-time. I think they make assumptions about your dedication, your commitment. It's very difficult to overcome. I think that a man who is working part-time temporarily because he has had a heart attack or a health reason isn't treated the same. As soon as he's released and working full-time, they are not going to make the same salary adjustment for a man that they would for a woman. And they won't punish him as long as they will a woman. Because somehow, choosing to work reduced hours to be a proper wife and mother is seen in the workplace as a weakness. That's my opinion.

"I also look at my peers in the law firm context. You have to make a choice. The women who don't make that choice, drop their baby in the field, and keep working and don't have a relationship with their baby. It's a tough choice to make. It's a harsh reality. It's a shame that's the way the world is. Part of being a relatively highly compensated individual is that in this kind of industry, in this kind of professional field, I think that it's considered a weakness. They take advantage of you for it."

While Holly and Sandy had a bad experience with job sharing, most women who get to this point do not. Most companies that go through the effort of developing and setting up a job share support the employees well. These organizations come up with creative ways to make the job shares succeed. While Gabi couldn't move into a management position in her job share at the Environmental Protection Agency (EPA), the EPA did increase her job share status to emphasize its support. "One thing that we found as a job share was a ceiling. We wanted to take the job up a notch to a management level. No one said, 'You can't do that, that's not how it works.' Our superior was leaving, and we put our résumé together as a team to apply for our superior's job. It didn't happen for a lot of legitimate reasons. They could slide someone of equal grade over to the position, whereas for us it would have been a bump up. Yet no one had the experience in the position that we had as we were our boss's deputies. But promoting us to management wasn't going to work, so we didn't get the job. But after that happened, the EPA gave us a vote of confidence by giving us grade increases."

When asked about the cons of a job share with a solid working partner, Debby felt there weren't many. In fact, she'd "do it again in a heartbeat, but needs to earn more money for college now."

Almost every woman in a job share stated that they bent over backward to make it work. Debby and her partner made sure that they could answer questions regarding each other's account. "We didn't want any lax on the desk. We didn't want anyone coming back to say, 'I'm not getting the coverage I need.'"

Key Learning—Job Sharing

- Don't be afraid to ask for a job share with your current employer. Your employer:
  - Knows your track record.
  - Knows your skills.
- Consider forming a job share that has overlapping time.
- Remember, setting up a job share takes time.
- Select your partner carefully:
  - Be able to trust your partner.
  - Have the same work ethics.
  - Make sure that there's good chemistry; this is your "other half."
- Analyze the commitment of your employer to a job share.

IT'S WORTH IT

Switching from a full-time to part-time position can help to bring balance to the lives of parents. While it may lead to a temporary slowing down of your career and not getting assigned to plum projects, it also leads to more time for your family and your kids. Most women are like Laurie and are thrilled to move into their part-time positions. She says, "When I came back from maternity leave, I had no idea the feeling of wanting to be with my child. Going back to work was hard, giving that up, giving up all that time with her. I felt I was throwing myself at the mercy of the court saying, 'Please, please, let me work part-time.' I was feeling so fortunate that they would do that for me."

    She as well as many others mention that they love being able to help support their families, working in a job they enjoy, and having time to be available for their families when they are needed.

Chapter 4

NO NETWORKS?
NO PROFESSIONAL CONTACTS?
AM I HOPELESS?

*"I think a lot of this part-time work is all about recognizing
what skills you have, what you can do, what you can offer, and
designing a job around yourself. It's getting out and advertising
what you can do."*

—Robin

You want to go back to work, but you've been out of the workforce for a while. You don't have the professional relationships and contacts that you did in the past. You're concerned that all that's out there for you part-time is the lowest-level hourly work, that if you don't go back full-time, you can't find meaningful work. Happily, lots of the moms I interviewed found that their fears were far worse than reality.

While it's true that you may not have the networks you did in the past, it only means that you'll have to work harder to get what you want. It doesn't mean that you can't get it. About *half* of the women interviewed went from being stay-at-home moms to working part-time. Some of them had kept up their contacts and easily reentered the workforce. But many had let their networks lapse or had moved and, therefore, had no contacts in their new geographic areas. This chapter explains how women with no professional networks and no professional contacts gained satisfying part-time employment.

RETURNING TO THE WORKFORCE

"I was really, really nervous. 'Can I go back into the workforce? Can I be good enough?' While I was at home, the computer world exploded. I had a little laptop with sales, but I didn't do Microsoft Excel or any of that. So for me, that was really scary. I didn't do any of that," claims Cheryl.

She wasn't alone. Ten percent of women were both nervous and exhilarated at the same time when returning to the job market; getting back out there with no contacts is frightening. Scared and anxious, but excited and thrilled all at the same time, that's how these women felt.

"I felt a lot of dread. Looking for a job is not a great thing. You have to find time for it. Looking for a job is a job itself. I had to coordinate babysitters when I wanted to look into things, find time to look on the Internet, refresh myself on what I did for a living, get my résumé together. Get in a different mindset. It was hard, and I had the emotional reaction that, 'I'm not going to be with my kids,'" says Brittany about her search.

"Relieved and anxious," says Kate about her feelings. "Relieved that I'd made the decision, anxious that my kids would be forever traumatized because I was abandoning them for a couple of hours a day."

Others also discussed their fears regarding how their potential employment might impact the family with the majority of concerns focusing on their children.

"I was nervous because things come up, like 'I have a sore throat, Mommy' or it's parent conference day and there's a half day of school," says Cheryl. Until she landed her job and saw how she could handle these things, thinking about those issues worried her.

Doreen agrees, "I was terrified because my whole reason to stay home with Catherine was that I didn't want someone else raising my child. I felt that she was too small to put her in someone else's hands. Remember, I had only been in the country two years [she moved from Canada]. I didn't have a lot of friends. It was a new environment, new everything. I needed to protect this little being, but as I was at home, I got really bored. It wasn't that I didn't love her, but I needed more."

As a mother of a three-year-old and an eighteen-month-old, Heather's feelings are similar. "I was a little anxious on how it would work for the children, getting up early in the morning." Heather was also concerned about getting everything done at home as her husband told her that he could not pick up any slack for her. She says, "He was very supportive of me going back to work. But he was also very clear: 'I can't help you. I can't do child drop off; I can't do child pickup. I'm not coming home any earlier in the evening to help you when you're tired. If this is something you want to do then I will support you as much as I can, but don't expect that I'll be doing more than I'm doing now. By you going back to work, you're going to be doing everything you're doing now plus that.' He wasn't being mean, that's his job. That's what you accept. For me, it's 'How are you going to do all of this? And is it worth it?'"

For many women, it is worth it. Remember you are the same person you were, just out of practice. Here's how to do it.

VOLUNTEER WORK TO PART-TIME JOB

You might believe that you don't have any professional contacts or networks since you haven't been employed for some time. But do you volunteer? I was surprised by the number of women who turned volunteer work into a part-time position. They obtained work at the very places that they volunteered, used volunteer contacts to gain employment elsewhere, or utilized the skills they learned from the work itself. The most important factor for these women was their success as volunteers. They leveraged their volunteer skills and contacts to obtain fulfilling, paid part-time work. As a bonus, most of them felt while earning income that they were also giving back to the community since many of the paid positions were in the same fields in which they volunteered.

Offering to Work for Free

Ilene is a big proponent of volunteering as a method to gaining part-time work. She actually offered to work for free at a New Jersey social agency in order to obtain the employment she desired, and it was a successful strategy for her.

"I wanted to do part-time social work, so I kept calling agencies for family therapy as that's what I had experience in. I hit on the idea of volunteer work. At that point in time, I wouldn't have been making lots of money as a social worker, so I wasn't losing a ton of money when I worked for free. I saw it as a good foot in the door, but I wasn't willing to do it for free forever," says Ilene. "The agency had just hired two people, and even with the offer to work for free, had no work. They said, 'Do you have experience in anything else?'"

Ilene did have experience in adoption as she had adopted her daughter recently. So she was put in contact with the director opening up a new, small adoption agency. Since she had a master's degree in social work, he let her respond to requests from adopted children who want to know about their birth parents with questions such as what they did for a living, what they looked like, whatever information the agency had on them except for their names.

"So I would write up these reports," she says. "My supervisor would oversee my work and was very generous with his time. Then he said, 'Do you want to start doing home studies?' And I said, 'Yes.' You need to do this for people who want to adopt babies. We sat down, discussed what was required, ten to twelve hours' worth of interviewing. It was a big deal and a lot of responsibility for a volunteer. I started doing that, and then three months later, he hired me."

From Ilene's viewpoint, you can't over volunteer. "Volunteer, volunteer, volunteer. It's a no-lose situation as long as you have a no deadline in mind. You get to try it out, get to know the organization, the culture. You get to figure out where you might fit in best. By the time you're hired, it's, 'Gee we're happy to have you.' That whole new employee period is waived. And you've done it under no pressure."

That's exactly what happened to Frieda, too. For three years, she had been volunteering to raise funds for breast cancer research in Minneapolis. While she knew she either wanted to work part-time or go back to school, she hadn't committed to either. During the time she was volunteering, she had begun vocalizing her options to her friends, but never settled on either one. The fall fund-raiser changed that.

"We had a big event in October where we solicit artists from the local area. At the event, we serve champagne and hors d'oeuvres and run a silent auction. By the end of the night, we raised $50,000," says Frieda. The dollar amount raised wasn't a fluke. Over the last couple of years, she solicited more art than anyone else by continually going back and back and back again to the artists for more donations to place in the silent auction. Three months prior to the auction, she spent so much time making arrangements for the event that it had been like a full-time job. Over these months, she got to know the director quite well.

And during the event itself, she got to know the scientific director, someone she rarely interacted with, better. He sets up the cancer research programs around the world after the money is raised. According to Frieda, the job then fell into her lap. "The next morning after the event, the director called and said, 'We really want you to work for us.' I jumped right on it." Since she had been thinking about working part-time for several years and already knew the organization well, accepting this twenty-hour-a-week paid position as breast cancer research fund-raiser was a no-brainer. Writing grants for breast cancer research fulfills her requirements of doing something productive with her time while also earning money for both of her children's college educations.

Monica also started out as a volunteer and moved into a paid part-time position that she has held for eleven years now, working thirty to thirty-five hours per week. She had a business background and a love of choral music. Since she had sung in college and knew she didn't want to return to the grueling world of certified public accounting, she decided to do something that combined both her financial and musical backgrounds. The Maple Chamber Choir, a professional a cappella choir and small nonprofit organization, was the perfect place for her. "I was first asked to be treasurer, on a volunteer basis, because of my business background. I was a board member and executive officer for three years. I took the financial methods of keeping books out of a shoe box to a real, double-entry bookkeeping system.

"Then there was an opening as the executive director. I was recommended for that job. They knew me, they knew my work ethics, they knew my commitment, and I felt like I could do that job. I wanted that job. It was time to dig into something really important. It was a very, very fine a cappella choir. So I felt strongly about the product. I knew I could help advertise it. I wanted to put people in the seats, and I felt like I had the background to do it."

Connections, Credibility, and Experience

While volunteer work itself may not turn into part-time jobs the way it did for Frieda, Ilene, and Monica, it can lead to employment in areas of interest. Two women interviewed, Mimi and Leticia, procured work based on their contacts and credibility obtained through volunteering.

"After having stopped working for a few months, I started going stir-crazy. My husband was connected with the events at a major performance center in downtown Chicago," says Mimi. "He heard that they needed volunteers and suggested that I consider going there. So I went in and started stuffing envelopes, faxing things, answering phones, general office work. After several months of going in, I got a letter in the mail asking me to be on their board of trustees. I'm attributing this to their getting to know me through my volunteering. While the board was volunteer work, it gave me great credibility in the community.

"The center sent me to a seminar to learn programming, producing, and investing in productions. I even got to help direct a play on Broadway, all through volunteer work. Then my children's school called and said that they were starting a drama program. Knowing my connections with the performance center, the school asked if I had ever directed a play before. I said that I hadn't, but would be willing to try. They were willing to pay me for running the school drama program six to ten hours per week. Then, based on my work with the school, I received calls from the director of a local community theater about more work. I directed and produced several musicals, all of which had big casts featuring about fifty people—fifteen kids and thirty-five adults—in each. This was intense as now I was directing adults. We rehearsed at night, but during the day I was taking care of all the other details: budgets, music, production issues, making sets. The phone was always ringing off the hook."

Mimi gained her employment through the credibility she earned from her volunteer work. On the other hand, there is Leticia, who used networking with her fellow volunteers as well as her volunteering experience to obtain the work she was seeking.

Leticia initially hadn't thought about part-time work. Her first part-time position virtually fell into her lap. When she was attending a Girl Scout coordinator's meeting, a fellow Girl Scout volunteer who worked full-time mentioned that she needed help with her publishing business, that she was falling behind with some of her publishing projects. Since Leticia likes helping people out and having a sense of self-satisfaction, she said that she'd help out. She ended up working twelve hours a week as a correlation coordinator for a textbook publisher. That job ended when the work was complete. At that point, Leticia was enjoying earning her own money and decided to find more part-time work.

Again, her volunteer work with the Girl Scouts led her to a position. Leticia says, "I was a trainer for the Girl Scouts. The leaders are all trained. I had a woman in one of my classes whose husband was in training professionally. I told her that I had always wondered if I could make the leap into being a professional trainer. She said, 'Oh, you're good enough to be a professional trainer.'"

So with the support of a fellow volunteer, Leticia conducted a few informational interviews and joined the Association of Training and Development. There she met and networked with fellow trainers.

"One woman didn't want a job offered to her, and she passed my name on to [the company]," claims Leticia. "They called me. The hours were evenings and Saturdays, and she wasn't interested in that. To tell you the truth, I wasn't either, but to get a start, I was more than tickled. This was for a bank holding company. They had six banks in four counties with a total of twenty-four locations. It was very progressive in that they were open Sundays and they had extended Saturday and evening hours. When you have those hours, you have people working those hours. They can only come those hours to be trained. So I took the full-time, two-week training program for personal bankers and rewrote it, making it a three-week part-time training program. I did that for thirteen months, and then I moved."

After Leticia moved to Indianapolis, she became active in various volunteer organizations again. Simultaneously, she began working twenty hours per week for a battery company upon answering an ad in the newspaper. After one year, she was let go because the company was downsized, sold, and her position was eliminated. So she ended up at the closest university career placement center to her house. She wanted to determine what type of part-time position would be best for her. Once the counselor there took a look at her résumé she said, "With all this volunteer experience, you'd be a good volunteer coordinator." Her volunteer experience now was one of her greatest assets.

Leticia then decided to use a tool that had brought her success in the past yet a second time. "Because of my success with the Association of Training and Development, I sought out a professional group for volunteer coordinators. When I called the membership chairman to say, 'I want to come to your meeting,' she said, 'Who are you with?' I said, 'Well, nobody. I'm looking for a job.' She said, 'There's a job here.'"

It didn't take Leticia long to accept the twenty-four-hour-per-week volunteer coordinator job for a meal program, working with thirty volunteers every day. After several years in that job, she moved to another volunteer coordinator position, recruiting, training, and placing volunteers. In this organization, the volunteers helped elderly people with chores around their houses so that they could stay in their homes. Leticia is happy with her track record and enjoys her job even more knowing that it allows her, as well as others, to give back to the community.

While I've given several examples of women moving from volunteer work to paid employment, I can't end this section without mentioning Brenda. Prior to having children, she worked in the field of mental health full-time. Then she had two children, became a stay-at-home mom, and did lots of volunteer work. She says, "Although I had not been working for pay for many years, I was very involved in the community and had been doing advocacy work. I was working quite a bit while my children were in school, and I was not getting paid a penny."

Right around the time she was finalizing her divorce, Brenda was approached by a small nonprofit organization, a Christian retreat ministry, where she had been volunteering, with an opportunity for a twenty-hour-per-week paid position as the associate director. Since both of her children were now in elementary school, the work was part-time, and the income was useful after the divorce, she accepted it. In the back of her mind, she had been toying with the idea of part-time work for a few years, so this was ideal. She did this for about a year and a half and then stopped working when she remarried.

Now some of Brenda's other volunteer and advocacy work focused on the death penalty and issues that surround the death penalty. After she remarried, one attorney in particular called and encouraged her to continue pursuing the death penalty work. She had toyed with doing this several years ago, but hesitated at the time since it meant going out on her own and becoming self-employed. At that point she wasn't ready to run the risks that self-employment entails. But after working for the nonprofit for a while, she knew more about what she was getting into and was now willing to run her own business. So she became proactive, going through specific training in order to become a mitigation specialist.

Brenda says, "I basically do a lot of interviews with anyone who knew the defendant. I also collect a lot of health and educational records. All the information is used to tell the client's story to the jury in hopes that we get a life-without-parole sentence rather than a death sentence. I'm most satisfied with my current job. I found what I'm meant to be doing."

Mimi, Leticia, and Brenda took the skills they obtained through volunteer work and translated them into paying jobs. Almost all volunteer positions can bolster anyone's skill set, whether it's the specific work itself, such as training people, or general skills, such as organizing people and offices.

Key Learning—Volunteer Work to Part-Time Job

- Offering to work for free can lead to paid positions. Have a time-frame in mind.
- Recognize the skills you've gained from your volunteer work. What skills have you gained that might not be obvious at first glance?
- Use your volunteer work to solidify your credibility. You've done the work; you just weren't paid for it.
- Network with the other volunteers you've worked with. They know your work and worth. Use those connections.

COLD CALLING

While some people obtain part-time work through their networks, contacts are not a necessity in succeeding in finding part-time work. You can get a part-time job as long as you are willing to put the effort into looking for it. What do you do if you've moved? You haven't worked in three or more years? You've lost all your support systems and contacts built over the years? You end up doing what 10 percent of the women interviewed did: cold call. Many of them used a simple yet effective tool, the yellow pages. These women, having no work-affiliated contacts and no networks in the areas to which they had recently moved, turned to the telephone book to determine what companies were close to their homes and within a reasonable driving distance for part-time work. The phone book, online or hard copy, along with a local map can be invaluable resources for future employment. Several women whom I spoke with were almost apologetic when they told me that they used the telephone book as a tool for finding employment. It was almost too simple for them to want to admit to using, yet it worked well for them.

Alternatively, you can search the name of your town along with the word "businesses" to obtain several websites that list employers in your area. Many often do searches by industry, a bonus for you once you've defined your area of work.

So how do you use these references? How can you pinpoint which companies are right for you?

Using Websites and the Yellow Pages

Lisa used the Internet in conjunction with the yellow pages to determine whom to call and then used the Internet to learn more about the firms. She flipped through the phone book to help her decide where to send her résumé. "Before I invested a lot of time and money on sending out résumés, I narrowed down whom to send résumés to by looking at their ads in the yellow pages and then viewing their websites. I even called before sending out résumés because you can tell a lot about a firm's atmosphere by the person who answers the phone. If they treat you like crap, you don't want to work there.

"It took me four weeks to obtain an interview. You know how you hate to make those calls. I set an objective for myself to make three calls a day. It took four weeks to find someone who was interested in hiring a part-timer. I went in for the interview and two weeks later got the job."

Lisa worked for two years as a part-time lawyer after that. Then she stopped and became a stay-at-home mom for nine years. When she decided to go back to part-time work again, the world of searching for jobs had changed radically. She says, "I did the Internet thing, sending out lots of résumés through the Web and got no responses for part-time work. I went back to the yellow pages. You just pick up the phone and sell yourself. If you get someone on the line, if they have any interest, they will talk to you. If no interest, they generally say, 'Send a résumé.' Calling is a good way to see who has a need. I did not receive one response on the Internet.

"The yellow pages work because I could identify the firm's area of specialty, the partners, and get a sense of the firm. I then checked out their website so I could get a flavor of their business. So to me, it wasn't a cold call. Their website also gave me something to talk about when I did get someone on the phone."

While Lisa didn't find anything on the Internet that was right for her, it is a good idea to search employment websites. She might have had success searching her industry by geographic region or town on the Web. Employers whom I interviewed predominately use two websites: Career-Builder.com and Monster.com. After cruising through their websites, I found that at CareerBuilder, finding part-time jobs by location is easy. But at Monster, sifting through all the jobs to get to the part-time ones is laborious. At Indeed.com I got excellent results for part-time positions. This website pulls from Monster, JobStalker.com, CareerBuilder, among others. Rather than going to all these websites, this one covers many of them for you. At TenTilTwo.com, part-time listings clearly define the hours per week, pay, and geographic location. Listings are geographically broad, covering many parts of the United States. There are lots of hourly part-time jobs listed, mostly in retail with a few at-home jobs as well at SnagaJob.com. Technology jobs that can specifically be worked from home are listed at PowerToFly.com, a site that connects women to jobs, enabling work-life balance. The job listings indicate whether the job is full-time or part-time.

Other websites that I have checked out include MomCorps.com, focusing on professionals who have opted out of the traditional work-place in order to meet family needs, and IvyExec.com, promoting flexibility and work-life balance. Neither identified part-time work easily at the time I reviewed them, but I am assuming once you sign up with them, they will contact you when something comes up in your industry. Also search for "part-time employment" on the Web as new and useful sites are always coming online.

Some firms specialize in finding temporary work for stay-at-home moms. One such project was with Lending Tree, an online lending exchange. The firm needed 600 job descriptions rewritten in one month after several recent acquisitions. Five stay-at-home moms jumped on the project after being connected through MomCorps.[1] A few other firms that also help stay-at-home moms find work are FlexibleExecutives.com,

FlexibleResources.com, FlexperienceConsulting.com, reacHIRE.com, and On-Ramps.com. Starting out on one of these temporary projects could just be the ticket to getting your foot in the door for something more permanent.

While the Internet is an excellent source of information, only one woman I interviewed *found* her part-time position online. In fact according to Penelope Trunk, author of *Brazen Careerist*, "Only three to five percent of job seekers find employment through online job searches."[2] Many women I interviewed used the Internet to help narrow their searches, obtain information on the firms they were considering, and/or identify potential employers. Using the telephone in conjunction with letters and the Internet resulted in high rates of success, whereas just placing a résumé on the Web for a part-time position generated almost no employment.

Paula, a physician, is a great example of utilizing the Web for information and then placing phone calls to get her foot in the door. "I went on the Internet to get lists of hospitals and physicians offices in the area. I just started calling them. I did not find that letters worked. I found the only way that really works, unless they specifically say 'no calls,' which some of them do, is either show up and say 'hello' or call. I forced my case in some ways. I called them and they said, 'Well, we're not really sure if we need anyone.' I said, 'I'm actually going to be in the area; can I just meet with you?' I did that in two cases, and they agreed to have coffee with me. I ended up sending both [places] my résumé, and they both ended up finding positions for me. If you really want a job, you have to let them know you want it. You've got to show up and plead your case.

"I called a lot of places," Paula continues, regarding the search for her part-time position in the pediatric emergency room. "Most people never got around to calling me back. I kept calling them, and I got the sense that either they didn't have openings or they weren't interested. If these two hadn't come through, I would have had to be more aggressive on another front. I got lucky. I called ten places, and I got at least three responses."

When Robin moved from England back to the US, she hit the yellow pages. She had tried looking in the classified ads, but couldn't find the data management service work that she was qualified to do. So she started combing the phone book. Her future employer had placed a small ad to entice customers in the yellow pages. It attracted Robin's eye. After calling the number, she received a warm response from her future boss. He was thrilled with a part-timer as he needed help, but not on a full-time basis.

Ilene, who has worked in family therapy and with adoption agencies for many years, says, "I called agencies to get the job. When I think back, I was using phone books to find jobs since I was fourteen years old. I grew up with a strong work ethic. I always wanted to work. You must keep calling, calling, calling. . . ."

"You just have to believe you're going to find something. You have to go after it," agrees Kelsey, part-time librarian. "For that matter, go in and say, 'I'd like to do something like what you do part-time. Do you get any kind of openings like that?' I mean, really, just go for it."

In case you didn't read chapter 2, check out the section on "Networking" for more ideas on gaining introductions for job searches in your area of expertise. Pay particular attention to the topic of "Social Media."

Résumés, Introductions

You've done your research, developed your list, and you're ready to contact a potential employer and forward a résumé. But it's been a few years. What do you put in your résumé? How do you format it? How can you be interesting and concise all at once?

Here's a quick refresher and update on résumés. For more detailed help on résumé writing, go to your local library or search the Web for "résumé." Two places where solid résumé help can be found for free are http://career-advice.monster.com/resumes-cover-letters/resume-samples/sample-resumes-by-industry/article.aspx (long to type but good information) and university websites, searching for "résumé."

- Write one page, unless you are/were a high-level executive. The point of the résumé is to get you the interview. You can expand your accomplishments when talking to a potential employer. Several books on the topic all highly recommend a one-page résumé. When an employer looks at your résumé, it's generally given ten seconds. It should be clear. It should be concise. It should be one page.
- Use bullet points, not paragraphs. They are faster to read and get information across quickly.
- Highlight achievements, not job descriptions. What successful accomplishment did you make in your last job? Achievements show you excelled in your job rather than that you just showed up for work. Each bullet should be an achievement. Using action-oriented verbs helps.
- Find the right words. Many recruiters and human resource personnel search for keywords. If you haven't looked for a new job in a decade or more, you need to update your résumé with the jargon that employers are looking for. For accountants, those words may be *Sarbanes-Oxley*. For marketers, those words could be *search engine optimization*.
- Beware of the personal interests line. If it doesn't make you look successful or relate to the job in some fashion, leave it out. Every line in your résumé should work to your benefit and not raise unnecessary questions. Remember, you've only got one page.
- Stick to tried-and-true formats. It's easier than developing your own style, which could easily backfire. You can go to various websites, such as BestSampleResume.com and Jobsearch.about.com to find easy-to-read straightforward formats.
- Test sending your résumé through e-mail. Send it two or three times to different friends to make sure that the formatting sends correctly.

After your résumé is complete, it's time to draft an introduction. This introduction may be used as an e-mail letter, as a phone call introduction, or as a cover letter in traditional snail mail format. This is your elevator speech to gain an interview. Each introduction should be written specifically for each individual company you are contacting. When making contact with the company of your choice, do so with a specific person in the company, preferably someone who can hire you. Check the company's website or call to get the correct contact person. This may take some research, but if you just call or address your letter to "human resources" and not someone in particular, your call won't get a response and your letter and résumé will end up in the trash. A few tips are listed below. Again, for more detailed information on writing introductions, visit your local library. Search online for "cover letter" and "letter of introduction." Many searches for "résumé" also include cover letters as well.

For a written introduction, some career counselors advocate the traditional four-paragraph letter. Others prefer a pithy, one-paragraph e-mail.[3] Researching your industry may help you to determine which is best for you.

- Develop a catchy opening. If your first sentence is dull, the employer will never make it to the second one. Express your interest in this organization.
- List accomplishments that you think match the needs of the organization. Keep it short. Your résumé is only a page; this should be much shorter. Each sentence should relate specifically to the job you're applying for at that company.
- Include why the company should hire you.
- Lay out the next step. Tell them what you plan to do next, most likely a follow-up phone call. Tell them when you plan to call.
- End with a statement of confidence. Overextending gratitude signals a lack of confidence. Don't use lines like "Thank you so much for giving me consideration." Use lines like "I look forward to hearing from you" instead.

For a phone call, have a persuasive and concise pitch ready. Refer to a newspaper article you've read on the firm or the company's website or friends that already work there as a catchy lead-in. Follow up with how your experience may be helpful to the firm in one or two sentences. Your goal is to generate enough interest to get your foot in the door for an informational interview. It could go something like this: "From your website, I see that your corporation is focusing on increasing accounting-related consulting jobs over the next few years. I have five years' experience in tax accounting that may be beneficial as your business increases. Can I come in and discuss potential opportunities that might open up with your firm over the next year?" This is asking for an informational interview that may lead to a job in the future. Since you're relating directly to the firm's stated public goals, chances of obtaining an interview are good.

If, instead, your call is a follow-up phone call to an e-mail or letter, you'll want to confirm that your résumé has been received and also make a strong connection. It could go something like this: "Hi, Ms. Smith. My name is Beth Brykman. I mailed you a letter last week concerning possible employment with your company. I am calling to discuss possible opportunities with your firm. Did you receive my e-mail/letter and résumé?" If she hasn't seen it, offer to send her another copy. If she acknowledges seeing it, offer to come in at her earliest convenience. If she can't set up an interview at the time, should you call someone else? When might someone call you? Your goal is to have definite next steps when you hang up the phone.

In either case, resist the urge to leave a message on voice mail. Your call most likely will not be returned. Keep trying until you get a live person on the line. This might mean varying the times of day that you call. Based on Elizabeth's and Doreen's experience (their stories included later in this chapter), early morning and end of the workday are the best times to reach contacts in their offices.

What about professional help? Some of you might want to get solid counseling on the résumé/introduction front, especially if you have been out of the workforce for quite a while. You can get help through the Professional Association of Resume Writers & Career Coaches or sites like ResumeWriters.com. There are many choices out there, but some may be people with little to no training and who have just hung out a shingle. Check references and credentials before hiring someone.

Informational Interviews

For Catie, informational interviews found her the work she desired. She had recently moved to Connecticut from another state and was looking for part-time work. Since she had previously worked in college admissions, she first turned to the phone book to learn what colleges were in the surrounding area. This gave her a clear list of potential employers to contact.

"I had worked in college admissions prior to moving to Connecticut. When I moved there, after being an at-home mom for a couple of years, I knew I'd be going back to work. So I started setting up appointments, having informational interviews with admissions deans and directors. I was kind of hoping in the back of my mind that it wouldn't have to be full-time. I didn't quite know if I could get a professional job part-time."

Catie explains what she did in those informational interviews. "Because I'm familiar with college, higher education, and admissions offices and how they're structured, I simply called the admissions offices and asked for the names of the deans of admissions and contacted them directly. One I called was a very approachable guy. I gave him my background, told him that I'd worked in college admissions, gave him my former title. I told him that I recently moved to the area. I'm looking to return to work, and I would like to get back into college admissions work. I would like to talk to him about positions he had now or potentially in the future. He was very receptive.

"I was at the right place at the right time. This was a new position that they created to have a person just over the academic year, four days a week. They wanted somebody they didn't have to pay benefits to. They felt lucky that they had found somebody with experience who was professional and didn't mind [the lack of benefits]. I took a sort of demotion at first. It was fine because it accommodated my life."

And since she's been there thirteen years, she's seen others come in for informational interviews. Catie says that having a bank of candidates is helpful when someone leaves. If she had to do it over again, she'd approach it the same way.

Another person who also used the informational interview approach was Ellen. As a lawyer, she could find work through government agencies as well as private firms. "I live in the state capital, so there are a lot of government agencies here. I looked at my state's website as they have all the job listings for every agency in the state. I also looked at any kind of city or government agency. I looked through law associations, specifically for women and for lawyers in general. I went to law school here. Since they have an outplacement office at the law school, I went there, too. I did word of mouth. I asked everyone I knew who was a lawyer [about jobs]."

Once she determined the best potential employers, she approached them for informational interviews, not for firm job offers. "When I asked, I didn't say, 'I want a job,'" says Ellen. "I said, 'I want advice on how to find a good job here.' I wouldn't approach the person for a job; I would say, 'Hey, do you think you could meet with me and sit down and talk about the best way to go about finding work for me would be here in town? How do you do that?' Especially with women who were successful, that I respected, I would ask them, 'How did you do this?'"

From these informational interviews, Ellen had a couple of different options. One was a state agency offering her a full-time position that they were willing to compress into a four-day workweek. She'd be working ten-hour days, four days a week, on a flexible schedule. She also was offered other opportunities at law firms. She turned those down in favor of a position at the public defender's office handling appellate cases with hours that are considered 75 percent time. She generally works four days a week and has the ability to work from home when necessary.

A few tips for the informational interviews. Research the company to know its business and how your skills will be beneficial. Prepare stock answers for commonly asked questions. Many books have been published on interviewing. If you need to brush up on your interviewing skills, grab one at the library. Then practice, practice, practice. Be prepared to ask for the job. Say something to the effect of "I look forward to working here. Do you have any reservations about me or my abilities?" If an issue is raised, it gives you the opportunity to address it on the spot and possibly alleviate it altogether.

Dianne, who has obtained three part-time jobs over the last eight years, has some advice for you once you've obtained the interview. "Stay positive, be genuine, be human when interviewing. Be professional, that's a really big one." She feels your total presentation, speech, manners, and clothes help the employer assess your value to the organization. "They're deciding whether you're going to be an asset to the company, someone who doesn't need to be checked on every minute, someone who can do the job and more, someone who can be a team player, someone that's not going to be whining about getting five extra files. Just put yourself in that employer's position. What makes you valuable to them?"

How has she obtained those three jobs? "Whenever I set my mind to it, I go out and get it. Once I set my mind to it, I approach it as a genuine effort to try and help, that's number one. And number two, I picture it in my mind as the outcome being successful. Three, I just think I have a lot of different skills that are useful out there. I'm not afraid of being turned down. I was prepared for them to say, 'Oh, I don't have anything right now, but maybe later.' I wasn't afraid of being told no."

References

Okay, you've written the résumé, gone through an interview, and now your potential employer is looking for references. Who should you turn to? The first place to look is your last place of employment. Who remembers you well? Who can speak highly about you? Don't limit yourself to just previous bosses. References can also be past peers or coworkers from other departments. They can be past customers, clients, mentors, vendors, or professional acquaintances who can vouch for your good character. Make sure not to use someone who barely knows you. The most important thing is that your references are willing to speak highly of you.

Sometimes it's helpful to draft talking points and even recommendation letters for references. Pass these items along for your references' final polish, personal touch, and use. These are gentle reminders about your work history, volunteer history, and your achievements as they relate to the desired job. Ask references to stick to professional comments and omit irrelevant information about your private life that could harm your chances at landing the job. Don't forget to thank your references after they have spoken on your behalf. This is easily done by sending a card or offering to take them out for coffee or a meal.

If you need to use the same person several times, let them know what happened with your last request. They'll appreciate knowing how the opportunity worked out. It may help them when speaking for you in the future.

Explaining a Layoff

If you've been dismissed recently, you may be asked difficult questions about your layoff. Knowing what to say about your situation can make all the difference. Start off right by not mentioning it in your cover letter. It is evident from your résumé when you stopped working. You can discuss the details of why in the interview. Use the cover letter to present your strengths.

Prepare an explanation for the interview. Maybe your skills were secondary for your previous employer and not necessary for the company's survival. These skills may be primary for the organization you are now targeting. Maybe your entire department was cut, not reflecting on you at all.

If you have been unemployed for a long period of time, have a solid reason why. Maybe you are being selective in your next move. Maybe you opted to spend more time raising your family or to update your skills by taking some classes. The key is to make time spent out of the job market sound like your choice, not someone else's.

Temporary Work

As exemplified in the volunteer section of this chapter, working temporarily for someone can lead to a permanent position. Many job hunters have discovered that "temping" permits them to explore working for a potential long-term employer and to display their capacity to do well.

Someone offers you three days of work per week for three months? Why not try it? In *Workforce 2020*, nearly 40 percent of temporary workers report that they have been offered permanent employment.[4]

Step-by-Step: How Two Women Found Work

Here are stories of two women, Doreen and Elizabeth, who came from totally different educational backgrounds, career paths, salary levels, and geographic areas. They both had recently moved and had no networks or contacts in their new locations. They both used cold calling as their method for obtaining part-time work. And they both had success in obtaining the jobs they wanted.

Doreen had moved from Canada two years prior to having her child in the Dallas area. While she only had a high school education, she had held a good job in human resources before having her daughter, earning $40,000 a year. Stopping work right after her daughter's birth, she did not anticipate going back.

Elizabeth, on the other hand, held a master's degree in business administration and retained a position in marketing, earning over $100,000 annually working at the same time Doreen did. After having her first child, she moved to New Jersey from the South due to her husband's career. She stopped working upon the move, as she was anticipating having a second child. Like Doreen, Elizabeth held no plans for returning to work.

After staying home a few months, Doreen began to feel she needed more intellectual stimulation. She also felt that she could help contribute to the family's financial situation. As she says, "At the time, I gave up a $40,000-a-year job. We went from $60,000 a year to a $20,000 annual income and had a child." Doreen told her husband, "Gee, Paul, I think I can make some good money consulting, and instead of you picking up more on the football side refereeing and killing yourself twenty-four hours a day, I can help out and make some good money." That's how her consulting business got started.

As for Elizabeth, she stayed home for three years. Over that time, she had her second daughter. Unlike Doreen, Elizabeth's financial situation was solid and the need to earn additional money was not a factor. But it was at this point that she reached the same conclusion that Doreen had: she needed something more. Both women decided to go back to work on a part-time basis.

Both women were voicing what Betty Freidan, founder of the National Organization for Women, wrote in *The Feminine Mystique* about suburban housewives' thoughts: "I want something more than my husband and my children and my home."[5] While Doreen could use the additional income, it was not her first priority in going back out into the workforce. Her driving force was the same as Elizabeth's: she wanted something for herself, intellectual stimulation.

While both women came from very different backgrounds with varying degrees of education, they both attacked obtaining part-time work the same way. Doreen, not knowing much about the United States, went to the Chamber of Commerce and obtained a tax identification number. "I created a name and then wrote a letter explaining my skills. I said that I was starting a consulting business. I was looking for clients that needed to outsource human resources work," says Doreen.

"Having just gone through a job search two years earlier, and understanding the dynamics in the US market, really helped me determine how to approach companies. I wasn't sending cover letters with a résumé. I was sending a different kind of letter with a different kind of spin. It was before the days of outsourcing. The idea was, 'Okay, think about it. You probably need human resource support in some sense. Here are the skills and qualifications I bring to you. Why not work with me part-time to meet your needs, as I'm affordable?'" Doreen says. She specifically targeted small companies that would have either few or no human resources employees so that her skills would be a welcome addition to a small firm. Her ideal hours were working two full days a week when her husband was off, so she was hoping to sign on a few clients that would want her to come in for one full day once a week or less. Her preference was to work at her clients' offices because she had her husband at home watching the children.

"People called me back," says Doreen. "My first client was a pharmaceutical company. They had a human resource manager. She was an administrative assistant who had grown into her human resource manager position. So they had me come in and coach her, design programs, write handbooks, just some basic things. They became my stable client. From there, I just kept writing more and more letters in the evening. I called and would leave messages on people's answering machines when the kids went to bed at night. I'd do my marketing at night. If someone had left a message on my answering machine about a job, I'd call them back during the day when my kids were napping. I really had to work it around the kids. That's how I built up my clientele."

Since Elizabeth, like Doreen, had no network or business contacts in her area, she also decided to start a consulting business as a way to obtain part-time work. She wrote letters as a method for initially contacting potential clients. Much like Doreen's letters, hers were not cover letters with résumés attached, but letters containing the marketing skills that she could bring to an organization along with a one-page list of accomplishments and corporations where she had worked. Her selling points focused on her ability to start and complete one-time projects that the potential client may not have the manpower to attack. She suggested that she could fill in for those on maternity leave, keeping the businesses moving forward.

Unlike Doreen, she targeted large corporations. Only big organizations would have the type of marketing work that Elizabeth handled. She says, "I preferred working for one client at a time from eight to one, Monday through Friday. This was a selling point for the types of businesses that I was pitching, being available every day of the week. It also enabled me to obtain consistent childcare." Elizabeth was willing to work either from home or at the client's office, based on the client's preference.

Both women used maps and public information to determine where to send the letters. Doreen went through the telephone book for her town and the towns surrounding her home so that any commutes would be within a reasonable distance.

Elizabeth also narrowed her search for clients within a thirty-minute driving radius from her home. She says, "If I was only going to work five hours a day, I didn't want to waste any more than an hour in commuting time so that I could maximize my time working and being with my children." Her clients had to be large organizations with significant marketing budgets in order to use her skills and afford her fees. Since she was new in the area, Elizabeth had no idea what firms surrounded her. Armed with the names of the towns she was willing to commute to, she hit the library. She used *Hoover's Handbook of American Business*, a book that is commonly found in the reference section of the library. From this, she formed a list of possible clients. Then she hit the Web for their addresses, phone numbers, and the names of the marketing department heads.

She then called each of the nine targeted companies to confirm the names of the vice presidents of marketing along with their addresses and phone numbers. Because websites are not always up-to-date, Elizabeth found that several of the people had changed positions. She also compiled the complete information that she needed to mail letters and make phone calls that wasn't necessarily on the Web. Each letter was sent to the vice president of marketing for each company. At the end of each of her letters, Elizabeth said that she would give the vice president a follow-up phone call in a few days. She mailed the letters, three at a time, waited a week and a half, and then followed up with a phone call.

Now because she knew that vice presidents would have assistants to answer their phones, and because she wanted to speak with them in person, she called after 5:00 p.m. This almost ensured their assistants would be gone for the day and that the vice presidents would answer the phone themselves. And it worked. She reached almost everyone personally.

As an aside, right before every phone call, she settled her daughters down in front of a *Sesame Street* videotape to ensure that she could get though the call without interruptions. Elizabeth says, "My first concern was to get my contact on the phone. The second was to set up my daughters so that I would be undisturbed for a ten-minute telephone conversation. That's not easy with a four-year-old and one-year-old."

While she anticipated rejection from a majority of companies, she received positive comments and interviews initially from two out of four companies. One company hired her for a three-month project to replace someone on maternity leave while the other one said that they might call her in the future. They did end up calling her a year later. After the three-month project was completed, she began the same process again, continuing down her list. This time she had success with two more companies, Ethicon, a division of Johnson & Johnson, and AT&T, obtaining interviews with both. She ended up working as a consultant for Ethicon for five mornings a week for almost four years.

The vice presidents of the companies that had no interest in hiring her were pleasant and courteous on the phone. One even asked her if he could pass her name along to another company. "I was surprised how nice everyone was when I called them, even when they turned me down. Sending the letter is easy, but getting up the nerve to make that follow-up phone call and speaking to potential clients is hard," says Elizabeth. "It wasn't that I was afraid they'd say, 'We don't need you,' as I was almost expecting that. It was more that I was afraid they'd be rude or mean. It was just the opposite; everyone was quite nice and almost apologetic if they didn't need my services."

For both Doreen and Elizabeth, once they started their businesses, word of mouth followed. "Some people left companies and said, 'Hey, Doreen, we could use you to do X.' So I went to their new company and helped them out. The business took off and grew a life of its own. I got a lot of work," claims Doreen. And while Elizabeth was at Ethicon, the vice president who hired her left to work elsewhere. When she left Ethicon, he called her and asked her to work for him at his new company.

While Doreen and Elizabeth did not use e-mail when they contacted their clients, it is another possible avenue. It may not be as potentially successful. After discussing this with several business associates, the consensus is that e-mails can appear to be impersonal because they can be sent out in mass quantities. They are also easily deleted along with all the other junk mail one receives daily. A personally addressed, regular letter with a follow-up phone call is seen as personal and well targeted in today's mass-marketing society.

Both Doreen and Elizabeth had to develop their own target lists and initiate their own businesses via cold calling. Both were successful, at not only developing consulting practices from ground zero, but also developing business networks/contacts for themselves. They had the drive, desire, marketing sense, and skills to obtain consulting clients and keep them. Five years after she started her business, Doreen received a full-time offer from one of her clients with a salary of $75,000. Remember that she left the workforce at a salary of $40,000? During her four years of consulting, Elizabeth was approached with discussions of full-time employment twice. Doreen decided to take the offer since both of her children were in preschool at this point and since the financial payoffs were large. Elizabeth never pursued the full-time work discussions as part-time work was what she desired. Not bad for two women with no contacts, no networks.

Key Learning—Cold Calling

- Prior to contacting potential employers, determine your marketable skills:
  - Why should they hire you?
  - What value do you bring?
- Using the Internet:
  - Obtain potential employer's names by doing advance searches on the Web using your geographic area and profession.
  - Identify potential employer's specialties on their websites.
  - Check out job listings:
    - § www.monster.com
    - § www.careerbuilder.com
    - § www.indeed.com
- Turn to the yellow pages:
  - Aids in finding potential employers/clients:
    - § Narrows employers by geography.
    - § View any ads to obtain their business core.

Key Learning—Cold Calling (continued)

- Making contact:
  - ○ Consider writing letters and following up with a phone call *or* just calling them.
    - § Set objectives on the number of potential employers you plan to write or call per day, and do it.
    - § Ensure you have current information on names, titles, and addresses.
    - § Don't e-mail, as those are easily deleted as junk mail.
- Informational interviews:
  - ○ Be assertive to get your foot in the door.
    - § Ask for advice on how to obtain a job in your area of expertise.
    - § Say you'll be in the area, can you stop by?
  - ○ Ask potential bosses how they landed their jobs.
  - ○ Discuss potential jobs in the future, if appropriate.
- When marketing yourself:
  - ○ Be professional.
  - ○ Be persistent.
  - ○ Make sure that your children are completely occupied so you can focus on your search.

FURTHER EDUCATION

Gaining more education can help you in one of three ways. First, it can be a great way to update your skills in your current field. If you've been out of the workforce for some time, this is an excellent way to update yourself on what is happening right now. According to *Workforce 2020*, "Individual workers will change jobs frequently over time. For those who maintain and improve their skills, the changes should bring increasing rewards."[6] Consider enrolling in one or two semester courses in your area. Look for courses that specifically focus on current issues to ensure that you'll be refreshing your skills. This will also help you learn about opportunities in your field. Don't be apologetic about your time off. Showing a passion for your field and obtaining further education will speak for itself.

Second, education is a way to change careers completely. When shifting from one industry to another, additional training is usually required. Do you want to work in interior design, but have a degree in engineering? Were you an accountant in the past, but now have an urge to counsel teens in college selection? What background or training do you need to pursue these areas of work? Several women who had been stay-at-home mothers shifted into areas other than those they had worked in previously. To switch into these new areas, they received further education.

Julie was one of them. Since her career prior to staying home full-time was in pharmaceutical sales, she needed training to work part-time in a nursery. Julie wanted to pursue her love of gardening, so she had to obtain education in the area of horticulture. She entered a Master Gardener Program at the local horticultural society and also took land-scaping classes at a local design school. This training was invaluable in her landing her current nursery position.

Others also used education to move into new areas of employment. Inspired by taking yoga classes for herself, Karen decided that she wanted to teach yoga. She received her yoga teacher certification by enrolling in teacher training classes. Carol completed real estate certification classes to ensure being a real estate agent was what she really wanted.

Third, education can validate what you are pursuing. You want to be a yoga teacher? Obtain certification to provide proof that you're trained in that area. Want to work in sales auditing? Show them that you're current by obtaining your Certified Information Systems Auditor certificate. Earn those highly recognized certificates in a given field. It shows that you have up-to-date knowledge in your area.

But Erica, a part-time ultrasound technician, warns women to be cautious when taking classes that promise employment. "Be careful of vocational schools and what their promises are. Really do your research as to what you're going to do. There are always openings in the medical field for part-time, per diem, and full-time people. Do your research. Go in and observe. In any job, whether medical or not, make sure it's something you want to do.

"My sister-in-law became a medical transcriber. She didn't like it. She thought it would be something great to do to work out of the house. It wasn't what she thought it would be. Talk to as many people as you can, go in, observe, and watch.

"I have friends who are recently divorced. They're struggling. They get sucked into the vocational schools. The schools say, 'We'll train you in a year.' But it's going to cost you $15,000," says Erica. "When you get out, you realize, 'I have this training, but I can't work just anywhere. I can't work in a hospital; I can only work in a clinic.'

"Make sure what they're telling you they're going to give you *is* what you want. Take the syllabus into places and say, 'Will you hire me with all of these requirements?' Don't rely on what the school says. Some of these colleges teach X-ray, but the X-ray they offer is only for working in a chiropractor's office *or* only in a clinic *or* only for certain X-rays. So you're really limited, and your pay is a lot less. You have to be careful."

Key Learning—Further Education

- Education and training enable you to move into new areas.
- Research and observe potential new jobs to ensure you'll like them.
- Double check the training:
    - Does it give you the qualifications you need?
    - Does it give you the ability to work in the location you desire?

SATISFACTION WITH RESULTS

When you lack contacts, gaining satisfying employment *is* hard. But it can be done, as exemplified by the stories in this chapter. Is it worth all that trouble? Is the satisfaction gained worth the effort? Based on the women I talked to, the answer is definitely, "Yes."

"I love it," says Julie. "I feel very confident about what I'm selling. I love these plants. I love this farm. I like the family I work for."

"Directing plays with over fifty adults and children was never a thought when I was a full-time news reporter. Who knew?" claims Mimi. "These opportunities that were opened up for me through my volunteer work are fantastic because I am self-fulfilled with my own work and still have time for my kids."

"Having to start from scratch, learning about all the potential employers in my geographic area, and contacting them cold, that was nerve-racking," says Elizabeth. "But after I obtained positive feedback and a few interviews, I felt empowered. Getting that work on my own gave me the confidence that I could do anything I put my mind to."

"I felt excited because when I'm at work people treat me like an adult," claims Susan. "I get to be in the car by myself for five minutes on the way to work. I can stop and get a coffee by myself. I was starting to see there was a 'me.'"

Chapter 5

STARTING YOUR OWN BUSINESS

"You are your own boss. If you're not a good boss, you're not going to be successful."

—Louise

Sometimes the best way to get the part-time work that you want is to simply start your own business. One-third of the women I interviewed ran their own businesses at one time or another. And according to Catalyst, an organization that addresses the needs of women in business, women-owned businesses have grown dramatically in recent years.[1] If women can't find the hours and flexibility they want in their fields, they are willing to develop a business of their own to get them.

And, while opening your own business may sound ominous, to many women it's not. When you are an independent contractor or freelancer, you have your own business. If you are a craft teacher, marketing consultant, reading tutor, artist, food stylist, freelance writer for a newspaper, researcher for a law firm, or architect consultant, you're running your own business.

The women I interviewed who have started a business never envisioned themselves doing so. Some did it because it was the only way to obtain the working hours they wanted. Others did it because after working for others part-time, they saw how easily they could work for themselves in the same capacity with the same hours making *more* money with *more* control and *more* flexibility. And still others did it because it enabled them to partake in work they enjoyed, not necessarily the jobs where they had previous experience. Catalyst's findings agree with mine as they state business ownership gives women more control over their time and their productivity.[2]

Were these women scared? Nervous? Anxious? Yes, yes, and yes. Did they have all the answers when they started? Did they anticipate all the issues that were before them? Did they start with thousands of dollars as a financial base? No, no, and no. Some developed businesses that took virtually no start-up costs such as tutoring, providing daycare, marketing consulting, and cleaning houses while others started businesses in law, family therapy, and political fund-raising that needed a minor amount of capital to get going. But they all did it, most going in slowly and building their businesses over time.

HOW THEY DID IT

The following stories illustrate how several women who had never envisioned themselves as entrepreneurs began highly successful businesses on their own. These stories have threads of consistency running throughout. They left their jobs in good standing. They started with what they knew and moved on from there. They initiated their own businesses for more flexibility and balance in their lives. And lastly, they all began on a shoestring budget using little start-up money.

Leave Full-Time Job in Good Standing

Samantha started her business by networking and ended up freelancing for her former employer. She wanted to become a freelance food stylist, preparing food for photography shoots in the New York City area. "I was tired, trying to get it all done," she claims. "I needed to cut back. My son was about to enter kindergarten, and I wanted to drop him off and pick him up at school. I decided to try my hand at being a freelance food stylist. So I left my full-time job at the test kitchen where I tried out new recipes for the magazines the company published."

While working for the publisher, Samantha had gone down to the photography studio many times. "Every month we got the magazines so we could look at the pictures of the food. I wanted to take the next step of food styling.

"My very first job on my own was from answering an e-mail: someone was looking for a food stylist. This e-mail was a lead; a woman wanted a food stylist for a cookbook author who was coming to town doing a TV interview for the Food Network. I thought, 'I have to answer that; it's now or never.' That started everything and has led to a lot of jobs.

"I did that author tour where we did a spread for the author cooking in someone's home. I prepared all the food. The newspaper was there taking pictures, and I started talking to the woman doing the article. Luckily for me, she gave my name to the food editor of the newspaper. Then the paper called me and asked me to do an Easter brunch for them. I said, 'Sure, I'd love to.' They actually came to my house, and I made the food. They gave me the recipes, I cooked them up, and we did a photo shoot right here in my home.

"Now the magazine publisher who I had previously worked for saw that I had done some food styling in the local newspaper. When they saw that, they called and said, 'What are you doing? Can you come and work for us?' Now I've come full circle because sometimes they take pictures of food that I've tested."

Since Samantha left her test kitchen job on good terms, the magazine publisher was more than happy to hire her as a freelance food stylist and now the company utilizes all her time. "I have not needed to self-promote. I could submit portfolios to photographers, but it isn't necessary as I could work full-time with the magazine publisher if I wanted to, there's that much work.

"Currently, they schedule month to month. They'll ask me my availability for the upcoming month. I tell them the dates I would like, and then they come back and give me dates they plan to use me. At that point, if something doesn't look quite right or something comes up, I contact them right away. They don't have to book me for those days, but I'm 'iced.' I'm 'iced' for those days, but they don't turn into bookings until they call me two weeks before. I've never had a problem with them not using me on days I've held for them.

"I'm making as much money, if not more, than when I was working full-time, but I don't have the benefits. I'm able to take my kids to school, pick them up, go on field trips, so it's fabulous. I love to see the end result of me getting photos in the magazine. I love the food benefits, too. I bring home the leftovers so we eat really well. I always say that you never know who you're going to meet, so you really need to follow up on phone calls and e-mails. That e-mail led from one photo shoot to another and another and finally to the jobs that I work today. That has led to so much, just that one e-mail."

Continue Current Job, But on Your Own

Initially, Jennifer worked part-time for someone else before realizing that she was better off on her own. "I had worked for nearly seventeen years as a teacher and then gave birth to my son," says Jennifer. "I was happy to take maternity leave because this was a new experience for me. I was at a baby group because this was popular at the time. I must have mentioned that I was a teacher on leave, and someone began discussing the SATs. Then one of the other mothers asked, 'Are you interested in teaching part-time?' It sparked my interest. She said, 'Why don't you come talk to someone I know who has an SAT business?' So this is how it began. I accepted the part-time job and started my training because I thought it would be a great, fun thing. I thought, 'What a nice sideline while I'm home with my baby; maybe I'll do it a few hours a week.' It wasn't about the money, at the time; there was no pressing financial need.

"The tutoring came naturally to me, and I was successful very quickly. My name became very popular with the tutoring crowd, and people kept calling and calling and said, 'Please tutor my child.' I used to refer them to the person who owned the business. She had quite a business with about twenty of us tutoring. After a few years, I began to think about going off on my own because the owner of the business was becoming resentful of my popularity. I was realizing if people kept asking for me, I could do this by myself. I remember asking for a minor raise, one or two dollars per hour, and [the owner] refused. That's when I decided to start my own business, creating my own materials and developing new methods.

"At this point, I decided never to go back to my full-time teaching position at the high school because my SAT tutoring business, which I had never planned, was quite successful. I was probably making similar money. The appeal of having my own business, working from home, and being around my son fulfilled all my needs."

But then Jennifer moved from Knoxville to Memphis. "After moving, I knew no one. I began by calling the high school, telling them about my Knoxville business. They weren't interested in me.... Another person moving to my neighborhood at the same time had a junior in high school. In a conversation, we must have discussed my past job. She asked if I could help with her child. I started with that one teenager; then there were three; then there were eight; then there were twenty. It spread in a very short time. Then the high school called and asked me to do an evening class for them because they were unhappy with the person they had. I agreed, and now they won't let me stop.

"Now I get all my students by word of mouth. I never advertise. I have kids from thirty minutes away. It's like recommending a hairdresser: if they like you, they'll recommend you to a friend."

Like Jennifer, Sonia worked part-time for someone else before realizing that she could do the same thing on her own. But unlike Jennifer, Sonia earns more money on her own than working for someone else.

Using her musical skills, Sonia went from opera singer to voice teacher to business owner even though that was not her original plan. "I went to New York to audition for an opera gig. I went to Cincinnati to audition for an opera gig. I traveled all around the country auditioning and singing. For quite a while, I was singing for the Indianapolis Opera. Then I had children and reality set in." At that point, Sonia reduced her singing considerably and picked up a part-time job as a database/systems administrator.

Just as Jennifer never envisioned opening her own business, neither did Sonia, especially one focused on teaching voice. "I told myself I'd never teach because I was going to be a diva, but children changed all that." Sonia adds that the art community was "opening a small fine arts center in town that was going to combine art, music, and a little bit of theater for young kids. They needed teachers for private lessons, so I interviewed there and began teaching out of this facility in Indianapolis. They needed to get more hours out of me than I could give them, so I decided that it made more sense for me to teach out of my home rather than work for them. This was especially true because a large part of my clientele is just ten minutes away from me. And the best part is I make more money. I set my own hours, set my own rate. They charged $22 per hour for lessons and gave me $11. Here I charge $40 per hour and keep it all.

"I didn't start teaching until about eight or ten years ago. I have to continue to do my database job, yet in an ideal world I would stop it and teach full-time. But I have children in college, so it's need versus want. I love teaching voice. I see myself as a grand dame at a baby grand piano with my shawl draped around my shoulders. I'll continue teaching as long as I can."

Take it Slow, Learn the Ropes

Starting out slowly is prudent. Plan on your income stream being low while you learn the business. By being cautious, you're potentially avoiding some big mistakes.

Joy went out on her own as a lawyer because her commute got to be too much. Initially, she wasn't sure if she would succeed, so she was cautious. "It got to be difficult and very stressful picking up my son as the last one in daycare because of traffic," Joy recalls. "It was not something that I wanted to see. Initially, I could depend on my husband for pick-up and drop-off. But then his work required travel. That's when everything changed. His schedule changed, so I had to make changes. I very hesitantly went out on my own. I didn't know if I could actually open my own business. It was an idea that I would take some clients with me from my current firm and see how it would work out. And if it didn't, I was going to look for a job in a firm.

"I took a few clients, and it was very slow at the beginning. It took three years to take off. Luckily, I was in a financial position that my working was good for us financially, but not a necessity. So if it was slow at the beginning, it was okay. I didn't feel the pressure."

Sheila, a marketing and public relations specialist whose first client was her previous employer, agrees on the preparation aspect. "While clients came to me from previous contacts, I needed help on starting up my own business. I took a three-month course to aid me in covering the self-employment basics. The course was helpful [to me] in shifting from working part-time for a nonprofit and having it become my first client."

Start with What You Know

While she was pregnant, Nancy decided that she wasn't going to go back full-time after her baby was born. So she took that nine-month period to think about what she could do from home with a small baby. Prior to having her son, Nancy managed five jewelry stores in Missouri. Being a certified gemologist, goldsmith, *and* having run her own flower shop, her qualifications could have led her down many avenues. She came up with a simple, straightforward idea that used all her skills.

"I had it in the back of my mind that somebody could bring fine jewelry into people's homes in a type of home party atmosphere. This would take the stuffiness out of buying fine jewelry. Not just offering the real high-end of the scale, but still offering things that are going to last forever and are quality products. Made with precious metals and precious gemstones in a price range where anybody can afford them." That was Nancy's idea.

"I always had that in the back of my mind when I worked for the stores. And I actually did kind of start at the stores. I had some people doing home parties after hours when the stores were closed. This was at the very end of my pregnancy, so I knew I wanted to do something different after I had my son. I didn't want to work sixty-hour weeks and travel as much as I had previously. I thought that maybe I would freelance and do bench work, that I'd just go to work for other jewelers and come in and do their repairs as they needed me. And I kind of did that for a while, but then I thought, 'Well, why couldn't I do this? Why couldn't I make jewelry and do home parties?'

"So I took $500, my initial investment, and purchased some items, and I made up some things. I purchased chains and whatnot to go with my handmade pieces. I called every one of my friends and said, 'If you love me, you'll do a home party for me.' I booked other parties from those parties. I always saved the money that I made and reinvested it in the business. I did that for about the first two or three years. I didn't keep any of the money out.

"I was also freelancing as a goldsmith for other jewelry shops because I wanted to keep my skills up. I wanted to stay in that atmosphere so I knew what was going on in the industry. It was mostly repairs, sizing, and soldering chains. It was the '80s, and everyone wore lots of chains, so we always had lots of chains to repair.

"And then a friend of mine, who has a child my oldest child's age, was stationed in Hawaii. Her husband was in the navy. She had an advertising background and was going crazy with boredom. I could totally understand. So I sent her a box of jewelry and said, 'Do this. It's fun; you get to meet women; you get to get out; you get to talk girl talk; you get to get dressed up. It's something to look forward to. You could do it at night, so you don't need a sitter. Your husband can be at home.'

"She started doing it in Hawaii. Pretty soon, I had people contacting me saying, 'I want to do this, too. How do I do this?' I went, 'Hmmm, I don't know. I'll have to call you back.' So I came up with a plan for them. There was a lot of hit-and-miss because I didn't know anything about direct sales. It took a while to figure that out, figure what they could live with and I could live with. Eventually, we got it right. I picked up more consultants."

Consultant is Nancy's term for her sales representatives, and she has 132 of them who sell her products today. "My sales reps are considered independent contractors, so they purchase items from me at wholesale prices and they sell them in their venue. They do sign something like a contract, so that they don't market my jewelry under another name." Her consultants sell in home parties, her company's heritage, and also in art shows because all of the products are handmade. Some of her consultants have wholesale accounts where they sell. "They can't market my jewelry with another home party company. They can sell it in a home party environment, but not with another jewelry product," Nancy explains.

"As my family grew, we started depending on my business more and more for income. I felt like I needed to grow my income, so I started going out and cold calling salons and day spas to carry my product." Nancy's jewelry is now in forty-eight salons and boutiques.

"There aren't catalogues or anything like that. I do most of the sales calls myself, so I stop and visit all of my shop owners, usually once a month; some of them don't need to see me that often." Her store base is split into three general groups. One is hotel gift shops and tourist-type shops. The second group is salons like day spas, nail salons, and hair salons. The third group is boutiques, places that sell other items that jewelry would accessorize, like clothing stores.

My question to Nancy is, "How did you go from your handmade bench work to selling through 132 sales reps and to forty-eight salons and boutiques? How did you make that much jewelry to sell with just an investment of $500?"

She replies, "I do all the designing myself. I make all the prototypes myself. From there, I enlist other vendors. I farm out tasks so I can do it in mass quantities. The line changes every four months. So the pieces are limited. I only manufacture a certain amount. And when I retire a piece, I never bring it back in its original form. I may bring it back, but there'll be a different twist on it.

"Initially, I used all of the same vendors as when I managed the jewelry stores. They all knew me. Luckily, they all trusted me. Everyone I went to extended me credit. I even had some gold vendors and silver vendors who would actually lend me their chain inventory when I needed it on consignment. Twenty-one years later, I still work with the same people."

Her sales reps purchase the samples they like and then go out to obtain orders. The interesting thing about Nancy's jewelry is that she can take any of those items and make them out of gold, diamonds, and platinum if a customer wants because all of the designs are hers and she owns all the molds. People can choose any gemstone and any metal, customizing the piece specifically the way they want it.

"A majority of the time, what the consultants do is try and pick up as many pieces in the new line as they can or as they care to. They don't always like everything. They purchase what they need, and those are their samples. Then we usually have a two-week turnaround once the order is placed. Sometimes, things can be executed a little faster. Sometimes, if it's something really unusual, we need a little more time. I let them know that as soon as they place the order with me," says Nancy.

As far as pricing goes, "there's a suggested retail price on everything that I sell. Whether they're a salon owner or a consultant, they get a discounted price based on quantities or based on a dollar amount. They can sell it for anything they want. I do have some shop owners on the shore who take off all of my tags and put their own on and mark it up more than I would suggest." Obviously, if someone customizes a piece, then the price is revised according to the metals and gems selected.

Was she concerned about taxes or legal issues? How did she handle that? "When I came across a roadblock, I just figured it out. I consulted experts along the way as I needed them. I knew how to do taxes because I had owned a flower shop. I knew that my sales representatives needed to be independent contractors because I didn't want to be responsible for filing taxes on them. Everything else was pretty simple. I did consult a lawyer about the contract that my sales reps signed. I have insurance. It's all pretty easy."

I was so impressed by Nancy that I asked her, "Aren't you proud of yourself?"

"I am. I love what I do," she says.

Spread the Word

When I asked how they got their firms off the ground, many women discussed how they not only used their contacts, but also advertised for themselves. I'm not talking about placing big ads in the local newspaper. I'm talking about using simple marketing tools that cost almost nothing.

Celeste started her craft classes by sending out flyers. After her business got off the ground, she began sending out e-mails instead, using her database that she had built up over time. "I wanted kids from second to sixth grade," says Celeste. "In the beginning, I sent flyers to all the elementary schools in town and my daughter's dance studio. Now I send e-mails to past students and referrals. When I send out the schedule, it's filled within twenty-four hours."

Edith used a similar strategy. She developed brochures for her mural painting business. Since her target market was adults versus children, she asked her employed friends to place the brochures in their offices and hang them on bulletin boards for her. It worked. She got jobs from these brochures. References were also important in her business, and she had those lined up for anyone who asked.

Even a tax preparer can advertise. Leigh initially received a few referrals from her mentor who was overworked and needed to reduce his client base. Then to grow her business further, she circulated flyers through her child's preschool. The following year, she mailed out post-cards through another school. Additionally, she placed magnetics on her van and circulated information about her business at church.

Celeste, Edith, and Leigh produced brochures and flyers that aided them in spreading the word. But you don't have to stop there. You can also use business cards, handing them out to people you see as you carry on your daily activities at the grocery store or on the soccer field. Handing people something with your contact information on it is a good idea. It makes it that much easier to find you, recommend you to others, and ultimately hire you.

Leap of Faith

Unlike Nancy who started her business slowly and methodically, Ava started her political fund-raising business on a leap of faith. "I was elated and scared to death. I was taking a running start and a huge leap of faith going out on my own. If I didn't do it, I would have always looked back and said, 'Why didn't I do this?' It was scary taking that last paycheck. I had $1,100 in my pocket and a notebook of contacts. I had one client and built it from there."

Regarding how she started her business, Ava replies, "People who are thinking of starting their own businesses probably have more money than I did. I rented a computer and printer. I found someone to rent me office space. I kept networking. I wasn't afraid to ask favors. I said to my friend, 'You know how to do this; you know graphics better than I do. If you mock up business cards for me, I promise I'll make you spaghetti and meatballs.' That's what I do. I said to others, 'If you can help me to set this up, I'll cook you dinner for two nights. I'll walk your dog.' I didn't have a lot of money. I was not afraid to go to people smarter than I was to say, 'How did you do this? How did you set up your business?'"

For her, the work itself is exciting. "I like projects that have a beginning, middle, and end. In fund-raising, it's very project-oriented. There are goals to meet. I have deadlines. I'm satisfied when I'm hitting my goals. I worked in Washington on two presidential campaigns. Usually my clients are specific political families or the Republican National Committee."

When asked about the best part of her job, she replies, "I love the fact that every day is something new. I get to deal with issues that impact this country every single day I work in this business. I'm so proud of what I do for a living."

Key Learning—How They Did It

- Keep your start-up business ideas simple.
- Know what you're getting into.
- Capitalize on your past experience. Can you use your experience with a new twist?
- Determine if you could make more money doing work on your own versus working for someone else.
- Realize that you can start a business with very little money.
- Leave your full-time job in good standing; the contacts may turn out to become invaluable.
- Be willing to take a chance, deciding ahead of time how much risk you're willing to take.
- Use your network/friends to help launch your business.
- Be willing to reinvest in your business.
- Go slow; be willing to take the time to figure out the business model that's right for you.
- Keep up your contacts and network in your industry.
- Cold call. It works. Don't be afraid of doing it.
- Use experts in areas unfamiliar to you, such as taxes or legal work.
- Be willing to do what it takes.
- Request recommendations from your clients.
- Love what you do!

INS AND OUTS OF OWN BUSINESS

Before starting your own business, it's good to take a hard look at the pros and cons. What will you gain by breaking off on your own? What will you lose? While being your own boss sounds great, you also do all the billing, you keep all the records. Some parts are exhilarating; others are tedious. Does the excitement outweigh the monotonous tasks? Only you can decide.

Pros

What's the best part about owning your own business? One thing tops everyone's list: the flexibility that owning your own business affords. Setting your own schedule, giving you the flexibility to meet your family's needs while earning income was mentioned by almost everyone. This is the single best part of running your own business, hands down.

"The flexibility I had in my schedule and the true balance between the part of me that wanted to work and the part that wanted to be a mom," that's how Janette, a home decorator, put it.

For Joy, flexibility means balancing her work running her own law firm with her husband's employment. "My husband travels a lot, so I'm a single parent Monday through Friday. I need this flexibility of part-time work."

According to the entrepreneurs, the next best part of running your own business is the people you meet. Becky, a dance teacher and dance studio owner, claims, "All the relationships that I have made over the twenty-seven years are wonderful. I've made good friends with parents of the children that I've had. I teach children of children now."

Many others had similar comments saying that they loved the variety of clients and new people that they meet through their work. This goes hand in hand with the stimulation that working with others brings.

Several women liked controlling their own destinies and felt that they did so much better by running their own businesses rather than working for someone else.

And for those whose businesses related to the arts, using their creativity to earn money ranked right after flexibility. "Nothing makes an artist happier than someone appreciating their work," says Karen.

Nancy adds, "I love the reaction I get from other people. It's a part of me; it's such a personal thing; it's really neat to share with other people and get such positive feedback."

Summing it all up, Doreen says, referring to her human resources consulting business, "I was able to earn money and help provide for the family, stimulate myself intellectually, and still meet my family needs."

Cons

While some women couldn't think of any downsides to running their own businesses and had no complaints, others came up with some salient points. These details are worth considering if you're thinking of starting up your own business.

"It's hard to do it on your own. It's easier to work in a typical work setting in an office because people can cover for you while you're not working, which is often what happens with part-time people in an office. It's hard to be on your own, especially if you want to build up a business. If the work is there, you have to take it," says Joy, regarding her legal business. "Working on your own is very difficult, because you take the work when it comes. So you're not really sure. Some weeks it could be fifty hours; you never know from week to week if it's going to be a busy week or a slow week. I do get overwhelmed sometimes, and I end up working at night. That's not what I signed up for; that's the downside of working for yourself."

Laura, who runs her own stationary business, says, "All the taxes and legal stuff is so laborious. I've done it myself, and my mom is doing the books. You've got to stay on your toes. There's a county license, a city license, sales tax license. It's yucky, and you have to muddle through versus going to work for someone else who figures it all out."

Others agree with Joy and Laura that it was tough having all the responsibility of making the business fly on your own shoulders. Because of that and not knowing where the next client or job will come from, some felt that their part-time business turned into full-time work more often than they would have liked.

Christi, who runs her own professional counseling/teaching services in conjunction with hospitals, agrees, "I have to totally rely on myself. There's no one else who's going to come along. I have to keep working; not a sick day, not a rest day."

Unlike Joy and Laura, whose work often took up more hours than they would have liked, Leigh has a different issue. As a tax preparation specialist, she works intensely February through April and then has no work. The seasonality of her business causes large swings in her income. She needs to come up with a counter seasonal business idea to even out her annual earnings.

Nancy also has an issue with seasonality. "I also don't like how it's such a roller coaster. I'm so busy for a few months of the year, I can't see straight. And then other times, I wish I had more work. That's the nature of the business. I find it's hard to be motivated and be creative when I'm not out there and busy, when I'm kind of stagnant. It's tough to go from being busy to not being busy."

Leigh has another issue, too. She works from her home to save money. Sounds smart, right? The downside is the clients come into her home or she has to go into theirs. When it's with people she knows, it's fine. But when she gets calls from people she doesn't know wanting to come into her home, that is less than an ideal situation.

Others mention that having sick children is difficult, since there is no one else to cover for you. You're it when you're running your firm alone; you do it all. This self-reliance along with the instability and difficulty in gauging the work bothered several women.

Remember Ingrid, the air force captain turned corporate part-timer? She closed her successful IT consulting business due to instability. "I had decided to start my own company after a six-month leave of absence upon the birth of my second child. I had a business phone in my house, and I passed that [number] along to past clients. I could solicit them after six months. I was very cool about it, and sure enough, I had two or three clients call me. . . . I started my own consulting firm. I ran my own company for six and a half years. I tried to keep it to twenty hours per week. I had a third baby during all of that. I had a very big client at the time. Literally, four months after I had [my daughter], they were begging me to come back. I was doing crazy stuff like bringing her to boardroom meetings, nursing her in the bathroom, running a meeting while burping a baby. It was good and bad all at the same time. But a couple of years after that, maybe when she was around four and a half, I said, 'This is too crazy.' When you're your own boss and your own secretary, IT support, accounts receivable, finance, marketing, it's too much. I was getting too tired doing all of it. I didn't have a big enough business to grow it enough to hire people. Nor did I want to. I didn't want to become an employer. My income started to vary drastically. I had highs and lows in income. I was tired of going after people. I just wanted something much more consistent. I wanted something where I wasn't always marketing myself and sending out bills. I just wanted to work part-time and get paid."

Isolation and loneliness came up with several women as another con. One woman mentioned never leaving the house and having little physical interaction with others. Joy says, "I'm in an office by myself, and, yes, I'm talking to people on the phone, but I don't have that support system. No immediate feedback. Yes, I can pick up the phone, but that person might not be there and it might take days before you connect."

And while she's obviously good at it, Ava dislikes cold calling, a necessary task for many entrepreneurs. Nancy adds, "I still don't like cold calling even though I've done so much of it. I've never liked cold calling."

Pricing

What's a fair price? How much do you charge? When do you charge? How do you decide? This is probably one of the most important factors in setting up a successful business. If you've moved out from a similar business and are now working on your own, you have their pricing as a base. But what if you haven't? What if you're starting from scratch? How do you determine the right price structure? So I asked these women what they did.

Sherry, the owner of a photography business, had a hard time determining an appropriate fee schedule because photographers have a wide range of rates. Due to her recent divorce, she needed the income. Since she left the business world as a chief financial officer, Sherry had the ability to go back into accounting, yet she loved her photography and wanted to make a go of it as a business.

"It was hard. I learned a lot about fee schedules," Sherry says. "When I first started doing it, I looked at my needs as far as income. How many hours a week or month I wanted to work, how many weeks a year I wanted to work. I broke that down. I judged based on what I could earn if I was working as an accountant, what the difference was between the two. Then I also looked at other photographers to see what the market would bear, based on the quality of my work. It's quite a varied market depending on what people do, whether they're in the studio or out of the studio.

"So I put all of those things together to make this worthwhile. I need to make X amount of dollars or it's not worth it. Then I based that on what it took me to do the work itself. People received it positively. I have a high-quality product: I'm not the cheapest; I'm not the most expensive. My work is high quality. I took some classes, and they said, 'Look when you start your business, make sure that you charge enough for your time because it's really hard to raise your rates.' I tried to start at a good point so I wouldn't have to raise them. If I had started low and had to raise them significantly, I'd have a different kind of clientele. I thought I wanted to attract a certain kind of clientele that could pay a certain amount of money. So if they couldn't afford my rates, they weren't my type of clients anyway."

Christi runs her counseling/teaching business servicing hospitals' needs out in the field. She made the mistake that many women starting off make: she didn't charge enough for her time. When asked about pricing she replies, "It has been a really hard thing. When I first started, I was very reticent to say how much I thought I was worth. I wasn't good at it. I initially negotiated for a contract that I had booked for a very low wage of $33 per hour, and, without benefits, that's not very high. Since then, I'm now comfortable asking for $100 per hour. I felt comfortable raising my rates by talking with others, sharing information about my supervision with people, and what others are charging in this area as well as in the state. I began to increase them.

"My teaching is a flat $100 per hour because there is a lot of prep. The $100 includes the prep time. I recently charged a friend $100 per hour to teach a course. He was behind on his credited hours, and he needed them. He had a deadline. I said, 'I'm charging you $100. That's what I charge.' It didn't feel good. He was a longtime friend. I said, 'Call me again sometime, and I'll do it for free, but right now this is my only income. I need to have this.'"

While Sonia set her own fees based on the going rates being charged by other high-level voice teachers, she decided to change how she scheduled the payments. "A lot of private voice teachers charge by the hour. I realized after paying our piano teacher a monthly fee that it made much more sense to charge a monthly fee. If students missed, you tried to make up a lesson. Otherwise, your income was going up and down, and up and down with children getting sick or having a test the next day and needing to study. So I have a monthly, not hourly, rate. If parents have paid for this, the students go. If they miss, it's up to them to schedule makeup sessions. Other voice teachers in town are so surprised at that."

Now Jennifer was fortunate because she could use a pricing structure from her former employer. But she has a secret for setting up appointments with new students that ensures success in her particular field. "I charge by the session. I never ask for money in advance. After my first lesson with a new student, I won't make the second appointment until the parent gets feedback from their child privately. I am that confident in my skills. And if a child is uncomfortable with me, I don't want to tutor them. I'd rather they get help from someone they can learn from. After that first session, I always tell parents the same thing. Your child will say one of two things, 'I hate it, it stinks,' or 'Oh, I can't believe what I learned; I can't wait to go back.' With that strategy, my schedule is always full."

For women in particular, it's key *not* to undercharge. Don't think of your clients as doing you a favor, but as *you* doing them a favor. People think more highly of services that they pay a fair price for versus what they get cheaply.

Key Learning—Ins and Outs of Owning Your Business

- Best parts:
  - Flexibility in scheduling yourself.
  - Meeting new people.
- Worst parts:
  - Potential instable work flow and/or income.
  - Drastic swings in income based on seasonality.
  - Use of home for client presentations.
  - Loneliness or isolation.
- Pricing:
  - Compare your fees to rates for comparable services in your area.
  - Charge enough for your time, taking benefits and preparation time into account.
  - Consider monthly versus hourly fees, if applicable, to stabilize your income.

NETWORK MARKETING

Maybe you're interested in running your own business, but you have no idea where to start. You have no business model, no product, just an urge to run your own show. Network marketing may be something you want to consider. You know network marketers as women selling Mary Kay or Pampered Chef or Longaberger Company products.

Network marketing, also known as direct selling, is defined as "a business distribution model that allows a parent company to market its products directly to consumers by means of relationship referrals and direct selling."[3] Independent, unsalaried salespeople in network marketing represent the parent company and are paid a commission based on the volume of product they sell. These salespeople may be referred to as associates, business owners, or consultants, among other titles. You could call it a "micro-franchising" business model. I talked to five women who earn their income via direct selling who are pleased and enthusiastic about their businesses.

Approaching Your Own "Micro-Franchise"

How can you decide if this business model is right for you? Obviously, you must be a self-starter, willing to work with lots of people, extremely organized, friendly, and most importantly, excited about the products that you're selling. If you have all these characteristics and think that this might be for you, how can you make sure that you select the right company to work with? By taking the time to thoroughly research whoever you choose and loving the product you endorse.

Leanne, currently with Arbonne, a health and beauty products company particularly known for skincare, is a great example. In the beginning she was skeptical of the entire business model. Her previous full-time experience had been in advertising and marketing. After staying home for six years, she felt she was losing her sense of self. At about the same time, she began to have a desire to bring in extra income to take the pressure off her husband as the sole wage earner. So when this opportunity came up, she was open to the idea.

"Another woman who was involved in Arbonne asked me to sample products for her and let her know what I thought," says Leanne. "So I did; I sampled the products. I heard she worked with the company, and I didn't understand what that entailed. I didn't think she worked that hard because I saw her at the soccer games and gymnastics and all the other things the moms were at. Then she and I met for coffee. I realized that she really did have a very big business, but it was scheduled around the needs of her family. I realized it was something I was looking for.

"She said to me, 'I think you'd be great in this business.' I said, 'I'm just starting to think about what I can be doing. I want to make enough money to make it worth my while to go back to work. But I don't want to be stuck on someone else's hours. I don't want to commute. I don't want to give up the field trips. I don't want any of that.' I remember laughing, thinking, 'That job doesn't exist.'"

Leanne's friend felt that Leanne would be a great asset to her team and asked her to attend a team meeting to see what she thought. Leanne mulled it over and distinctly remembers telling her husband she was going to go to the meeting, but thought it would probably be a little cheesy. She planned on returning early.

"I went to the meeting where I was able to listen to other people involved with Arbonne. It's a once-a-month meeting involved with her organization; they did training and were getting recognized and promoted for different things they had done with their businesses. I was really blown away by the professionalism of the women and the diverse backgrounds. All kinds of great backgrounds, but like me, [they] didn't want to continually trade time for money. They wanted something else, but didn't want to sacrifice time with their family.

"So I looked at that and looked online at the company's website for a while." And, after some thought, she decided to do it. "The worst thing that could happen is that I would jump into the business and realize that I didn't want to do it anymore. I would have invested in three sets of skincare products that I use every day anyway, so it really didn't matter."

Leanne was willing to make the upfront investment to get her business going. After building her business twenty hours a week over three years, she is currently a regional vice president. "The next level up is a national vice president in the next year. My own activity doesn't change a lot, my own sales. But it's bringing more people into my organization. That aggregate sales number equals a volume that puts you in a national vice presidential position. Just to give you a background, some people think it's a fun little skincare hobby, but the average salary of a national vice president is $22,000 a month. That's a significant amount of money for a part-time job. I look at that and think my reason for doing the business is much bigger now. It used to be that I wanted something for myself and a little extra money. Now I look at it and realize this can actually change our family, in terms of my husband. If he doesn't really want to do his financial job anymore, if he wants to do something else. If he wants to start his own company, I'm giving him that flexibility and freedom to be able to make some different choices. I don't want him to have the feeling that he can't walk away from the high-paying job to support us. Additionally, when you get to the national vice president level so much of what you're doing is leadership and coaching; that's what I love best."

Like Leanne, Leigh thought through what company would be the best for her before joining a scrapbooking company. "I've always loved scrapbooks," she says. "I had some rudimentary ones, magnetic albums, the ones that peel back, yellow, and fade. My friend and I wanted to start baby albums for our children, and I said, 'I want an album I can give them when they get married someday that won't yellow and fade.' She said, 'Yeah, I do too. I don't want to waste my time. Mine that I've done for myself are all terrible-looking.' So she ended up hearing about this company on *Focus on the Family*, a radio show. She went to an event and said, 'Leigh, I'm going to do this.' I said, 'What do you mean you're going to do this?' She said, 'I'm going to sign up and be a consultant.' I said, 'I'll have your first class for you.' So she came over and had a class. I thought, 'Oh my gosh, I love this.'

"When this came across my doorstep, I could have gone into selling toys because some of those opportunities were really neat. I had children, a one-and-a-half and a three-year-old. But I thought, 'When they're nineteen, am I still going to be passionate about selling blocks and toys? Maybe not.' So I thought about Tupperware. Once I own everything I need, I probably won't want to do that anymore.

"But photos, you're always going to take photos. I always advise people if you're going to get into some type of part-time job, get into something that people are going to use up. They'll always take more photos. Once they start scrapbooking, they're going to need more pages, they'll need more product. That would be my advice. I love baskets, but once you've sold to somebody, it's kind of a closed door. Once you have customers in this, you have customers for life." Leigh would know, since she is currently a director for the scrapbooking company. "I had a big event on Saturday here. Some of those mothers have been coming here for seventeen years. They buy every month. That's nice!"

Louise got involved with network marketing through a beverage distribution company because she was so enthusiastic about the product itself. She was recovering from cancer when she heard about this fruit beverage from a friend who sells the juice. It reportedly has anticancer agents in it that sparked Louise's interest.

"I read the policies and procedures, actually read them," says Louise. "People don't. I listened to the CD and read online as much as I could. I was up at 4:30 a.m. reading everything. I was so excited. Then I started on the product, and it made a profound difference for me within a week. I started looking for ways to market it and started it as a business, really quickly. It's a $35 fee to become a wholesale customer. That's how you get your juice. It also gives you rebates to introduce it to others so it gives you rights as a distributor as well. The company offers some training by the people who bring you into the business. You are in partnership with the company. You get paid for results, not hourly. You basically educate people and connect them to the company. The company handles all the shipping and customer service issues. You get a bonus for the initial order." As with many of the other direct sales businesses, Louise is paid based on her volume and the volume of all others she brings into the organization.

Louise feels this aspect of network marketing is right for her. Unlike the others who directly sell products to customers, Louise doesn't. Her customers have seen an ad on national television or have gone to a website and are calling for more information. She then calls them back at a time convenient for them and answers their questions. If they place an order for the product, she gets credit for it. She says her business is easy because it comes from the referral market.

Here's how she explained it to me. "The cold market is calling people who have filled out a survey and they don't know, have no idea, what you're calling them for. They haven't called specifically about your product. They may have filled out a survey to win a television. That's completely cold. The warm market is family and friends. That's a great way to build your business because it's people that you love and they love you. They trust you, *but* you don't have creditability with them as far as business goes. You're changing your relationship with them from a friendship or family relationship, and you're trying to make it a business relationship. That can be touchy. There's a club called the 'NFL Club,' No Friends Left, because they know you're in one of those [selling] things. So I've avoided that. The referral market is the best for me because people who are calling you are interested in the product."

Network marketers don't all start as stay-at-home moms. Many begin their businesses while also working a full-time job. This enables women to see how much money they can make in a part-time position. Some women even leave their jobs altogether, focusing solely on their network-marketing businesses as sales increase to a sustainable level.

Roxanne is one of those very women. She became a scrapbooking network marketer while also teaching school full-time. "When I was teaching, I had a parent whose son was in my class, and she was a consultant. I started purchasing my scrapbook materials from her and doing my scrapbooking with her. Eventually, I decided it made sense to become a consultant under her." Once Roxanne knew she could make enough money selling these scrapbooking products, she cut her teaching hours and began a job share, teaching first graders half of the week and selling the scrapbooking products one night a week. While it would be easier for her to teach full-time rather than to try and juggle two jobs, Roxanne wanted the flexibility working these two jobs offered.

I asked earlier, "How do you select the right company to work with?" Even after researching the company, you may sign up with one that doesn't fit with your lifestyle. Many times issues arise that you simply didn't consider. This happened with Roxanne. Over the years she sold the scrapbooking products, the market shifted. Scrapbooking products were popping up in many stores and locations. Roxanne felt her competitive edge was waning. In addition, while she loved her company's products, she hadn't thought about how carrying inventory would take up space in her home as well as tie up her money. She also learned each company offers different incentives for hosting a party. Some incentives are clearly better than others, making the consultant's job easier.

So after working with the scrapbooking company for seven years, she became a consultant for another company, a candle company, as well. Roxanne sold for the scrapbooking company, taught school, and sold for the candle company, too. Yes, she held three part-time jobs, working about sixty hours a week, for one year. The high-quality candles drew Roxanne into the third job. "I talked some of my friends into selling candles before I did. We needed a new consultant because our consultant was pretty flaky. I had a friend who was at a dead-end waitressing job, so I talked her into it. She loved candles. She started selling it. Another friend of mine started selling it, too. We were out to dinner one night, and my husband said, 'I don't understand why you don't just give it a try.' So my husband prompted me to decide to start. I had tons of friends who were already addicted to the product, so I thought I might as well serve their needs. And the money; I feel like I make a lot more money."

Roxanne sold both products for a year until she knew she could make enough money selling candles to drop the scrapbook line. Moving into the candle business had advantages for Roxanne. "I didn't like having to store inventory with the scrapbook line. I felt like I had $2,000 worth of product at all times, but not necessarily what my customers needed. I didn't like taking up the storage space, and I didn't like my money sitting there. I also wanted a product that didn't have a lot of competition. I wanted to sell something that I loved and was passionate about, that was consumable, and that didn't have a lot of competition. I really loved the candles personally. I was working shows of my own every other month for another consultant. There was no money to get started, no start-up costs, no risks. So I just thought, 'I'll give it a try.' And I did. I didn't have to stock any inventory. I had paychecks deposited in my account every week. With the scrapbooking products, you bought the inventory outright and then sold it."

With Roxanne no longer carrying inventory, her income stream became much clearer to her. "It helped me to show my husband how much I was making. I did a show, and money got deposited. I did another show, and money got deposited in my account. Whereas with scrapbook products, I bought everything outright and it sat on my shelf until I sold it. I didn't like that."

She also feels that the candle company has programs in place that make her job easier. "One thing I love about the candle company versus the scrapbooking company I worked with is we have the best hostess plan around. Hostesses get so much more in free product and benefits when they host a show. People call me to rebook. With the scrapbooking company, I had a hard time getting people to do initial shows for me and make a commitment. I feel like hostesses just love getting so much free stuff. They constantly reward us as consultants. And they constantly come up with new things to make the hostesses more excited about hosting shows."

Unlike the other three moving either from being stay-at-home mothers or working full-time, Eileen switched from one part-time job to selling Mary Kay products. After realizing that the earning opportunities with Mary Kay were greater than with her part-time food brokerage job, Eileen jumped into the business. Like Roxanne, she liked the flexibility direct sales offered her, allowing her to choose whether she wanted more time with her children one month or more income based on her family's needs. She also believes in the product line and enjoys sharing it with others. "The flexibility, geographic, and income advantages with Mary Kay exceed what I had with the food brokerage job. I can take the things that are important to me, streamline them, and be home when I want to be. I can determine what I want the income to be based on how much time I put into it."

Since Eileen's oldest child is going off to college, leaving just two at home, her home dynamics are changing. She sees this job as offering the transitional opportunities that she'll need over the next several years. "A friend of mine invited me to join the business. That's the concept behind this business; you're invited by someone else to become a consultant. She paid incentives upon my joining the business and building inventory, how much I order and maintain. Bonuses come on a monthly basis. I am paid on building team members. You start earning bonuses once you've brought three people into the company, then get paid a percent of commission for whatever inventory they order. What you order correlates to what you sell. You replace inventory as you sell. The more people you add to your team, the more opportunity you have for bonus increases as well."

Think about these women as you decide if this is the right path for you. If so, make sure that the company you select is with the Direct Sales Association (DSA), online at www.dsa.org. It's like the Better Business Bureau of network-marketing companies, accepting only legitimate businesses. Consider the following:

- Are you excited about the product line?
- What do you know about the person who introduced you to the company?
- What are the start-up costs?
- When will you start making money?
- What are you stuck paying for if you decide you don't like the job?
- What are the inventory policies of the company?
- Do you need storage space or a selling area in your home?
- How do you get paid?
- What is the bonus structure?
- Are there any special incentive programs such as trips?
- What are the hostess incentives?
- How comfortable are you selling to friends and family?

Succeeding at Direct Sales

Succeeding in network marketing takes skill. It takes someone who is willing to hear "No" and not take offense. Direct selling is tough and is not a job for the meek and mild. It takes a self-starter who is well focused and above all, a persistent worker. What other qualities are necessary for these types of businesses?

I asked these women what they attribute to their success. Since Leigh has had as many as 800 people working for her at one time in this business, she knows what she is talking about. "I have always been diligent," she replies. "No matter what, I would always schedule two events a week. I stay on a real pattern. I tell my gals, 'Tell me how many hours you can commit, if it's two hours a week or ten hours a week. But during those hours, you can't go in and load the laundry. Once you go to load the laundry, you'll see something else that needs to be done. You load the dishes and then the whole women's world thing starts in. Then you go out and make one call and you feel like you've worked two hours on your business, but you didn't.' So I tell them you have to not do all that little stuff, even though it seems to make sense. No. Just pretend you've left and gone to an office."

Having risen to vice president, Leanne is another role model to emulate. "I followed the path of the girl who got me involved," she says. "That's key with this type of business, network marketing. We have models of success; people already know what works. It's trainable and teachable to others so it's, 'This is what you need to do to be successful.' You just do it. I've attached myself to people who I think are doing it well and asked them what they did and follow the direction that they gave me. I copied, followed the leader.

"I share Arbonne's products and business opportunities with lots of people." A big part of Leanne's job is bringing people into the business alongside her. "I help get their businesses going. I do a lot of leadership training and coaching in addition to building my own business. I can work ten hours per week. If I find three other people who only want to work ten hours per week, I get paid on my ten hours per week and all their ten hours per week, ultimately getting paid on forty hours per week when I'm only working my ten hours. So ultimately, when I bring people in, I am credited for the work they do as well as my own. The beauty of it is, the way Arbonne works, it only behooves me to help others. Because if I help others, then I'm successful. If I worried just about myself, I won't be successful because I need others as well. It's kind of a nice change from the corporate environment, which wasn't so nice that way.

"A lot of what I do falls into my day-to-day life," Leanne continues. "If I'm in the park or at a soccer field, just normal chitchatting is sharing products. Someone may say, 'I need to go back to work' or 'We need another income' or 'I'm looking into several options' or 'I can't believe I've got to go back full-time.' I chitchat a little bit about what I do. At that point, I say, 'You might want to take a look at what I do. Would you be interested in getting a glass of wine or a cup of coffee and hearing a little bit about it?' So that kind of stuff is working, although I'm not sitting at a desk in my house."

Since Roxanne has earned over five incredible trips through the candle business, I wanted to hear how she did it. "I've been to Aruba, Atlantis [the resort], Hawaii twice, Mexico, and I just got back from a week-long cruise through the Caribbean. I run two to three shows a week at night. I'm calling during the day, compiling packets, closing shows on the computer. I do all the office stuff on Monday and Wednesday."

While she feels starting with a company is less of a risk than starting up your own, she believes that you need to work with products you're passionate about. Sell something you love. Additionally, select a company that has clear goals and guidelines. "My candle company sets up guidelines. You have to do X amount in sales; you have to do X amount in sponsoring. It's always on a point system. You get a point for every dollar you sell, and you get 1000 points for every person you sponsor and bring into the business. So it's achievable to all. You can't say you win it because it's not a competition where you draw names out of a hat. Everybody who meets the qualifications gets to go. You earn it. It's very achievable. I'm very consistent.

"I definitely make more at this than I do teaching." Remember, Roxanne teaches part-time along with selling candles. "It's sad; I taught for twenty-four years and have my masters in teaching. I love my real day job; I love teaching. But to be honest with you, I went to college for five years, got my master's degree, and never have they paid for an all-expense paid vacation for me. They don't even pay expenses for conferences where I'm going to learn more about my job. I have to pay for those. Yet the candle company pays for exotic vacations for my husband and me every year."

It's *Your* Business

Running a network-marketing business has its advantages. It has a low cost of entry with the potential for high revenue. You are the owner. You decide how much you want to work and when you want to work, giving yourself the flexibility you need. When you build your business, it directly increases your income. Most of the upfront equity comes in the form of your own hard work. You can try it out while maintaining your current job, and there is the potential for tax breaks as well.

"If you're going to work part-time, why not have ownership? Why not build your own business rather than working part-time basically working for somebody else?" asks Leanne. "In studies you see over and over again, the key to wealth is ownership. With network marketing, you have your own business. But you're not putting in a lot of equity up front, just sweat equity, your own hard work. Women are such natural networkers, especially if you think about how we buy shoes or go out to eat or find a contractor. Everything is 'who do you know?' or 'where did you get that?'

"Even women working full-time, who want to get out of full-time work, can build a network-marketing business on the side. Then ultimately make enough money to get out of full-time employment. For a lot of people, it's scary to give full-time work up. It's 'I need the money.' What's nice with an opportunity like Arbonne, they don't have to give it up. They can work it alongside in the nooks and crannies of their day. When they've built it to where they're getting a significant amount of money each month, then they can step away. It gives them a safety net. You don't have to quit one to start the other."

Roxanne sees tax break advantages in her direct sales business. While she hopes to eventually go back to teaching full-time, she feels she will always continue selling candles and accessories. "I think that anybody in America would be foolish not to have a home-based business for the tax write-offs. I feel that when I go back to teaching full-time, I'll keep my part-time business as long as I can for the tax write-off. I can write-off so much that I wouldn't be able to otherwise, the space in my home, my new computer, my postage, my mileage. When I'm making my deliveries, I always do my own errands at the same time if they're in the same neighborhood, writing my gas off. In this day and age you need that. It's smart to have some sort of home-based business; even if it brings little obvious income, I think it saves you in the long run."

But while network marketing is a legitimate business model, it has a bad reputation. Could it be due to its tiered compensation structure? Most large sales organizations pay their sales reps, directors, and vice presidents in much the same fashion, so it shouldn't be that. Could it be due to the purchasing of your own inventory? That's not unusual in the standard franchising model.

So why do people see it as an offensive business offering? Probably because some people attracted to the model don't have the qualifications to implement it. Maybe they don't have the money saved up to properly invest in the business or they have no previous sales experience or they have little experience developing business relationships. The women I interviewed feel the people who don't succeed in network marketing have unrealistic expectations of how quickly they should be earning large incomes. Those who fail don't give their businesses a chance to grow; they expect instantaneous results. They have unrealistic expectations of the amount of work involved compared to the income earned. Some simply aren't good salespeople. Selling is a skill that everyone does not have. Others become desperate to succeed quickly and then push themselves on family, friends, and mere acquaintances.

Pam, an area manager for a network-marketing company, says, "The biggest downfall for most people working part-time is they don't use their time effectively. You really have to be structured, organized, and have time management skills. If you really have a lofty goal, it's going to take time. Many times in network marketing, people think they're going to get in and get rich fast. It's really not about that. It's called network marketing. You do have to work."

Scott Allen, writer for *Entrepreneur*, says, "The point is to make sure you're going into it with your eyes wide open. Many people have made a lot of money in network marketing, MLM, and consumer direct marketing, but many more have ended up wasting a whole lot of time and money chasing a pipe dream. You can ensure your success best by being sure you're getting into the right opportunity in the first place."[4]

"Network marketers who are serious about building a *business* should be reading and learning about business fundamentals, the latest sales and marketing techniques, strategies for networking and business development, etc., not just swapping tips at your team's weekly or monthly meeting. Act like a small business owner, and people will treat you like one," Scott adds.[5]

Key Learning—Network Marketing

- Research the company:
  - ○ Do you have what it takes to succeed?
  - ○ Are you well organized?
  - ○ Do you have good time management skills?
  - ○ Are you persistent and persuasive?
- LOVE the product you sell:
  - ○ Can you be passionate about it for five years?
  - ○ Is it consumable, allowing for easy repeat sales? Does that matter to you?
- Are you comfortable establishing a business relationship with your friends and family?
- How much inventory do you have to carry? Consider storage and finances.
- Are you willing to help others start up their businesses to enrich your own?
- Tax benefits with write-offs are possible.
- Financial independence can be gained with hard work over time.

START-UP IDEAS

After reading this chapter, you're psyched. You want to start your own business. But you don't have a big, grand plan, a vision for a multimillion-dollar product. You have the drive, but no specific idea in mind. Scott Allen developed a list of ideas for businesses that are easily started with under $20.[6] I have included many of his ideas here along with a few of my own. They will probably start off small, but have the potential to earn good money on a part-time basis if you treat them with the same professionalism and enthusiasm you would treat a full-time career:

- **Dinner Caterer:** Prepare dinner for those who don't have the time to do it for themselves. Most people who do this prepare two to three entrees per week, per client.
- **Pet Sitter/Dog Walker:** This requires a love of animals, particularly dogs and cats. Reliability and trustworthiness are a must along with personal references.
- **Professional Organizer:** Most people keep saying that they want to clean out their closets, but never get around to it. If you're a neatnik, here's your opportunity to help out others with your skills. This job takes organizational skills and a familiarity with containers/shelving at your local stores.
- **Consultant:** I've referred to several women in this chapter who have become consultants. You just have to know how to do something better than most people, such as work in accounting, IT, human resources, or decorating. You can either teach them how to do it or, better yet, do it for them.
- **Tutor:** Several women in this chapter started their own tutoring businesses and some weren't teachers. The only downside is you're tutoring when your kids are out of school, so you'll need babysitting services if they are young.
- **Administrative Services:** Are you good at designing and typing presentations using PowerPoint? Good at proofreading or transcribing? Good at laying out charts and/or graphs? Many small

businesses need these services, but only on occasion and not enough to hire someone permanently.

- **Website Designer/Maintenance:** Everyone from churches to schools to small businesses to community organizations have websites. Once they're up, they need to be maintained and updated constantly. If you're good at website design/maintenance, this could be your calling.
- **Advertising:** Along the same lines, if you have a good sense of design, a computer, and high-quality printer, this may be for you. You can develop ads, flyers, logos, etc. for small businesses that don't have the time or creativity.
- **Personal Services:** Run errands, shop, and/or dog walk for others who don't have the time. It's fun and really works around the holiday timeframe. Dependability, timeliness, and trustworthiness are key attributes for this job.

Spread the word on your newly developed business by posting on Facebook, posting on LinkedIn, putting up flyers on local bulletin boards, passing out business cards, talking to your friends/neighbors, and possibly placing a small ad in a local neighborhood paper. Hook into any appropriate networks such as small business associations. These start-up costs are minimal; your biggest investment is your time.

BECOME PART OF THE SHARING ECONOMY

Similar to the ideas above, another way you can help others access goods and services is by becoming part of the sharing economy, capitalizing on marketing and distribution support from various platforms. The sharing economy matches goods and services that customers want with people who can provide them. Examples of this are Uber (ride-sharing services), TaskRabbit (small-jobs provider), and Airbnb (overnight rooms provider). These platforms match "needs" with provider "haves." According to a PricewaterhouseCoopers survey, about 7 percent of US adults are working on sharing platforms with more likely to follow.[7] Of those aware of these types of jobs, 51 percent say that they can see themselves being providers in the next two years.[8]

What makes these platforms so enticing? Simple, jobs with flexibility and the chance for providers to be their own boss. Rachel Botsman, a global expert on the power of collaboration and sharing through technology, calls providers "micropreneurs" and claims that they fall into four distinct groups with specific benefits for each group.[9]

- For the "flexers," stay-at-home parents (perhaps like you), retirees, students, and anyone else who can't (or doesn't want to) work a nine-to-five job, flexible hours is the driving factor getting these people into the workforce. They can work when they want and how long they want.
- For those who can't find a regular job, due to difficult regional economic conditions, the sharing economy is a way to generate much-needed income while continuing a search for a traditional job.
- The "pros" have utilized one or more sharing platforms to develop full-time jobs for themselves. These platforms have enabled them to expand their businesses much further than was possible on their own.
- Lastly is the group of full-time workers who use sharing platforms to generate extra cash by working in the sharing economy during their off-hours. As an example, Airbnb hosts can work full-time jobs and rent out rooms from their homes simultaneously.

The sharing economy is flourishing because workers can control when they work, how long they work, where they work along with how much they charge for that work. If this sounds interesting to you, explore one or more of the opportunities that I found below. These platforms are growing by leaps and bounds, so search for "sharing economy" online for the latest new start-ups.

- Airbnb: renting rooms or a whole house
- DogVacay: leaving dogs with hosts at rates cheaper than kennels
- RelayRides: renting cars from neighbors by the hour or by the day
- TaskRabbit: hiring people to do jobs and tasks from deliveries and pickups to handyman and office help
- Getaround: borrowing and lending cars to and from others
- Zaarly: providing services such as home repair to iPhone repair to homemade meals
- Lyft: ride-sharing services
- Liquid: renting/lending bikes to and from neighbors
- Lending Club: coordinating borrowers and investors
- Fon: Wi-Fi-sharing network
- Handy: home-cleaning and handyman services
- Poshmark: buying and selling clothing
- NeighborGoods: sharing stuff with neighbors
- SnapGoods: lending and borrowing high-end household items
- Uber: ride-sharing services

ADVICE FROM ENTREPRENEURS

I asked these women what advice they would give someone thinking about starting up her own business. What are their words of wisdom? Their watch-outs?

"I would say, 'Don't kid yourself.' I've had a couple of groups that recently asked to be their motivational speaker. One was Avon. And you know so many people want it to happen, they know how to make it happen, but something holds them back. Either it's fear, fear of rejection, or 'I just can't get off the couch' fear. I'd say, 'Don't be afraid. Don't give yourself excuses,'" replies Nancy.

Ava says, "There's nothing in this world that you can't do. If anyone tells you so, quit asking them. We all have an internal voice. All of us know the right answer. Usually the first answer that comes to us is the right answer, but we never trust it enough. Don't listen to people who tell you it can't be done. Anything you put your mind to can be done. I'm living proof of that."

Ava also wants to pass on the best advice she was given. "Look, if you don't do anything else, make sure that you have six months of expenses put away. Know where your money is. I know where every dime of my money is." She also recommended not being afraid to ask questions. To her, "No question is stupid."

In hindsight, Christi wishes that she had researched the business aspect of it, the paperwork, a little bit more. She didn't think about it for too long because she was really unhappy with her prior situation. "I jumped out. I said, 'I'm not doing this anymore; I will find something.' It was one of those leaps of faith," says Christi.

She had a mentor who has been on her own for twenty years, so she's someone Christi looked up to. Knowing this hard-working woman took some of the fear and anxiety out of starting up her counseling services. And based on her experience, she knew that she could find work since she had three offers on the table. But she knew that she didn't want any of those three and was willing to try and make a go of it on her own, using acquaintances to help her understand the ins and outs of running her business. "I talked with people whom I admired and respected who were doing it on their own. They were generous women who gave me time and energy, answered questions, either via e-mail or in person or on the phone, and really supported me. It was a nice network of women who said, 'This is how you do it, this is what I did, this is what I learned.' It was unusual for me to ask for help. I was embarrassed about what I didn't know.

"Somebody recommended a good accountant. The accountant couldn't have been kinder or more gentle, didn't laugh at my questions. She also walked me through stuff that I didn't know, I needed to know. Deep down, I knew I had the skills," Christi explains. But despite that, she felt she could have prepared herself a bit more before she jumped out, doing the research before she went out on her own rather than afterward.

Remember Elizabeth, the consultant from chapter 4? Her advice dovetails with Christi's. She suggests putting a business plan in writing. Writing it down clarifies your thinking, helps point out the holes in your plan, and outlines your upfront expenses. Items she recommends putting in your plan include the following:

- Name the Business.
- Outline Your Business Goals: What are your goals, short- and long-term? Make them measurable. They can be as simple as annual hours you hope to work, monthly income, or weekly sales targets.
- Describe the Business: What business are you in? What's your role? Who is your customer?
- Describe the Product or Services: What's your product or service? What benefit does your customer receive from your product or service?
- Develop a Competitive Analysis: Who is your competition? Why would someone use your product or service over your competition's?
- Outline Execution Details: How do you plan to sell your product or service? How are you going to produce and deliver your goods or services? Do you need to hire others, such as subcontractors, to help you? What other resources do you need?
- Determine Financial Needs: What are the start-up costs? What are your sources for funding? Can you cover those costs and still make the income you desire?

Angie's experience reflects why a business plan is useful. By working through the numbers upfront, she may have altered her goals or plans. Angie sublet office space through a network group for two days a week, committing to a year upfront. While her husband, who has been self-employed for years, helped her with taxes and paperwork, she never had much income left after paying off her firm's bills. "I don't think that my part-time experience in private practice was as lucrative as it needed to be. I probably really needed to work closer to full-time to make the kind of money I needed to make. You need to look at what you're spending to be in the business part-time, to make sure that you're actually making money and not losing money. I didn't lose money, but I think I really needed to work almost full-time to make the kind of money to make it worthwhile working."

While writing your plan, don't forget to include your network. As a migration specialist, Brenda feels that it's important to continue relationships with those who can offer support and advice. She believes that maintaining a network is as important as the work itself.

Nancy has tips to meet your goals. In fact, she sets daily and weekly goals to keep herself motivated. "One little game that I play with myself is that I have to make five cold calls before I can stop for lunch. It's amazing as soon as your tummy starts grumbling, you say, 'I'm just going in and doing it.'" She also has daily goals. "I write a to-do list every single day. Two days out of the week, I make cold calls, whether they are on the phone, whether they are on e-mail, or whether I'm physically pounding the pavement. Two days a week, that's what I do. I don't work for eight hours a day, but that's what I do. You have to be strict with yourself; you have to be motivated. Don't give yourself excuses, because there are lots of excuses. That's the thing: if you want it, if you really want it, do it."

Key Learning—Advice from These Entrepreneurs

- Do research before jumping in on your own.
- Don't be afraid to ask for help when needed.
- Analyze income versus expenses to ensure you come out ahead.
- Put six months of expenses away.
- Know where your money is.
- Use your network for support and answering questions.
- Don't give yourself excuses; either do it or forget it.

Chapter 6

PURSUE YOUR PASSION FOR LOVE *AND* MONEY

"I love what I do."

—**Nancy**

W hat could be better than doing what you love *and* making money while doing it? Not much. Since a passion relates to feeding your soul, women usually defer to the arts when describing their passions. In fact, the examples in this chapter focus on the arts: dance, photography, yoga, jewelry, voice, and painting. But they certainly aren't limited to that. Defending social issues in court, designing the perfect garden, raising others' spiritual consciousness are all passions that could lead to paid employment. No matter what the topic is, women have learned to turn their passions into paying part-time positions, and the first example below even turned into a lifelong career.

PASSIONS THAT BECAME CAREERS

What started as a summer lark for Becky turned into a twenty-seven-year career in the Madison, Wisconsin, area that she can pass on to her daughter. She taught dancing at school for one summer, thinking that it would be fun and could earn her some extra money. When the summer was over, she had the parents and children encouraging her to continue teaching dance lessons in her basement. Becky says, "I told them that my basement was such a mess there was no way." But then she thought about it, and said to herself, "Why aren't you seizing this opportunity?" She realized that she could have a good part-time job teaching what she loved. With current contacts, she had thirty-two students right off the bat. If she started networking, she'd have several classes filled in no time.

Attributing the reason she started the business to the parents that helped her, she claims their support and assistance motivated her to get going. "So the parents came in and helped me fix the basement up. One gal was an artist and painted murals on the wall, and then my husband put a floor in, a bar, mirrors, and away we went," she says. Her basement was transformed into a dance studio. She ran her dance classes from her basement for ten years, working about twenty-two hours a week. Then she moved.

"It was not conducive to teach in the new home. My first home was on a busy street. The second house was in a forty-home neighborhood; that wasn't going to work either. So I opened a commercial studio that I rented. I would teach twenty-five to twenty-six hours a week, then spend mucho hours on paperwork: getting out checks, writing letters, setting up recitals, purchasing costumes. I've moved into an even bigger studio now. I've hired additional teachers." Over the years, Becky's part-time passion evolved into a full-time one. The hours grew as her daughter did, and her family could accommodate it.

Becky adds, "A local costume company asked me to be on their advisory board. What a fun deal is that? I kept telling them to change this and change that, so I guess they thought they'd shut me up and put me on the advisory board. I love it.

"I want to continue the dance studio as long as I can. It encompasses my entire life. I've been doing it for twenty-seven years now. I still enjoy being at the dance studio. I can be tired and not feeling good and go to the studio and feel great when I get home. Each class brings a certain joy. All bring different rewards. My daughter will take over the studio one day."

Remember Nancy, the jewelry designer/business owner from Missouri? The reason she started her own business was because jewelry has always been her passion. "I love jewelry work. I have been fascinated with gemstones and jewelry since I was four years old. We had a family jeweler; my family's Italian, so they were really into jewelry, [and would] come to my great-aunt's house on a Saturday a couple times a year.

Everyone would gather there. All the kids would go play. Not me. I was glued to that man [the jeweler]. I've always had a passion for gemstones.

"So I didn't want to give up what I loved doing when I had children. I love the creative aspect; I love the reaction I get from people. So many times my kids will be in a new environment, either with new friends or in a new class. All of a sudden the teacher or the friend's mother puts it together and says, 'Are you Nancy the Jeweler?' My kids are, 'Here we go.' But I love that! I'm excited. I love the reaction I get from other people. It's a part of me; it's such a personal thing; it's really neat to share with other people and get such positive feedback.

"When other people can't sleep at four o'clock in the morning and they're up reading a book or watching TV, I come downstairs and draw or carve waxes. Or I might be stringing something, doing things that don't make noise. That doesn't *feel* like I'm working. I'd be doing something else creative, if I wasn't doing that."

ONE JOB FOR LOVE, ONE FOR MONEY

While pursuing our passions for money is a good concept, it can't always be the only income brought into the family. I've discussed Sherry's and Sonia's businesses before in the previous chapter on starting your own business. But what I didn't mention was that the roots of their businesses were their passions. I also didn't mention that neither Sherry nor Sonia can currently support their families on their businesses alone, so they augment them with another part-time job. By maintaining *two* part-time jobs, both totaling to under forty hours per week, these women earn enough income to meet their families' financial needs *and* meet their personal needs of fulfilling their passions.

As you may recall, Sonia was an opera singer turned singing teacher. While singing is her first love, she realizes that she can't support herself singing. She specifically works a flexible, thirty-hour-per-week database/systems administrative job so that she still has time for her singing, both through teaching and singing in a choir herself. This works for her. "For some reason musicians have some aptitude for computers. It's like a right-brain, left-brain type of thing. There's the creative side, then there's the analytical side, and music encompasses both. Computers just seem to compliment music. That said, while I enjoy the secretary and computer work, I consider it a job, a way to support my family. I consider the singing what I have to do for myself. If I could have supported myself singing, that's what I would have done," she says.

"There are two things that are really important. One, people need to be able to satisfy their creative person. If they can do work they absolutely love and get paid enough to support themselves, bless them. Two, there has to be a certain amount of realism to one's approach to life. If you're going to have children, you have to pay the bills. If you're going to have children, you have to be responsible for your children.

"One thing I realized over time: if I don't have time to explore my own creativity, everything in the rest of my life suffers. I need to retire at some point. Ideally, I should be working full-time, but I just don't think that I'm going to because then I wouldn't have time for voice lessons. Once I retire, I'm going to continue teaching voice for extra income and will probably try to expand my voice studio at that point. I don't expect to stop teaching voice until I can't do it anymore."

Sonia has learned to balance her need for singing with the reality of earning money. Spending eight hours a week teaching voice and then thirty hours a week at her administrative job keep her creative juices flowing and her family on solid ground economically. Similar to Sonia in her pursuit of self-fulfillment through the arts, Sherry also balances two part-time jobs, one for love and one for money.

Sherry started her photography business as a hobby, taking her own kids' pictures then taking other people's photographs. But then it turned into a business out of necessity. She said, "I got referred to another person and another person and another person. I did it for a long time before I took any money for it. I would do it for friends because I liked it. It was four years before I actually asked for money. It was hard to take the money because I loved to do it, and taking money for it seemed odd. I was getting divorced, so I needed to turn it into an income.

"I schedule sessions with clients, mainly families and children. I shoot them; then I meet with the clients to preview, edit, and print," says Sherry. "I feel I give people something. I like my creative side. It feeds me."

But the photography business wasn't enough to support her family and herself, particularly considering the seasonality. She shoots photos during the day and edits at night, sometimes working up to fifteen hours per day during her high season, fall, and early winter. Then it drops off in the spring and is nonexistent during the summer months.

To augment her income, Sherry also does some accounting work for about eighteen hours per week. She does it not only for the steady income, but also for the flexibility of being able to work from home, allowing her to keep the photography business. The accounting work is a necessity that makes her photography business, her passion, feasible. And since she has been growing her business for over five years, Sherry said that she hopes to turn her part-time photography work into a full-time business in the future, enabling her to drop the accounting work.

CHANGING PATHS, SHIFTING GEARS

"I needed more value to my life. I needed mental stimulation," says Julie. "I love my children, but there were days I thought I was going to lose my mind, being at home. I had been on the road in pharmaceutical sales. And before pharmaceutical sales, I was a flight attendant, so I was always out and about all the time. Now I was at home with three children. They were six, four, and two years old at the time, so there were days that I never left the house. I wanted to go back to work for mental stimulation.

"When my children were at school, I needed to find something to do with my life. I didn't want to go back to the corporate world because my kids come first." Julie wanted flexible hours that part-time work brings so that she could see her kids in school plays and attend their sports events.

"While I was home, I've always had a love of gardening. So I said to myself, 'You know, I don't want to go back to corporate work; I'd love to work in a nursery.' Gardening had only been a hobby for me, so I went back to school. When the kids were at school during the day, I signed up at the local horticultural society in their Master Gardener Program. That was September through December. Then I had to do sixty hours of volunteer work, either in a greenhouse or on the grounds of a nursery or answering phones on gardening questions, on people's garden problems, to get certified."

Julie completed the program and became a Master Gardener. "I also took landscaping classes at a local design school. Once I did that, I started looking around. Now there are two nurseries near me within ten minutes of my house. But I came to the nursery where I now work, even though it's farther away, because [the owner's] a horticulturalist, because it's a family business, because he grows his own plant material. I heard so much about it. I said, 'I've got to go; I've got to get a job there.' So I came here. My boss said, 'I'll give you a call.' I said, 'Okay.' Then I called back and I called back. I said, 'I'll learn the plant material. If you need more knowledge, I'll learn it. I love being with people, and it's really about sales. I can show people your property and all these plants. Not everybody has this.' So he said, 'Okay, we'll hire you.' It's worked out great."

TWO PART-TIME PASSIONS

Like Sherry and Sonia, Karen holds two part-time positions. But unlike them, she holds a passionate devotion for both jobs, making it hard for her to pick which position she prefers over the other.

"I went to a health resort and spa with some girlfriends about ten or so years ago. They talked me into trying a yoga class, which I pretty much laughed my way through; it wasn't for me. When I got home another friend asked me to try a power yoga class at our gym, and I liked that style much more. I did a few classes here and there and then found a teacher who inspired me to take the practice more seriously. Fairly quickly, I began studying yoga, both the physical and spiritual practices on a regular basis," says Karen.

Prior to practicing and studying yoga, she taught art classes to children on a part-time basis. But as she became more and more inspired by her yoga, she decided to stop teaching art and, instead, chose to obtain certification to teach yoga. At about the same time, Karen's current yoga teacher left and was replaced by Henry, who was also an artist making jewelry and sculpture figures.

Henry was having a sculpture/jewelry show in Los Angeles. Because he knew that Karen taught art and because his walls were currently empty, he asked her to paint something to put on them. She recalls, "Henry had this big canvas. I put some paint on it, and then he put some paint on it and it became a big collaborative piece. I also had other paintings that I brought over and hung. Much to my surprise, lots of pieces sold. But the most buzz was about the collaborative piece that we did. People heard about it and reacted well to it."

So from that initial showing, Karen and Henry began painting abstract art collaboratively on canvas panels to exhibit in galleries and in their studio. "We started out by renting a small space in town. It was more productive if we could work in the same space, rather than each of us working in our own separate studios, even if we were not there at the same time. It was so much easier than me carrying the work back and forth from my studio at home. In fact, 99.9 percent of our pieces are collaborative. I choose the colors, and he applies them. He has a sense of movement, and I have a history of photography and framing, so together we make a good team. We are obviously successful as we have upgraded to a larger space." That's her first part-time position, taking about sixteen hours per week of her time.

Her second part-time position is teaching yoga about ten hours per week. That brings her total working hours to twenty-six hours per week, still giving her enough time to drive her kids to sports practice and attend all their games. "I was offered to teach a class at the same gym where I was certified. I was also teaching kid's yoga at my son's school for the after-school enrichment program. Word of mouth in the yoga world goes a long way, and within a month offers started coming, and in six months I was teaching in some terrific local yoga studios."

Asked how she foresees the two part-time positions balancing out in the future, Karen adds, "My intention is to continue with both the yoga and art. I don't know how long I'll be able to teach the yoga if the painting keeps up at its current pace. It's a tough choice between the two, but I have art inside coming out. Nothing makes an artist happier than having someone else's eyes light up when viewing your piece. You do a painting and you like it. But when you do a piece and then another person gets that same glow that you have, it's worthwhile."

Key Learning—Pursue Your Passion

- Do what you love, what keeps you excited.
- Take help from others when they offer. It might take you further than going it alone.
- Consider taking on a partner. It may help to make your endeavor economically feasible or optimize your choice.
- While filling your creative side, look at the reality of your life and balance your creative wants with economic needs.
- Be open-minded to all opportunities that present themselves to you; you never know what might succeed.

Chapter 7

WORKING FROM HOME: GOOD OR BAD IDEA?

"I love working out of the house. What is tempting is getting stuff done around the house. It's a double-edged sword."

—Ingrid

W orking from home is the best, right? Getting to throw a load of laundry in the washer in between checking e-mails, or putting dinner in the oven while making phone calls. It sounds great until you think about the doorbell ringing with a delivery in the middle of a critical phone call or looking at your unfinished research sitting on the kitchen table on a Saturday afternoon at 2:00 p.m. Using home as a base for your business can be wonderful or it can be a disaster. It depends on the individual home situation, the type of work being done, and your temperament/mindset.

THE BEST

The absolute best part about working from home is the flexibility. This flexibility translates into being there for the family, the whole family, whenever someone needs you. If your daughter wakes up with a fever, you can handle it. If last week's Little League game was rained out and is rescheduled for today at 3:00 p.m., you can juggle your schedule and be there. If your mother can't find the documents for her noon appointment with the accountant, you can run over there to help her find them. Working from home gives you the ability to move your hours around to accommodate whatever the day brings.

Sherry, a home-based photographer, feels it helps her manage school holidays. "There are a lot of days the kids are not in school. When I was still working full-time, I had a nanny. Then when I stayed home, I was thinking of going back to work full-time after the divorce. I started to figure out how many days a year the kids are actually out of school. It's pretty shocking. It's about eighteen weeks a year once you add summer and all the breaks including Christmas, Easter. It is a lot of the year they're not in school. The positive aspects of working from home are accommodating your children when they're out of school.

"My kids go to private school, so our calendar doesn't match up with the public school calendar. So for public school kids, when they are off for spring break, there are a lot of programs provided for that week to accommodate them for working parents. But when your kids are in a private school situation where their days don't match up, there isn't anything offered. So you have to find childcare, which is hard. There're only so many days you can take off in an office environment. So by working from home, you can still work and your kids can be at home."

Agreeing with Sherry, Noel likes that if her children are sick, she can still work. Noel says, "I like working from home the days when my kids are home sick because I don't like being too far away from them; if midday, I want to call the pediatrician."

Flexibility isn't needed only when the kids are off or sick. It's used daily by many of the women. Angela, a freelance food stylist, can drive her kids to school and pick them up because she's in charge of her own schedule. As a lobbyist, Christina says, "If it's more important to go to the kids' practice at 3:30 p.m., you can go do that and work at 8:30 p.m."

Brenda, a mitigation specialist, says, "I can continue to work when my children are at home playing with their friends or doing homework. Most importantly, I can work when the kids are at school, work in the evening after they've gone to bed—hours I can choose, can fit around family schedule."

And being home is good not only for the kids but for husbands, parents, and grandparents, too. This was particularly true for Nancy. "I've had all kinds of situations over the years that I wanted to be there, at home, for what's going on. I've been able to do that. My husband's been very ill for the last five years, in and out of the hospital, had a couple of heart attacks and heart surgeries. I've been able to still work and be there for him when I need to be. I also took care of my sick grandmother before she passed away. I was able to balance that. I'm an only child. My parents are up there in age, so they need me quite a bit. The flexibility is priceless, absolutely priceless. I've never, ever missed a concert, a baseball game, a football game, anything. I've always been able to figure it out."

Several women brought up the time efficiencies that working from home brings. Celeste runs her washer and dryer while developing her medical presentations. Lisa prepares lawsuits during the time she would have been commuting. Laura cooks dinner while designing stationary. Erin reconciles bank statements instead of fighting rush hour traffic. And Elizabeth is there for phone calls and service people while she's writing marketing plans for her clients. Almost all the women who work from home multitask, handling home chores and business duties.

Ashley sums it up well. "There are so many pros. I'm able to be here for phone calls. I'm here for service people if I need something done; they can come to the house. I can tend to the dog. I'm able to take the kids to school and pick them up. I'm able to throw in a load of wash. I can talk on the phone or listen to audio books. I'm totally in control of everything happening here. I can be here with the children and complete my work."

Another benefit of having a home-based business is the cost savings it affords. Lisa mentioned the reduction of wear and tear on her car because it sat in her driveway versus moving down the highway. Laura commented on the fact that there is no overhead for her home-based stationary business.

There's also the benefit of your children seeing you work, making you a mentor as well as a parent. Eileen says, when she works from home, "The children get to see a parent in motion working. As opposed to saying, 'My dad leaves the house for X number of hours, and then he comes home.' He's gone to this place called 'work.' But they've seen me meet goals, meet deadlines. They've actually participated in some of it with me. I've been able to give them some jobs where they can sharpen their skills: alphabetizing, organizing papers. They've seen and under-stood project work. I've provided a role model. The visual aspect and participating, they've been part of what I've done."

Several women mentioned concentrating much better at home than they would in an office. Having everyone out of the house during their working hours gives them the ability to concentrate and work more effec-tively than if they were in a busy office. "I have as much billable work as full-time people in the office. It's real easy to get work that needs to be done, done. You can get as much done in three or four hours at home as the eight hours it would take me in the office, but you have to be a self-starter," says Christina.

As a human resources consultant, Janette agrees with Christina's experience. "I loved working from home. I couldn't be interrupted. When I was working 9:00 a.m. to 1:00 p.m., I was working 9:00 a.m. to 1:00 p.m. I had a tiny little office; I was undisturbed. I really worked. I was extremely self-motivated." An added benefit of working from home is getting to wear whatever you want to wear. Four women specifically mentioned that they liked the ability to wear their pj's and slippers. Why not be comfortable when you work?

THE WORST

While flexibility is the best part of working from home, isolation and physically working alone is clearly the worst. Women miss human contact and interaction. Many of the women discussed the constant struggle that they have with isolation. Interacting with people is how many of them get their energy, so staying home alone all day is draining.

"I miss the camaraderie and collegiality of an office," says Christina. "In the kind of work I do, it is gathering information, ideas, and thoughts out there for the people to react to and develop. It's pretty collegiate. I miss those relationships and the camaraderie. If something great comes to you, you think it's great; you just can't holler or run to the office next door or sit down at lunch and say, 'Hey, guys, what do you think about this? Am I crazy or will this work?' You can't have those political discussions. 'Do you think this would fly with leadership based on yada, yada, yada?' They say, 'No way.' Then you say, 'Well, what about this?' Then they reply, 'Yeah, yeah, that's more like it.' That's the part I miss, all that collegiality."

Gina, who does contract management work, agrees. "I enjoy seeing people. Part of what I like doing is managing, discussing, and planning with people, personal interaction. Being in the workplace enables me to network, get better information. I can pick up information that I might otherwise miss. I don't have that at home."

"The downside is the isolation of working out of your house because it's usually just you. You might be on the phone with someone, there might be some interaction, but most of the work is pretty solitary," claims Sherry. "Even with my photography, my interaction with the clients is probably 20 percent of the process. Most of the time, I'm working alone."

"It's not as much fun to work alone from home. It's not exactly glamorous; it gets lonely," adds Christina. "I can do errands; I can take conference calls while I'm out. I hate to be sitting here at home all day. It's a lonely way to do your work. You would think that I can get involved in community activities, back into tennis. I'm trying to by scheduling around my conference calls. I get to work part-time and should be able to do all of these other things, but it doesn't always work that way. Conference calls get scheduled when I usually go to yoga."

As a physician, Patti mixes it up, seeing patients at a teaching hospital and developing presentations for medical students from home. She says, "I wouldn't stay home all the time because I am a social person and like going to the hospital and meeting people. If being home was more than brief, the social isolation would be hard."

Doreen had the same reaction as Patti. "Two days I was not in the office. I'm an extroverted person, so it was a big adjustment at home with dead silence. I shut the door and was in my office. It took a couple of months to adjust."

Other downsides of working from home are the distractions and being able to keep focused. "You have to realize that you're working.

You're not vacuuming; you're not washing the dishes. You can't have any distractions," claims Lisa.

"Setting healthy boundaries is essential," agrees Brenda. "You can come to the end of the day and not have gotten any work done. You did the laundry, responded to the top 100 personal e-mails."

"If you work from home, you have to develop a different attitude about your home," claims Leticia. "When you go to the bathroom and you see it needs cleaning, you have to say to yourself, 'Maintenance, we'll get to that tomorrow.' So you don't get bogged down and get distracted, so that you can honestly say to yourself, 'I spent X number of hours on my work today.'"

"You must be self-motivated to do your work. You're at home, and there are always things to be done," adds Sherry. "You have to be very disciplined. Discipline is the hardest part. Because when you go to an office, you forget about everything at home and concentrate. At home, it's definitely harder. And the fact that you do have your kids home with you a lot of days makes it worse. The days the kids are home, I work at night. I work late at night rather than during the day because it is hard to get in a groove and stay in it. You sit down; then you're up; then you're down. They're constantly wanting something. So those are days I usually work at night."

This leads us to the single-biggest distraction, the children, the major reason many mothers work from home. "It's difficult to do everything at the same time," says Noel. "When you're in your office and you hear your child in another room crying or fighting or misbehaving, it's hard to *not* be a parent while you're working. I find it very difficult for the children to see me wander in and out of the rooms that they may be in. I think it's confusing for them. I'm either at work or I'm at home. It's hard for them to see me and know they can't have my time at that particular moment. Working from home is the last resort for me."

Ashley views it the same way. "It's very difficult to get anything done. Unless my son is asleep or in front of a good movie, it's tough to get a couple of hours of work done. You need a sitter or need to work when they are in bed. There are constant distractions."

Connie brings up another con, respect for her work. "Because you're working out of your home, you don't get respect, the respect of working for a company. If you're a woman working out of your home, you're not respected as really, really working. Because your neighbors knock on the door and expect you to be able to answer it and do whatever, whenever or your friends call when you're home and expect you to be available to have lunch.

"You don't get the same respect, and people don't take it seriously that you're working a job. Even my husband would say at the beginning, 'My wife's doing this little thing.' For men, money talks. Once you start earning up there with the big guys, it's like, 'You should see what my wife does.' It's a completely different demeanor. That's usually the case with men."

Another downside is separating home from office. Unless there is a specific room or desk designated as "the office," some women feel as though they never go "home." "The office" is always there, making it difficult to stop working and to find balance between work and family each day. "A home-based business can be a blessing and a curse," says Alice. "I try to keep office hours 8:00 a.m. to 2:00 p.m. I can do it from home, but at the same time, I put my little guy to bed and I'm back in there."

"Sometimes I feel like I never get away from work because it's in my house," Nancy reveals.

And if there isn't a space dedicated to the business, interruptions are higher. Since Gina doesn't have a large enough house to designate a room as her office, she is constantly being interrupted. Her work computer is in the same room as the television set. "Any job needs to have a home base where you put your stuff. You need one of those rooms you can be in with all your stuff and shut the door. It would be ideal."

"If the kids or the dog are rambunctious, you can get interrupted. It's hard to stay focused, hard to get things accomplished. I'm in a small house; there's no place to go!" says Melissa.

Noel agrees. "It's not an ideal condition for me. I don't have a sprawling mansion where I can go in another wing of the house and not hear it. My husband and I also share space in our home office, so I have to compete with him as well."

Key Learning—Working from Home

- Best parts:
  - Flexibility to accommodate family and self
  - Time efficiencies due to multitasking home chores during working hours
  - Cost savings on automobile, gas, and rent (if you own the business)
  - Act as a role model for your children
  - Potential to get more work done in less hours
  - Potential to concentrate better because no one else is around
  - Can wear whatever you want
- Worst parts:
  - Isolation and loneliness
  - Distractions at home
  - Potential to feel like you never leave "the office"
  - Potential lack of respect for profession
  - Interruptions high without a dedicated, separate work space

---

TIPS

Career counselor and executive coach Clay Parsons advises people to prepare themselves psychologically. Working from home is a job and not a day off. Just as the women above mentioned, he feels creating a work area or home office helps. Additionally, creating a schedule that you follow aids you in getting your tasks accomplished.[1]

To prevent the isolation issues that were discussed above, meet a friend for coffee or lunch. You'd do that in an office, so why wouldn't you from home? Or take a break sometime during the day and go to a health club. Schedule these things as part of your routine so they don't become distractions.

Celebrate when you have a success. If you were in an office, you'd go out to lunch or dinner. Go out and buy that new sweater that you've been eyeing. Reward yourself when you sell that new idea, gain a new account, or surpass a stated goal.

And don't forget to maintain your professional network. Stay connected with your contacts by meeting them for coffee, lunch, or having discussions on the phone with them. If you're working for a corporation from home, stay connected with events at work.

Working from home can be great if you set yourself up right.

Chapter 8

DAYCARE:
IT CAN MAKE OR BREAK YOU

"I've made myself crazy with daycare."

—Jodie

Daycare for part-time employees can be more complex than for full-timers. When women don't work forty hours per week, they aren't following the norm for daycare models. It's hard enough obtaining good daycare when mothers work full-time, but when they work ten, twenty, or thirty hours a week and have infants or toddlers, it's even more difficult.

The biggest issue is obtaining part-time care for a part-time price. Many daycare providers, whether in your own home, someone else's home, or in a center, require being paid for full-time daycare. This is even the case when they are only providing care for a portion of the time.

Another, yet lesser, issue is consistency of hours. Some part-time positions don't have the same hours day to day, week to week, or even month to month. Obtaining daycare can be difficult. Rosemary claims, "With part-time work, it's typically just you. I have not found myself to be as nearly organized with part-time work. I'm not sure why that is as I tend to be a fairly organized person. The days vary with part-time work. Sometimes you have a conference call at 9:00 a.m.; sometimes you don't have a conference call. Sometimes you're traveling for two days; sometimes you're not. For me there's not a consistent schedule. That has been more difficult to manage."

Once the children hit school age, part-time childcare becomes a little easier. If you can find work during school hours, most of the childcare is covered. One quarter of the women interviewed take advantage of school hours when scheduling their employment. Finding care for a few hours a week after school, if necessary, seems to be easier than finding infant/toddler care. If women have to work later on some days, they place the kids in after-school programs, hire high school or college students to come in, or ask one of their own parents to watch the kids for a few hours a week. And while there are still vacation days, summer, and holidays to consider, the bulk of time is taken care of by school. Having the kids go off to school is just the boost a few women need to go back into the workforce. Some women find jobs that are different from their former careers, specifically to work within the school day.

Here's how the women I interviewed handled part-time daycare. Some of their experiences may help you to decide what type of daycare is right for your children. There is no one correct answer, and it's constantly changing. It takes creativity, flexibility, and persistence to find the right situation for your family.

COSTS

One of the biggest inhibiting factors for part-time employment, as with full-time employment, is the cost of daycare. Can you cover your childcare costs and still be ahead? Is it worth making almost nothing after childcare expenses when the children are toddlers to stay in your field? That way when the children enter school, you can make more money than if you had stopped working because you've had continuity. Maybe continuity's not a factor in your field as long as you can keep your skills updated. What's best for your career? What's best for your children? What can you handle financially? These are the questions mothers ask themselves.

"I was fortunate enough to make enough money to cover childcare costs for three children," says Gabi, referring to her job share in the Environmental Protection Agency (EPA). "The tipping point for many women is when they come home after childcare costs with barely $20 in their pocket. Some women don't come out $20 ahead and then can't go part-time. If there's not good childcare, then there's double stress, paying for mediocre childcare and not being paid enough money for the hassle."

Gabi was lucky. Several women I spoke with were more like Sonia, paying for full-time childcare providers when she was only using them part-time. This was the only option that she was comfortable with for her children.

Tessa was fortunate the first year she taught part-time. Her sister babysat for her. But then she had to find daycare beyond her family. "People don't like part-time, and so you'd find people who would say, 'You can bring them here part-time, but you have to pay full-time.' And of course, we couldn't afford full-time. We kept finding people; then they'd move. That was the one drawback. We didn't do a center because they charged more than half. For my third son, I found a preschool that counted half day as four and a half hours, so they did give you a break on the price. A lot of daycare centers said four hours per day was half, but that doesn't give you time to get to work and back. I cut lunch out to gain fifteen minutes. I continually pieced things together. I had at least six different sitter situations."

Despite most daycare providers wanting to fill their slots with full-timers, it's worth asking about part-time slots. In some areas of the country, it's full-time or nothing, while more can be negotiated in other areas. Renee, a software engineer from Oklahoma, says, "I researched daycare that allowed part-time attendance, both in centers and homes. It was a matter of negotiating, and it wasn't advertised. I asked, 'Will you work around these hours, and will you accept this amount for the time?'"

Sandy chose to hire a full-time nanny until her child was two. She knew that she was passing her paycheck over to her nanny until her child was old enough to go to a nursery school. "We didn't cover our expenses during those two years. My income went down and my expenses went up. With a young child like that it's incredibly hard to get out the door, out to work, and focused. I spent more money than I earned."

And even when the children are in school, there's always the cost of finding coverage over the summer months. Vicky, project manager at a construction company, lives in a school district in Wisconsin that has a great summer adventure program for the older kids. But it's not cheap. "It costs just as much for the older kids now at camp as it did when they were babies," she adds.

"I had to pay for childcare during the summer months," says Eileen. "I had college students for at least three or four summers. That didn't sit well with me. I was leaving the house, making a fair salary, but I made the salary and handed it over to someone else to watch my children."

As an office manager, Alice has a similar feeling. "My infant went to a private home for daycare. When they were on spring break or summer vacation, they had after-school programs or day camp. Days I would work I'd put them in daycare, and frankly, it wasn't worth it. My paycheck paid for the daycare for them."

USING FAMILY MEMBERS

While a quarter of the women use school hours to complete their work, 30 percent take advantage of either their husbands' or parents' offering to help out with childcare. What could be better for your children than to have their own father watch them? Other than yourself and your husband, who's better than either your parents or your husband's parents to watch your children?

About 15 percent of the women interviewed coordinate their work schedule with their husbands' to ensure that one of them is with the kids. While this takes effort, it avoids daycare costs and the guilt of leaving the kids in someone else's care. The women who have their husbands watch the kids feel blessed that they have that option.

"Luckily, my husband, Bill, could fill in at the end of the day," says Sheila, who was working a compressed workweek in corporate communications at the time. "The spousal support was there for me, so he could pick up my daughter. That is what made it all possible."

"I could not do this without such a good husband," exclaims Suzy, who works her hours opposite her husband's so that they avoid using a sitter. "My husband cleans house, I come home at 9:30 p.m., and he has food for me. The kids are in bed at 8:00 p.m. He's good at being a dad. We've managed to keep my little crazy rules in place."

"At the beginning, I worked when they napped," says Connie, talking about how she handled daycare when she was starting up her scrap-booking business. "My husband and I would alternate. I would work Tuesday and Thursday nights; he would watch the kids. He would cold call on Monday and Wednesday nights. It started slowly."

Angie's part-time therapy and counseling job was made possible by her husband's hours. "I had almost a one-hour commute. I had to leave at 6:30 a.m. My husband did everything that I would do if I were there. He worked part-time, and I worked part-time. So he was on duty from 6:30 a.m. on, and I was on duty from when I got home at 4:30 p.m. In our area in California, we didn't have school bus service, so he actually had to drive the kids to school. So that meant that he had to be avail-able to drive them to school or drive the carpool. If they were sick, we would take turns taking time off. He ended up having a very part-time life because of my part-time life. After a while, we determined that both of us working part-time were not really providing us the income that we wanted. We decided that I would become a stay-at-home mom and he would become a full-time wage earner. So then there was a transition step. I was working during school hours or Saturday. I kept working part-time while he was ramping up."

As an ultrasound technician, Erica works weekends when her husband is with the children. Her husband is off on Fridays, so she works then as well. As a food stylist with a husband who runs his own business, Samantha lets her husband take the kids to school while she's off working, and then she picks them up after school. Trish also has a husband who juggles his schedule alongside hers. She claims that he enjoys having the daily interaction with his children.

As with all these women, Nadya feels fortunate that her husband can help watch her children by working from home. She believes that many women who would like part-time employment don't go after it for the lack of a helpful husband.

Another 15 percent of the women interviewed used their parents at one time or another. Rosemary used her mom, who lived a few hours away, when she traveled. Since her travel was limited to a certain time-frame, this worked well for everyone. As a dance teacher, Becky taught children in her basement while her mother was upstairs watching her children and cooking dinner.

Fran feels that her mother is willing to help because it is part-time versus full-time. "I lucked out on all ends. My mother watches my children. I have this ideal situation. She comes to the house, takes care of my kids. I'm not worried about them. Part-time makes it work; she would not want to baby-sit full-time. Who would? I'm not asking too much of her."

DAYCARE BEYOND FAMILY

Some mothers want their children watched in their own homes, while others prefer taking their children to providers where there are other children. They feel that playing with others helps to socialize their children.

Whatever the preference, finding good childcare is one of the major factors in maintaining a part-time position. This takes time and effort. Several women had the same experience that Bonnie did when searching for daycare. As a therapist, she had specific ideas of what she envisioned for her daughter. "My daughter was a one-month-old when I started looking for daycare. I visited lots of places and came to the conclusion that I wanted a home daycare provider with a small number of kids, a nurturing daycare provider. I looked at a lot of places; they made my stomach hurt. There was a point that I thought, 'I'm not going back to work if this is what it looks like.' My husband kept saying, 'You will know when you find the right place.' And sure enough, I found wonderful daycare, a fabulous, kind, nurturing mom who raised two kids of her own.

"I'm of the firm belief that if kids are in nurturing daycare where they have a positive attachment to another adult that enhances their lives. But if they don't—I still think of some of those places I saw while looking for Emma. They broke my heart. I actually think the relationships that our kids formed with other kids in daycare and the parental relationships that our family has formed with the other daycare families have enhanced our lives. We have richer friendships because of it. It's a group of families we still socialize with and see regularly. It creates a sense of community. I feel fortunate about that."

Bonnie had her best friend watch her children until they were old enough to go to school. "My best friend is two houses away. She was a stay-at-home mom who did childcare. She loved my babies, so anytime, day or night, she would take them. She had mostly older kids. They loved my babies."

About 8 percent of the women I interviewed used nannies. The obvious advantages are having someone in your house to dress, feed, and bathe the children. In addition, they also do small child-related chores such as wash the children's clothes. The major disadvantage, of course, is the cost as mentioned earlier in this chapter by Sandy. Elderly women who want extra money or just love kids are good people to tap for part-time nanny positions. They like the part-time hours, not only for the extra money but also because working about twenty hours per week is perfect. It allows them to keep up with the children without putting a physical strain on them. Everyone is happy.

Leslie found two part-time nannies. "I had one woman for three years. I met her through a friend. She was an older lady who needed some money, loved children, and had done it all her life. She was semi-retired. The other woman was my neighbor. She was an older lady who was retired, but wanted to keep busy and loved kids."

Laurie was lucky to also find a great part-time nanny for her daughter Ashley. "She would come to my house for a couple of hours and get Ashley dressed, do a few chores around the house, take Ashley to her house, and do things with her there. Her husband came home, so it was like an ancillary family as we didn't have any family in town. This was three days per week. My daughter loved Olga. As a new mom, it was hard. I look back at Olga and thank her for being such a patient person with us and in regards to me. I was so type A. I wanted everything to be perfect. It had to be a certain way, and Olga was so relaxed, let her hair be messy, and didn't care if her shirt matched her pants. I wanted everything to appear perfect. Olga was 180 percent different. She's a down-home kind of country gal and was the perfect complement to me. I don't think I fully appreciated Olga while she was our nanny."

"I've made myself crazy with daycare," says Jodie, a physician, recalling life before hiring a nanny. "When we were in medical training, we couldn't afford a nanny. We had a cute, tiny old house in Columbia, South Carolina, that would never be safe in terms of baby-proofing. We didn't have a nanny. It was hard on us, the traffic, commuting, and working around daycare hours. It was tough.

"As the kids got older, and as my job got more flexible, it was much easier. My daughter is at school with an after-school program. My son is at the same school in a preschool program. With my newest child, I decided to get a nanny. We did a nanny share with the neighbors, who are also two doctors. They have an infant. We share costs, so it comes to the same amount as daycare. She helps out in the house, is reliable, and on time. It gives me more flexibility when the kids are off from school so I can still work. With her, it's made me realize how much easier it could have been with the other two who were in daycare when they were younger."

While there are services that can help you if you're looking for a nanny, they may be prohibitively expensive. These are designed for full-time nannies, not for part-time care. Networking (see next section) or posting flyers around town can work. Kate used a small, local town newspaper ad to help her find a nanny. "I put the ad in. Someone told me to do it. I interviewed a bunch of people. I got a college student from Brazil going part-time at the local community college.... She needed twenty-five hours. I paid her twenty-five hours whether I used them or not because I liked her so much."

In fact, 10 percent of the women interviewed used college or high school students as nannies. Several women mentioned that they obtained nannies from the closest elementary education program around them. Ingrid found three nannies from her local college.

Since she had been an English teacher, Margo liked using high school girls while she was tutoring part-time in her home. Since her daughter had kidney reflux, she wanted someone who would ask lots of questions about her daughter's care, checking in before giving her medicine. "I had two girls who wanted to make money. I had taught one of them. We sat down and interviewed them formally and said, 'Look, if we hire you and pay you a nanny's wages, you have to do the stuff we'd expect a nanny to do, like walk the dog once a day, do baby laundry.' They loved the idea. So I hired two high school girls, one Tuesday and Thursday and one Wednesday, all year long. When I had extra kids on Monday and Friday in the fall, I hired one of their friends."

NETWORKING FOR DAYCARE

Networking for daycare? It sounds odd, but a few of the women I interviewed found their daycare in just that manner. When you talk with neighbors, friends, and relatives, explaining your potential part-time status may help you to find daycare. That's what Heather, Brook, and Bonnie did.

After Heather left full-time employment as a registered nurse case manager, she kept hearing from her former employer, asking her to return. Daycare was her big drawback, and networking solved her problem. "They kept begging me," she says. "I was one of the very first case managers in a new role. I was one of the strongest case managers when I left. They were very happy to have me come back. They kept calling me up. They'd leave me alone for a few months. My husband, being a physician in the hospital, is always running into somebody saying, 'When is she coming back?' I never stopped thinking about it. The appropriate timing never presented itself.

"Then one day, one Sunday morning, I was sitting in Sunday school and one of my friends across the way from me was chatting. We were having fellowship time. I said, 'Yeah, I'd like to go back to work, but I don't know what to do with the kids. I can't pay daycare. They won't let you do it on an as-needed basis. I live way out yonder, and I have no family to help me, and it can't be too expensive because I don't want it to cost me to go to work. I need to be able to say, 'This week, I'm working Monday and Wednesday; next week they don't need me at all, but the following week they need me three days. I need something very, very flexible.' And she said, 'I'll watch your kids for you.' She was already keeping another baby. I went, 'Really?' So I had a conversation with her and sent the kids over there. Let me say, I live forty minutes away from her. For me to get to work by 8:00 a.m. or 8:30 a.m., I was willing to travel forty minutes to get to her house so that I knew my children were well taken care of. I live only fifteen minutes from the hospital. I left my house at ten after seven to go all the way around to her house so that I could clock in usually by 8:00 a.m. or 8:15 a.m. I was very willing to do that, willing to go the extra miles. Then I left the hospital, going all the way to her house in the afternoon and back to my house again."

Brook asked around her neighborhood to find childcare. She ended up using her next door neighbor to watch her kids. "We had a senior citizen who lived next door, had none of her own grandchildren. My kids were just like her grandchildren. She would come to my house; I would pay her. She was worth every penny and then some. Faith would bake, cook, sew, plant gardens, and read books. I was blessed to have Faith."

While networking, Tessa, Joan, and Eve found other mothers in a similar situation as themselves. This opened up the opportunity for "childcare sharing." Childcare sharing is taking turns babysitting each other's children. While one mother goes to work, the other one babysits. Then they swap. The key to success is how often you're watching other people's children. If you have someone else's kids part-time every day, it can be tough and wear you out over time. Based on the women who have done it, babysitting twice a week seems to be more manageable than daily and works out well. It goes without saying that the children should get along and play well together. That wasn't an issue for any of the mothers who shared childcare.

As a part-time teacher, Tessa shared babysitting with her neighbor daily. "With the second child, I had neighbors move [into the neighborhood]. One was also a teacher in the district who was going to go part-time. So I talked her into childcare sharing. She worked mornings, and I watched her two kids. Then I worked afternoons, and she watched my two kids. That worked, but at the end we were both ready to be done with it. It was hard as sometimes our kids were together eight to ten hours per day. It got to be a long day. That lasted one year. The next year we got daycare."

Joan, a banker, only babysat twice a week, yielding more positive results. "I have a friend who freelances writing books. She had one child at the time. I watched her son two days a week while she worked. She watched my son two days a week while I worked. It worked out really well. I went to her house at lunchtime and nursed; she lived close enough."

Childcare sharing two days a week also panned out well for Eve. "One of my husband's college friends lived near us. His wife was trying to work part-time at the University of Texas Medical Center. She just had a baby a couple of months before I had mine. So the two of us said, 'Why don't we watch each other's child on our off days? We'll swap; it won't cost us anything. Both of our kids will have someone else to play with. We're both moms who care about who are watching our child.' So we started swapping days. The two days a week I didn't work, I watched her little girl. The two days I worked, she watched my son. This worked out fine. It gets a little hairy when one kid gets sick, or the mom's sick, but it worked out."

Key Learning—Daycare

- Take advantage of school hours and after-school care when possible.
- Ensure that you earn more than you pay out in daycare costs unless you are working part-time for continuity.
- For part-time hours, using an in-home provider may be less costly than a daycare center.
- Try to negotiate part-time hours at a full-time childcare provider if that's your best option for daycare.
- Consider working while your husband is at home to watch the kids.
- Are your/your husband's parents available to help out?
- Consider using local college or high school students as part-time nannies.
- Networking can help you find the best childcare provider for your situation.

LIKE A PUZZLE

Putting daycare together is like a puzzle. Monday and Wednesday is one schedule while Tuesday and Thursday may be totally different. During the school year, the kids use after-school care, but in the summer it's a patchwork of camps, friends, and family taking care of them. And, if a child is sick, that's when backup support is needed.

"We never did traditional childcare," says Michele. "We always pieced things together. Previously, it was one of us at home and an in-home sitter or a combination of preschool, in-home sitter, and us juggling the schedule between the two of us. As a therapist, I can work evening and afternoon hours. [The kids are] both in elementary school, so now it's much easier. I try to work while the kids are in school. I work two after-noon/evenings a week to 6:30 p.m. or 7:00 p.m."

Janette pieced her childcare together with a lot of help from her husband. "When I went part-time, my husband, Lee, was a partner in an employee benefits consulting firm. Lee worked his own schedule. When he went in, he worked from 7:00 a.m. to 3:00 p.m. and picked up my son from school. When Pam was a baby, Lee stayed home two days a week. I worked from home one day a week and hired someone to cover the rest of the time. Then when she was older, Pam went to a little daycare center at a local college three days a week."

Nancy was lucky enough to get help from several family members with an occasional use of paid sitters so she could run her jewelry busi-ness. "I worked around my kids' schedules. I had to rely on people from time to time. It could be family members. A long period of time my father was available to my kids. A long period of time my mother was available to my kids. For the most part, I worked around them. I did have situa-tions during my busy season where I did have to hire daycare. But for the most part, it was seldom. Now I don't do very many home parties myself. I do more work from the design aspect and work more as a salesperson to my shop owners. But in the beginning, I was doing all the home parties myself. I'd be gone at night when my husband was home. I designed during the day. As the kids got older, they were coming to the shop with mom. My little one, I used to put him in the infant seat when he was a few weeks old and prop him up on my bench, and he'd watch me work."

And Ellen used all types of daycare to cover her needs. "I advertised at colleges, and I had two sisters. Then I got a series of ladies via word of mouth, older ladies needing part-time work. I put the little one in two days of preschool. My mother-in-law helped in the summer when the kids weren't at camp. I linked up with friends, and we helped each other out."

Articles have even been written in the *Wall Street Journal* discussing extreme childcare maneuvers. Husbands and wives have been bending schedules, squeezing in freelance work, and shuttling children all at the same time. Families are choreographing calendars down to the minute in ways they never have before.

BE COMFORTABLE

I can't say it any better than Kate, a psychotherapist. "My words of wisdom are really be comfortable with the daycare situation, whether it's someone in your home or not. Really investigate it. If you don't feel good about it, you're always going to feel guilty. But if you feel, 'Wow, my kids really enjoy themselves,' then you take some of that guilt away from yourself. Mothers are stuck with that guilt. 'Is my job being taken care of in the best possible way while I'm not there?' Make sure it won't come back to bite you in the bum later."

Chapter 9

WORD OF WARNING: PART-TIME ISN'T FOR EVERYONE

"When I think back, would I have done something differently?"
—Debby

I would be remiss to write a book on part-time employment without discussing those who stopped. If it's so great, why do some women choose to either move back into full-time work or become stay-at-home mothers? What caused them to leave a situation that many consider "the best of both worlds"?

This chapter only covers those women who had issues with part-time employment. There are many women whom I interviewed who moved from part-time work to full-time employment once all their children were in school. Having everyone gone most of the day made full-time employment feasible for them again. Others who also enjoyed part-time work returned to a full-time position either for economic reasons or to obtain benefits.

BEING STIGMATIZED

Some part-timers feel a stigma attached to their work related directly to their hours. Bias comes from within the companies for some women and from outside factors for others. I heard from several women about a lack of support from within the organization that agreed to part-time hours. In one firm, not only was there a lack of support, but an attempt at sabotaging the position itself. Stigmatism from outside the job can also pressure part-timers. Friends may question why you are taking a certain job. Maybe they feel the position is below your skill level. Maybe you are working in a job that they themselves would never consider doing. Peer pressure can cause dissonance when a part-timer might otherwise be quite content.

Several part-timers describe the prejudice they experienced from the very company that agreed to the position that they held. While the employer obviously supported and approved the job, the boss's true feelings about part-time work came to light once the agreement was underway. When the prejudice comes from your employer, each day going to work can be miserable rather than enthralling. Sometimes the prejudice can be so strong that it eventually causes women to quit.

On the other hand, some women, like Suzy, feel it from outside their jobs. Suzy sees prejudice coming from her neighbors. To obtain the healthcare benefits that her family needs, she is a deli clerk at Fresh Market, an upscale grocery store.

"When people look at what my husband does for a living (a lawyer) and then they see what I'm doing, they look at me like I have three heads," says Suzy. "They're so confused. I've had so many neighbors and friends go, 'Gosh, is everything okay? Are you guys financially okay?' It's one of the most insulting things that has happened. They think that we are in dire straits. Maybe it's something they wouldn't be willing to do. I shouldn't have to explain it. Be my friend, don't judge. Maybe it's the hardest thing I've had to deal with at this job. My neighbors going, 'Gosh, I didn't know you were working here.' Like *eww*. That's the strange thing; we live in a nice house in a nice neighborhood, and they expect us to go bankrupt. I have filtered a lot of people by doing this. I'm fine with that. It's not the end of the world."

Suzy has not quit her part-time job despite the insults she has received from her neighbors, but a less secure person might. Unlike Suzy, several women did quit due to negative influences outside their employment. These women received flak from their immediate family members about working too much, even though their hours were only twenty-five to thirty hours per week. When the pressure built up in addition to the constant criticism from family members, these mothers folded and left the workforce.

Over time, however, views *can* change. For Nancy, her friends and neighbors are finally seeing her as a "wage earner" in her household, not a stay-at-home mom with a cute hobby. "Now that my children are nearly grown up and I'm still doing this, people are getting it, that this is *really* my job. My husband has been out of work on and off for years because of his illnesses. I've been the sole provider. People are finally getting it. But that's been hard to deal with over the years."

FAMILY TIME

While part-time work brings relief from the forty-hour workweek, sometimes it's just not enough. Several women stopped working outside the home when their third child was born. Having three children, one being an infant, put them over the edge. Other moms, prior to resigning from employment, felt that their minds were still at work, even when they were at home. It just wasn't worth it for them, so they decided to stay home altogether. And a few moms had issues finding part-time daycare and had to move back into full-time employment to obtain consistent, quality care for their children.

Leslie is one of the moms who left the workforce upon the birth of her third child. "To tell you the truth, it was perfect and great with two kids. But with three kids it was too much to juggle," she says. "If you have two kids, I highly recommend it. If you have three kids, it's much harder. Once all three are in school I plan on working fifteen hours per week, from 8:00 a.m. to 2:00 p.m."

She isn't the only one planning on returning. I had several other mothers voice their plans for going back once their children were at a certain age. Laurie is one of the moms who left work because her mind was always there, even when her body wasn't. "Even part-time in a company like Procter and Gamble, you're not working 60 percent," she says about her part-time research position. "If you look like you're not working, you're working through things in your head. You're not present to your child, at least I'm not. They hire mostly type A people, making a very stimulating environment. Even when I was doing stuff with my daughter, I wasn't always present. I was thinking through research designs. Sometimes I'd have to work late, pick her up from daycare, and take her back to work with me. Everyone loved having a kid in there, but I couldn't do that for very long. So I ended up working more than 60 percent. I can't say that it was P&G's fault or my supervisor's fault because if I said, 'No,' that would have been fine with them. It was me, that type A person. So I couldn't keep that balance; I wasn't good at it. I would be one of the last parents to pick her up. I'd be running over to get her, I mean really running, trying to get there in time to pick her up.

"It would have been detrimental to my marriage if I had continued to work part-time," she adds. "I did it for me, not for my husband. I would have been a resentful person by ending up doing everything for my daughter. Hopefully, mothers are preparing their sons to be in a marriage of equals."

Laurie is now considering going back to part-time work. "In retrospect, I look back and say, 'Should I have stopped?' I'm going through a loss of power and confidence that I could go back working and be effective, that I've forgotten a lot. I'm afraid that I'd embarrass myself. P&G has seen that there's a value in retirees for part-time work. Now they see value in having people like me and retirees do something for a little while, for a three-month project. Right now they need my skill base. I have to say, I tend to get very intense and throw myself into something 100 percent. I'm afraid I'll lose sight of my priority. I have a fourteen-year-old; I don't have much time left with her. I'm feeling, 'What's next?'"

As a registered nurse case manager, Heather loved her job. But she left it after working part-time for three years. The flexibility working sixteen to twenty-four hours a week gave her was good when her kids were young, but worked against her when her children grew older and had lots of activities. Planning a solid schedule when she needed it was hard in her part-time position.

"It became too much for me," she explains. "Now my children are older. My son is now doing soccer, after-school activities. Before it was easy: drop them off at 7:15 a.m.; they play; they have lunch; they have a snack; then mama's there. Once they got older, it got difficult. I can't work on Wednesday because my son has soccer practice at 2:00 p.m. My daughter has dance on Tuesdays. I never know if I can leave. Can I get in there and get all my work done and not have any families knock on the door at 4:00 p.m. wanting to see the case manager when I've got to go to soccer practice? It became much more difficult for me.

"There were days that I left at 2:00 p.m. I left early, but I'm responsible until 5:00 p.m. I was feeling guilty. Someone else would have to fill in for me if something came up. And that's not fair. As the kids got older, it became harder to maintain the flexibility. They started having homework. I started getting a taste of what full-time moms have to do. They come home at 6:00 p.m. and have to make dinner, do baths, and so on. I had no help. Nobody's doing the grocery shopping. My husband was working every third weekend. No one is doing that stuff for me. It became more difficult to justify taking that time away from my family and being cranky, putting stress on the family.

"I could see it, not wanting to make that decision [to quit]. I was always in a good place, work when I wanted to work, making $25 an hour. I'm in nirvana. How many people get to do this?"

Then Heather and her husband decided to put an addition on their house. "The addition on our house was the breaking point. My husband said, 'I want you to consider not working while this is being done. One of us needs to be there, and it can't be me.' I didn't think that was the case, but he was right. I did need to be here to make daily decisions, to oversee what they were doing. Me doing all this work, getting up at 5:30 a.m., getting dressed, making sure everything was done, rushing [the kids] out the door, yelling, and screaming, 'Get your shoes on, we've got to go,' doing all this stuff, working all day, coming home, being tired, traveling—and I made forty bucks. I pay in my husband's tax bracket, so I'm paying 35 to 40 percent in taxes, so by the time I pay taxes, pay childcare, buy gas, buy a pair of comfortable shoes—it's like if you're not getting a whole lot out of this, you better rethink what you're doing.

"My husband said, 'What you're doing is putting a big strain on the family, so you need to get a grip. So you need to figure out if, to make it worthwhile for this family, it would almost be better for you to go back to work full-time, get a housekeeper, and take that load off of you. You can't do it all. Can't be mommy, have the house 100 percent, can't blame the children for being kids.' So I made the decision, at this time, that I needed to be home."

Because Heather loved what she did, she is torn. She is considering going back. Here are the pros and cons as she voiced them to me. "Summers were always a problem. I had to find childcare when they were older, which meant summer camps, which are very expensive. Summer camps are for a whole week. Am I going to pay for a whole week of summer camp when I'm going to only work for two days? Now I'm paying to go to work. It's a crossroad of some sort, and I'm paralyzed. But I'm not able to make the decision [to go back] at this time. It becomes very challenging because the longer you're out of the workforce, the harder it is to go back, especially when you're a nurse. Things change. I once worked a night on a night shift in the critical care unit, people who come right out of open heart surgery. I couldn't go back to that now. The more you stay out of it, the harder it is to go back. If I am going to go back, I need to do it soon. If I'm not going to go back, I need to get that in my mind. The kids are going to need me more the older they get. I'm only going to be chauffeuring more the older they get. Are we making a decision that I'm staying home? I'm not going back to work when I'm fifty-eight."

But for Missy it was clear. Handling daycare over the summer vacation became a big issue that was too difficult to overcome. "I had [the kids] in camp July through August. I had them in one camp after another. I actually felt like I was spending all my money on camp. I spent all my money on daycare, when they're not physically in school. They have lots of time off. That's the real challenge because I don't get that much time off. You've got to have somebody who can be with them because you're not going to get the time off. You can't be home week after week. I did think about it; there were times that I took breaks from working because it got to be too much. It got to be a big hassle, a big responsibility."

Roseanne lives in Detroit and managed investments for a high net worth individual twenty-five to thirty-five hours per week before leaving the workforce. She was nervous about giving up her identity as a career woman, having to depend financially on her husband. It was hard for her to let go of her job. She resigned because of daycare issues.

"What prompted me to leave was the situation with my nanny," she explains. "We had a live-in. . . . She had invited her boyfriend into our home without my knowing it. A couple of nights a week, my husband and I would go out to exercise and this would happen while we were gone. The kids would be asleep by the time I got back. My husband would take them to school, so by the time I would see the kids after this event, it was old news, almost twenty-four hours later. I still don't know how many times it happened. He was in our home. That disturbed me to no end. I said, 'I need to be here 100 percent.'

"Looking back, so many times I wouldn't see the kids for three days at a time. I feel that I prioritize my career; I feel I was trying to keep up with the men. If I had to do it all again, I would have prioritized my family more. I would have done part-time hours far earlier than I did, and I wouldn't feel guilty about giving 100 percent. I always gave 110 percent. I was never satisfied with that.

"Also once I stopped working, the one thing that benefited me the most was the relationship with my husband. I always put myself last on the list, but he was second to last. The kids came first, the boss came second, then school, then my husband, and me."

In retrospect, Roseanne now feels that she should have tried to shift that hierarchy a bit, moving her husband and herself up higher on the list. "They weren't going to ever fire me because I was such a dedicated individual. We, as women, have to give ourselves more credit." With many of us, that's much easier to see in hindsight.

WORKING FROM HOME NOT IDEAL

After working part-time from home, a few women either stopped altogether or went back to the office in full-time positions. The issue was more about working from home rather than the work itself.

Did you wonder what happened to Holly after she left her job share with Sandy? She ended up working from home. "Our decision-making process was that we were going to have to cut everything in half. We were still fine. I stayed home; I was retiring. Then within six days, I started getting phone calls from new clients. So after turning two or three people down, my husband said, 'Okay, you're going to have to open your own office.' I said, 'I don't want to do that.' And he said, 'Just open a law firm, hang out a shingle, and you don't even have to have any space; do what you want to do. If all you do is refer people to other people, the lawyers in your community will think you are still here.'

"I started a law firm haphazardly and did that for two and a half years, working from home. I usually worked in the middle of the night between 1:00 a.m. and 4:00 a.m. I'm a night owl. Usually I'd talk to my clients, judges, do deposition work, had to make court appearances during the workday, taking maybe ten hours per month. The balance of the work was drafting documents, doing e-mails, letters, or research. I would do that whenever I had free time. When my daughter was napping at age one, I had a two- or three-hour block in the middle of the day. But for the most part, I'd go to bed with her at 8:00 p.m. and wake up at one or two in the morning, thinking about what I needed to do. I'd go do it and then go back to bed and sleep until she woke up. My entire legal career I worked at least two or three mornings a week from 1:00 a.m. to 4:00 a.m. because the stress of the job would wake me up and then I wouldn't be able to go back to sleep. I got more done with no distractions.

"Then my husband started his own company, working out of the house, too. We were tripping over each other. When I was working at home, I kept the house stuff moving along. But I didn't stop in the middle of work to do something in the house. When he started working at home, all of a sudden I noticed I felt like my workday was being interrupted with him being there. I used a large bedroom, so we decided to take two small bedrooms and combine the kids in the large bedroom. Then we each had our office. We did that, and it still wasn't working. So I said to my friends, 'I think that I need to come back because this isn't working.'"

Holly went back full-time as a trust officer at a large financial institution, letting her husband work from home and become the primary caretaker.

Key Learning—Part-Time Not for Everyone

- Prejudice toward part-timers can come from within the same organization that approved the position.
- Bias can come from friends and family who don't understand your objectives in working part-time.
- Family constraints to part-time employment:
  - Third child's birth.
  - Strain on keeping the family organized and all children's activities in place.
  - Summers off of school for the kids.
  - Unreliable daycare.
  - Working from home too difficult.

Chapter 10

EVOLVING OVER TIME

"Life is about change. It doesn't end until you want it to."
—Ellen

When deciding whether to pursue part-time work or not, some women feel that they are making a lifelong decision. But women, unlike most men, have careers that change and evolve over a lifetime. They move from full-time to part-time to stay-at-home situations and back again. They can rise to high-level positions in Fortune 100 corporations, become stay-at-home moms, open part-time consulting businesses, become stay-at-home moms again, and then go back into corporate America working either full-time or part-time.

Because women have to be flexible and adaptable to raise children, they carry those traits into their personal lives. They modify their lives when they need to for financial reasons or when they want to for self-satisfaction. They lead fluid lives.

Sylvia Ann Hewlett, an economist and founding president of the Center for Work-Life Policy, says, "Sixty percent of highly qualified women have nonlinear careers."[1] Obviously the push-pull of family life explains the difference between male and female career paths, but Hewlett claims it's even more than that. "Women's ambitions, it turns out, are different from men's. While money is a prime motivator for men, it is much less important for women. Several other factors—including high-quality colleagues, recognition by bosses, and flexible work options—trump compensation as reasons women go to work."[2]

Delving into the lives of four women, Stephanie, Joan, Laura, and Jesse, whose careers have changed over time, you'll see how women modified their lives. They made sure that their employment choices were consistent with what mattered to them most. Each had worked for large corporations full-time and was on the male model career track prior to becoming a mother. Each of them stepped out of a full-time job to begin her personal career track upon having children. And each one is successful today.

STEPHANIE, BANKER TO BOOKKEEPER TO INTERIOR DESIGNER

"When I had Nicole, my daughter, I didn't know how I'd feel being home. I took three months off for maternity leave and didn't know if I was going to like it or not because it was a huge change," says Stephanie, a commercial loan officer at the time. "If I could have stayed home financially, I would have. I loved being home."

When Stephanie came back from maternity leave, she worked purely for the money. Her husband wasn't a partner in his law firm yet, so she needed the income. "My perspective changed; I wanted to be home with Nicole. Not only had I been working for twelve years, I also worked all through college. I was really enjoying being at home. I had never done that before, and I had wanted to have a baby."

Stephanie knew that she wanted to return to work on a part-time basis. She says, "I told the bank, 'When I come back from maternity leave, I want to go on flextime.' The bank has banking hours, so flextime to them means reduced hours. They look at hours as being when the bank is open." They let her continue in her former full-time role on a part-time basis, thirty hours per week.

"I was exhausted. I enjoyed the client contact; I enjoyed that very much. I did not enjoy the grunt part of the job, and there's always that aspect to a job. But I disliked it so much more than when I was working full-time because I was so pushed for time. They doubled my workload, and I got it done. I realized how inefficient you are when you have the luxury of working all day. Then you come back working flextime; you are so under the gun. It's human nature, when you are so pressed you are much more efficient to get it done. You've got to leave. You won't spend the extra six minutes gabbing with someone on the phone, won't linger or chat in the doorway. You are so focused to get something done, and you only have a limited amount of time. It annoys you how much time you waste. It's like when you have nothing to do; you can take all day to make a pot of tea. That is human nature. And when you have a ton of stuff to get done, you get a ton of stuff done. I like to have things to do. I was very, very efficient. They told me they'd let me have that schedule forever. I could have done that until [my daughter] went to high school if I had wanted. It was good for them; it was good for me. We got what we wanted. My clients at the bank were wonderful about my schedule.

"I liked the hours, but I was doing two full jobs. I managed a loan portfolio of $35 million; that's a big portfolio. I had to maintain all of that with all the depository relationships and the volumes of paperwork within the bank that comes with that. I felt like they were taking advantage of me. But it was a win-win situation as I wanted the schedule the most. And I was the only one who had ever done that in this office, so I was breaking new ground. It was a trade-off," she says.

Then when her husband became partner, Stephanie left the banking world and her commercial loan officer job behind to become a stay-at-home mom. She was home for about a year when her former bank clients called her and asked her to work for them in a bookkeeping capacity. She hadn't thought of going back, but she kept on getting phone calls with more work.

Stephanie worked while her daughter was at preschool, from 9:00 a.m. to 1:00 p.m., working about twenty hours per week. "It was perfect because I was in control when I worked. All my clients knew me because I had been their banker, and they were so good about my hours. In fact, it made me realize how willing people are to work with you when they understand your family situation. They offered to let me do their bookkeeping at home, and I didn't want to do it that way. I said, 'I need to come to you.'

"A former client called me and said, 'Stephanie, are you bored yet?' I said, 'No, what's the matter?' They replied, 'My bookkeeping's a mess.' I said, 'Okay, I'll come in and look at it.'

"I set up accounting systems on a computer. That's how it started. Some businesses, like the local brewing company, put me on a regular schedule once I set up their systems. I went in and did their bookkeeping: payroll, paid bills, recorded bills, did financial statements, budget, taxes.

"When I was bookkeeping for the brewing company, there was a wine store across the street that wanted my services. Then I would run into the owner at the bakery and told him what I was doing, and he said, 'Oh, come work for me.' So then I did that. I said, 'This is so good.'"

She told another former client what she was doing. Stephanie adds, "That client said, 'Oh, I need you to come work for me.' I started letting people know what I was up to, but I didn't want to have too many clients at a time because it got very intense over the three- or four-month period while setting up everything. Then I'd train them so they could do it themselves. And then there was the manufacturing distributorship job. [One woman] just overheard me talking about my 'play job.' She said, 'What is your play job?' and I told her. She said, 'You need to come work for my husband.' I didn't look for them; they all came to me."

Because her husband was leaving his previous job to start up his own law firm, Stephanie was again working for the money, not self-fulfillment. "A year after I was home, right when I started my bookkeeping business, the bank called me up and asked me to come back to run the private banking department in town. I would be working the schedule I wanted. And I turned it down.

"I thought about it for a week. With a lot more money, it was very hard to turn down. I knew how much time it was going to take, and it wasn't the right time in my life. If Nicole had been in elementary school, I would have taken it. I thought about it, and my husband wouldn't tell me what to do, which was infuriating. What made it hard to turn down was that they were offering a really sweet deal. That was really a nice way to end [my relationship with the bank]. I was on an ego trip. I wondered about that for a while, if I should have turned it down, but I don't regret that decision ever."

While banking to bookkeeping is logical, how did she go from bookkeeping to interior design? Stephanie had been doing bookkeeping for

Joanne, an architect in town. So it only made sense for her to use Joanne as her architect when she decided to finish her basement. "I have learned that only 50 percent of the time what you design as an architect gets built. So when the project was finished, I called her up and said, 'Do you want to come over?' And she said, 'Yes, we don't get to see the finished product very much.' She came over and said, 'You come work for me in interior design.' I thought she wasn't serious."

But Joanne was, and Stephanie let her bookkeeping business with everyone other than Joanne wind down as her interior design work went up. "So I was working for Joanne some and still doing my accounting. I just worked my way out of it. I didn't have that much interior design work at first. It came in spurts. My first client had just designed their house, and it was being built. That's when I come in, at the end of a project, just as the building is finishing up in the last two months. It's really intense.

"Money has never been part of the interior design business," says Stephanie. "I never put a lot of resources into it. I'm making money now, but it wasn't even enough to cover childcare then.

"I'm still working with Joanne. She looks at it as though I'm an additional service. I am no overhead to her. I'm paid only when I'm billable to her, and we split the fee. The regular hours I keep are for her bookkeeping. She pays me a flat rate."

Stephanie loves the hours because they are very predictable. If she can't get to work, it's okay, too. "If we had a snow day, unless it was a payroll day, it wouldn't matter. There's nothing that I do that someone else can't back up. If Nicole got sick, Joanne's husband can come in and help. There's never an interior design crisis, only in their minds. What happens is people wait too long to make a decision and they're being pressed by the contractor. That happens all the time."

Stephanie is pleased with her current situation and encourages women to pursue part-time work to obtain the working hours they want. "I'd never planned it out like this. You must have confidence to go after it. More and more, people in the workforce are baby boomers and, unless they're really sheltered people, will work with you. If you're a good worker, they'll work with you when you're available. Women are the best because they've done it. And if they haven't, they've had to deal with it. I had a client from Atlanta who wanted me to work on weekends. Joanne and I told her we don't do that. We thought that was above and beyond. She said that people in Atlanta work those hours. We said this is a small town and we don't. I wouldn't have approached it that way myself, but Joanne said that this woman is going to be difficult. I wouldn't question that now, but I questioned it then. I said, 'Oh, I don't have that much this weekend.' But in retrospect, Joanne was absolutely right. Sometimes you choose not to take a client.

"By having done all these weird part-time jobs, I'm not stuck. If something awful happened and I had to go back to work full-time, I think going out and getting employment with benefits would be easier because I've had my hand in the pot. It's a perceived advantage. I'd be a better employee because I know what it's like to run a business, unlike someone who has worked for a huge corporation and hasn't run their own business."

JOAN, BANKER TO TEACHER TO ACCOUNTING POSITION

As a vice president for an Oklahoma City bank, Joan wanted to stay home with her new baby boy. So she asked her employer if she could cut back her hours in her current role. "I was thrilled the bank would let me do it in the capacity that I was in. I don't think they would have given me the opportunity if I had started part-time. Having a track record made all the difference."

After two and a half years, she stopped working to stay home for five years. Then when both her boys were in elementary school, she was ready to go back. "I wanted something more to do; I'm not a homebody. So I went to the banking world because that's where I came from. I went to an organization here that does continuing education for bankers. I said, 'I want to teach a class.' It took probably at least a semester or two before they had something for me.

"I started teaching Accounting I. I've taught ten different classes for them. Then I started developing my own coursework, creating the coursework. And I did in-house work for the banks. I would teach their employees. Since the banks knew me, they'd say, 'Could you teach about blah, blah, blah?' I'd say, 'Sure.' And I'd go to the bank and teach it. That was pretty cool *and* lucrative. I had the same students; they would look for my classes. They'd say, 'When are you going to teach XYZ?'

"In a few cases, the banks contacted me directly. But I had them go through my employer, the American Institute of Banking; it was only fair. The benefit of going through my employer was they provided all the materials. If I needed a book, they ordered the books. They'd reproduce syllabuses for me. It was a great thing.

"And once you get hooked in, you're hooked in. I did a seminar for one bank; I did it once. Then I did it again and again. Eventually, everyone in the entire holding company had to take my class. So that was a two-year stint. They had three shifts around the clock. I did the first shift, then the second shift, then the third shift. That was a very cool situation except for the ones that I had to do in the middle of the night, the third shift. I was willing to do it because they were so nice to me and willing to accommodate my schedule. I thought, 'Okay, I can do this.'"

She continually juggled her schedule to match her children's, taking on more and more weekend work and working less during the week. Then, when her third son entered kindergarten, she decided that she needed yet another change. "My time would be free again. It was major déjà vu. I was ready. I was getting tired of teaching. I did not want to be working on weekends anymore. I wanted a different schedule, Monday through Friday, no evenings, no weekends. So now I had mornings free. I put out my feelers. My next door neighbor started a bank. He called me up. . . . He said, 'Joan, I heard you are going to go back to the workforce and work for a bank.' I said, 'Yes, I am.' He said, 'Why don't you interview with us?' I said, 'Okay.'"

While in this position, Joan moved from being a part-timer into a full-time role. "I'm contemplating a job change," she says. "I polished up my résumé two weeks ago. I started part-time and then went full-time; it's like being a paralegal and then becoming a lawyer. I'm not sure you can stay in the same place moving from part-time to full-time, whereas the reverse worked great for me. They're not giving me everything I want in terms of responsibility. They see me as a mommy first.

"I'm not as satisfied as I would like to be. I'm not a very good follower. I am more of a leader. I thought I would be satisfied with that because I just wanted to get back into the workforce. I needed to sharpen my skills, like utilizing the computer. So I took a part-time job [at the bank] in an accounting department that only had a CFO. I was the accounting clerk. I did all of the accounting functions, which in a way was great as I had to sharpen my skills. I had to sink or swim. I quickly realized that I needed more responsibility. It wasn't satisfying. It's been very hard to get that. Here I am; I've been here five years. I do have more responsibility now, but I still don't have enough.

"The bank has grown around me. They're not recognizing that I'm working eight- or ten-hour days now. I'm doing what the others are doing. But they still see me as how I started. I may have to change for that reason, and I regret that."

LAURA, BUYER TO BABYSITTER TO HOUSEKEEPER TO STATIONARY BUSINESS OWNER

One day Laura came home from her full-time job as a buyer at Macy's department store and told her husband that she couldn't do this anymore. She couldn't work full-time. Her son had had three sitters, and he wasn't even nine months old yet. "It was too stressful finding babysitters, so I quit," claims Laura.

Since the family needed the income, her husband was questioning how they were going to make ends meet. "I said, 'Don't worry,' to my husband. I put the word out that I would keep children at my home. I became a little daycare provider. It just worked out that [the parents] worked part-time, so I didn't have anyone past three o'clock in the afternoon. It was a beautiful thing. It was all toddlers. We put together a little playroom, and they all napped at the same time. Everyone was on varied schedules between 8:00 a.m. to 3:00 p.m. If I had three [kids] or less, I had double strollers. I could then put three kids in, and we went for walks every day. We played in the backyard, had a little pool, a sandbox. I had lots of mommy friends in the neighborhood, so we'd get together in other people's backyards. It was such an intimate setting that I could call the moms and say, 'If we're not in my backyard, we're in so-and-so's backyard.' They would just come over there to pick up their kids.

"It started by word of mouth; knowing mommies helped. We were all in the same situation with daycare. The only reason that the situation changed is because my little guy needed to go to preschool. So there I was trekking back and forth to preschool with kids in tow. That was too much, having their kids in the car.

"So then again, I told my husband, 'Don't panic.' I started cleaning homes. I did both for a while. I kept kids Monday, Wednesday, and Friday. Then I cleaned homes Tuesdays and Thursdays. I had a sitter come in for my son. I segued into that by word of mouth and telling people I was a housecleaner. I still do that part-time. I started with eight hours a week, and it went up from there. I worked the entire time he was at preschool, from 8:30 a.m. to 3:00 p.m. every day. I had eighteen cleaning clients. I did that for about a year and a half, and then we moved.

"At that point, I was driving too far to get to my cleaning clients. My husband's financial situation has improved over the years, making more money. When we moved, I cut cleaning houses down to two days per week.

"I started a stationary business prior to moving. My girlfriend and I were getting together scrapbooking. She's a friend of mine who is super creative and works full-time. We started making handmade cards, actually punching little things, and at Christmastime, making little wreaths. We sold them at craft shows," she says.

In addition to working full-time, Laura's friend also lived thirty minutes away. That meant getting together during the evenings, which was hard with a young family. "It was hard to plan the business together. So I, on the side, was piddling around with the printing aspect. Then I started doing invitations for people, and one thing just led to another. I said, 'Wow, I can do cards.' I was also designing notepads and having a printing company make up the notepads for me. One of my girlfriends said, 'You can do that. You can "pad" it.' I said, 'You're right. I can!' So I Googled 'how to make a notepad,' and there I was, making notepads at home. People kept putting little bugs in my ear."

So Laura printed, cut, and "padded" the notepads herself. They sold so well that she began to use a small mom-and-pop company across the street from her. She e-mailed the designs to them, and they did the laborious job of printing, cutting, and padding. "So it's nice because that laborious task is out of my hands. I can now focus on creativity. I'm a self-taught graphic designer, and I use that term very loosely."

Selling her products was easy since Laura decided to start with at-home parties like Pampered Chef, Tupperware, and Longaberger Company. She'd attended many of these parties herself as a guest and believed that it would be a good venue for her products. She designed paperware for parties as well as a line of notepads and cards. After completing the products for one particular party, she hired her first consultant. "I did one of her daughter's sweet sixteen parties. She was so impressed with the level of service. I went to her home. I designed the proofs for her, all custom. I did candy wrappers, invitations, and the whole bit. She loved it so much, she became a big advocate. I said, 'I've been thinking about having some consultants, would you want to be one?' She just jumped in. She was my guinea pig."

Laura was off and running. She had well-designed paper goods to sell and her first consultant. But how could she afford it? Money was initially tight for Laura. Remember, she was cleaning houses to make ends meet. "If we had a show, then I had to make samples. There were some months I said, 'How are we going to do this?' We started with nothing. We made bag tags, and we had to get those laminated. I'd go to Kinkos and pay a dollar a tag to get them laminated. Now I own a laminator. We slowly built it up. And now we have cash flow. My friends all say that they can't wait to see me on the stock exchange.

"I'm reading the Martha Stewart rules and trying to be smart about things. My son is cute. We were at the shopping center, and there was a vacant storefront. He goes, 'Mommy, that can be your store.' I said, 'It could.' I do have a degree in merchandising, so it could be. I said, 'It could be, but then we'd go to the store every afternoon instead of coming home.' He goes, 'Oh, yeah.' I said, 'I don't know if I ever want it to be that big.'"

In a typical party, her consultants may sell $500 of product. The consultant keeps 30 percent, and Laura grosses $350. If she can get all four of her consultants running a party a week, Laura would be doing very well. She is contemplating an incentive plan for her consultants to boost the number of parties they hold. This in turn boosts sales.

During her high season, October to December, Laura personally ran eighteen shows one year, more than one a week. That's quite a bit when you consider that she is also producing and filling all the orders as well. One of her goals is to run a show a month, not a home party, but a multi-craft show. That way it's easier on her and she still can obtain large orders. Another goal of Laura's is to hand out a business card a day. It can be at the grocery store, the dry cleaner, the post office, wherever she happens to be that day. Like any good business owner, she's always on the lookout for more clients.

Starting from a craft closet under her stairs, she longed for a bigger space for all her production. After all, this woman was selling $3,000 worth of product a month that was being produced in a closet. "It's where it started, the craft closet. I put a desk in there and painted it all cute to make it fun. I had been begging my husband to make our dining room a studio because we never used our formal dining room and it was close to the closet. He kept saying no."

Then one year, while her family was traveling to their vacation destination, Laura was recapping her fourth quarter numbers. On the return flight home, she says, "I showed it to my husband and said, 'Look what I did fourth quarter.' He said, 'Wow.' The next day he said, 'Why don't we go shopping for your desk; I think you need your studio.' It was a big surprise to me.

"So . . . we made over the dining room to become my studio. It's nicer, because it's right by the front door. If I do have clients come in to have consults on invitations, it's right there; they don't have to go all the way through my house. It doesn't have doors, but I do have a dedicated space, which is really nice."

So what does her business look like several years later? "We make notepads, note cards, all kinds of stationary items. My four consultants do the home shows. They have sample books and display boards. They take orders, and we fill them. That has been all-encompassing recently. We did $50,000 in sales. Out of my home! I still clean, which is insane. In the fourth quarter, I said, 'Why am I doing this?' but the catalyst is that my son goes to a private school and it's very expensive. While my business is very good, it's not steady cash flow. I can't count on it as it's cyclical. We're really busy with Valentine's Day. We did $3,000 of business in January. In February, it could die off a little bit. In June, it gets really quiet. The cleaning is year round. The stationary business can be as high as fifty hours a week and as low as fifteen hours."

JESSE, NURSE TO JAZZERCISE TO INVENTORY CONTROL

Initially, Jesse was a full-time nurse. But once she began working in hospitals, she saw greater career opportunities for herself by moving from nursing into medical sales in hospital information systems. Even though she rose to the position of vice president of Sales, she decided that she would not return to the job after the birth of her child. She then stayed home for a few years tending to her daughter. And she got restless. Being an at-home mom wasn't enough; she felt something was lacking. So she went looking for part-time employment.

By answering an ad for a pharmaceutical sales position in the *New York Times*, Jesse began her pursuit of part-time employment. "In pharmaceutical sales, I was bringing a new drug to market. It wasn't as interesting as I thought it would be. After having done high-level, mul-timillion-dollar negotiations for sales contracts and getting someone to sign on the line, this was just not as interesting. Pharmaceutical sales was very different. It's as if I was a talking advertisement for the doctors. I had to convince them to write a prescription. But if they don't have a patient who needs the script, then they can't write it. Even if they do write the script, the point of sale is at the drugstore when the patient turns in the prescription. You're really not part of that sales process, so it just wasn't that interesting to me. The job was a one-year assignment from the start, so I knew that it was a short-lived project.

"Then I did Jazzercise. It was great," says Jesse. Finding the job was easy, since one of her friends was the owner. "I love to exercise; it's the first part of my day. It was a way to incorporate something that I love into my day. I started off as a student and became interested in becoming an instructor. I substituted for my friend who was running the classes at the time. When she moved to Japan, I bought the franchise from her. The problem with the Jazzercise was that I couldn't do any other type of exercise. My days with Jazzercise kept me busy either teaching it or preparing for class. I like to be outdoors, and Jazzercise kept me indoors.

"If my kids got sick, I couldn't cancel class because I had twenty women waiting for me. I had to take my sick kids in sleeping bags at the side of the class for an hour and then go to the doctor's office from there. You can't find a substitute at the last minute, so it evolved into something where after five to six years I was ready to move on."

Jesse adds, "So I obtained a sales position at a local publishing company." She had a friend there who was in human resources. Her friend told her about the position, and she went, interviewed, and landed the job. "I sold to professors. I was cultivating professors to buy textbooks to put on their curriculums. Textbooks are expensive. I was brought in to expand the high school sales base. I sold textbooks for advanced placement high school classes. This was all telemarketing work as you need to get hold of the professors and talk to them; you don't need to see them in their offices. I made all the calls from the local office in town, so no travel was involved.

"In all these jobs, I worked it so I had August off. The sales manager who hired me left a year later. The new person didn't know about my August deal. He came in, and he wanted to know why I got August off. This wasn't how he wanted to run his department, so I moved into customer service where I could continue working part-time. I did filing and special projects. Eventually, the publisher wanted the hours to be from 10:00 a.m. to 4:00 p.m. so that they could run specific reports at the end of the day. I didn't want to work those hours because my kids got home at 3:00 p.m. and they were my primary focus. They changed my hours, so I left and answered an ad in the local town paper for a part-time job.

"I was hired at a company that sells regional gift items and sports collectibles. I was as an assistant buyer, processing purchase orders, sending faxes, confirming purchase orders, and running reports. I did anything that the buyers needed to have done. I helped out with the plans for the next year because in retailing you have to buy things far in advance. Then the same thing that happened at the publisher happened here. There was a changing of the guard, and a new director of buying was put in place. This new director didn't like part-time workers. It took about a year, but she replaced me with a full-time person.

"When I returned from my August vacation, she said that there wasn't enough work for me anymore and she'd put me 'on call' for part-time work. She was changing the model for the buyers. I called the CFO right away and asked if he needed support in the warehouse. He said, 'Absolutely.' So I started on the Friday after Labor Day instead of the Thursday, missing only one day of work, even with the change in job assignments.

"In the warehouse, I counted every piece of clothing for inventory purposes. This is not glamorous stuff; it's task-oriented. Right now, I'm working for the hours and the commute. I want to be close to home, and I want to do what I want to do. So I don't get to do the glamorous stuff. I work really hard when I'm there and don't have to think about work when I leave. Not everyone could do this. I don't care what I do; it's the hours and location that matter to me. I've had the career. I have nothing to prove to anyone. I can call and say that I need to come in between noon and 4:00 p.m. today instead of my usual 10:00 a.m. to 2:00 p.m. with no problem. I've got good flexibility. It's interesting to see that in my last two jobs, I was hired by one person and that model changed, causing me to adapt myself from one department to the next, twice.

"There are two different things to address as far as satisfaction goes. In my full-time work, I was intellectually simulated with a high-powered job. But I also got all the stress that went along with it. With my part-time work, I get a location minutes from my home, the hours that I want, and flexibility with those hours. I'm satisfied because I can get those things along with every August off to be with my kids. You can't have it all. The trade-off is that I'm willing to do anything. I don't care if it's not glamorous."

Jesse continues, "It's a privilege for me to work part-time versus full-time. I don't look at that lightly. I'm thankful for the income from my husband so that I can work part-time. I am sandwiched between taking care of my mother as well as doing stay-at-home mom chores. I'm the only local child and have to fill the needs for my mom who has dementia. It's a quality of life that I'm able to afford. I can give back to the community as a volunteer, too. I have it all: exercise, extending time to my mom, giving to the community, marriage, time for the children, and a job. It works for me."

GO FOR IT!

As women marry and have children, there are times their careers may shift to the background or move out of the picture altogether. Mothers need flexibility and time for their families. And that's okay. As their children grow, their professional lives can come back into focus. Part-time employment helps mothers to bridge the gap between the worlds of "mom" and "career woman."

Women love part-time employment because it either prevents them from stalling out professionally or aids them in redirecting and redefining themselves while also remaining involved with their children. Part-timers possess a sense of self-fulfillment by participating in the career of their choice, enjoying control over their daily lives, being intellectually stimulated, and successfully filling the role of mom.

"I think every person has to find their balance," says Ellen. "It changes through life. Finding good part-time work can be difficult. If you want it, be persistent and do what it takes to make it work for you. I make less money overall, but at the latest law school reunion I was one of the happiest people there, and I saw governors, justices, those from the San Francisco DA."

Let's face it, life isn't linear. Mothers are willing and able to adapt their time and careers to fit their needs for specific timeframes in their lives. When those needs change, women evolve, moving to the next phase. There is no set path, no right or wrong way to go. Each woman must follow her own objectives, her own goals. And those change over time as children are born and grow. Because part-timers earn income, hold a professional identity, and still have enough time to be at home with their children, they are happy and extremely satisfied. As I said earlier in the book, *two-thirds* of the women interviewed "love it" or claim it is *better* than full-time employment. What endorsement could be better?

ACKNOWLEDGMENTS

Writing *The Best of Both Worlds* was fun for me not only because I enjoyed the exploration of the topic but, more importantly, because of the interesting and engaging conversations that I was privileged to hold with women across the country. If it were not for these women telling me their thoughts, feelings, and stories, there would be no book, no story to tell. My sincerest thanks and deepest appreciation goes out to the over 100 mothers and numerous employers who were interviewed.

I also wish to thank my two sisters, Kathy Engelmann and Margo Searson. Kathy helped me in recruiting interviewees on the West Coast, and Margo helped with interviews in the South. Without those interviews, the geographic dispersion of the book would have been incomplete.

I'd also like to thank my daughter Ashley for helping me develop the social media section of the book, also Kelsey, my other daughter, for her support.

And finally, my thanks go to my loving husband and good friend, Kurt, for inspiring me on the topic. He asked numerous questions about the thoughts and feelings of part-time working women after reading my first book, leading me to this one.

Appendix

RESEARCH DETAILS FOR
THE BEST OF BOTH WORLDS

I developed a questionnaire to answer not only why women pursue part-time work, but also how they do it and how successful/happy they are. To ensure that I was obtaining candid answers, I conducted each interview individually with the promise of anonymity for those who wanted it.

Initially, I started interviewing a few women whom I knew personally in various parts of the country and then asked them if they could give me the names of two or three other mothers whom I could call. By using this process, I was referred to relatives and friends across the country. Other than ensuring that I was obtaining a geographic dispersion, I randomly selected the referrals to call. By using this methodology, I talked to women with a wide diversity of professions and backgrounds.

I called each woman to ask if she would like to be interviewed for a book that I was writing on part-time employment. Upon receiving a yes, I set up a thirty-minute appointment at a time convenient for her. Despite the appointment being set up for only thirty minutes, the majority of interviewees talked forty-five minutes to an hour. Most of the interviews were conducted via the telephone. I started the interview process by obtaining the demographic information, including items such as name, address, highest level of education, household makeup, full-time work experience, part-time work experience, etc. I assured each interviewee that her demographic information would be kept confidential and that I was using it for sorting purposes only. Then I launched into the questionnaire detailed below.

QUESTIONNAIRE

"While I am taking notes on this, I am also tape recording it to ensure that I capture all of your information. Is that all right with you?

"I am writing a book regarding part-time work. My definition of a part-time position is working under forty hours per week for money or benefits. The goal of the book is to use experiences much like your own, good or bad, to aid others in obtaining part-time work. I will be asking the same questions to over a hundred women across the US. I would like for you to be totally honest and spontaneous with your answers. All of your answers will be anonymous unless you would like to be quoted. I will ask that at the end of the interview. Ready?"

THINKING ABOUT YOUR DECISION TO WORK PART-TIME:

1. What was the single-biggest factor causing you to pursue part-time work?
2. What was the second-biggest factor?
3. How long did you think about part-time employment before you started pursuing it?
   What were you doing during that time?
4. How did you feel when you made the decision to go part-time?
5. How did you feel once you started doing the part-time work?

THINKING ABOUT THE WORK ITSELF:

6. What exactly do you do part-time?
7. How satisfied are you with your part-time work? Compare that with when you were employed full-time.

NOW LET'S THINK ABOUT HOW YOU OBTAINED YOUR EMPLOYMENT:

8. How did you obtain your part-time employment?
9. What resources did you use to obtain part-time work?
10. Did you follow a path of other part-timers or a role model?
11. Did your previous full-time experience help you to obtain employment? If so, how?
12. What did you do about daycare?

LOOKING TO THE FUTURE:

13. Where do you see yourself in the future regarding employment?
14. What do you like best/least about your employment?
15. Is there anything that you would like to add that you feel we haven't covered?

    Any watch-outs? Any words of wisdom?
16. Do you wish for your answers to be anonymous or can I use your first name associated with your answers?

    Anonymous _____

    Name associated with answers _____
17. Do you have any friends whom you could recommend that I call? Who? And what are their phone numbers? Can I use your name?

    Thank you for your time.

NOTES

PREFACE

1. Roxanne A. Donovan, Andrew L. Pieper, and Allison N. Ponce, "Walking the Maternal Tightrope: Work and Family in America," *New England Journal of Public Policy: Special Issue: Women* (University of Massachusetts Boston, John W. McCormack Graduate School of Policy Studies, Spring 2007), p. 197.

2. Beth Brykman, *The Wall Between Women: The Conflict Between Stay-at-Home and Employed Mothers* (Amherst, NY: Prometheus Books, 2006), p. 104.

INTRODUCTION: WHY NOW?

1. Patricia Aburdene and John Naisbitt, *Megatrends for Women* (New York: Villard Books, 1992), p.100.

2. "Our History," *Catalyst*, http://www.catalyst.org/who-we-are/our-history (accessed July 11, 2016).

3. "History," *Work Family Directions*, http://www.wfd.com/aboutus.html (accessed July 11, 2016).

4. Brad Harrington, "The Work-Life Evolution Study," Boston College Center for Work & Family (2007): 4.

5. Ibid., p. 5.

6. US Department of Labor, *Women in the Labor Force: A Databook*, September 2007, p. 8, http://www.bls.gov/opub/reports/womens-databook/archive/womenlaborforce_2007.pdf (accessed October 11, 2008).

7. "Current Employment Statistics," *Bureau of Labor Statistics*, http://www.bls.gov/web/empsit/ceseeb5a.htm (accessed April 25, 2014).

8. Sabrina Schaeffer, "Business Must Stop Coddling Women in the Workplace," *Forbes*, December 4, 2013, http://www.forbes.com/sites/sabrinaschaeffer/2013/12/04/business-must-stop-coddling-women-in-the-workplace/#6dddce65552f (accessed April 25, 2014).

9. Harrington, "Work-Life Evolution Study," pp. 2–12.

10. Ibid., p. 9.

11. Ibid., p. 7.

12. Penelope Trunk, *Brazen Careerist: The New Rules for Success* (New York: Warner Business Books, 2007), p. xii.

13. Deloitte, *The Initiative for the Retention and Advancement of Women* (2006 Annual Report), p. 35.

14. Joe Echevarria, "The True Economic Value of Women," *Fast Company*, May 11, 2012, http://www.fastcompany.com/1836989/true-economic-value -women (accessed April 25, 2014).

15. Ibid.

16. "Life at Deloitte," *Deloitte*, http://www2.deloitte.com/ui/en/pages/careers/ articles/inclusion-work-life-fit.html (accessed April 25, 2014).

17. Deloitte, *The Women's Initiative 2006 Annual Report*, http://www.deloitte .com/dtt/article/0,1002,sid=2261&cid=cid=151244,00.html (accessed September 20, 2007).

18. Deloitte, *Initiative for the Retention and Advancement of Women*, p. 35.

19. Leslie Kwoh, "McKinsey Tries to Recruit Mothers Who Left the Fold," *Wall Street Journal*, http://www.wsj.com/articles/SB10001424127887323764804578314450063914388 (accessed April 25, 2014).

20. "Employment Opportunities: 'Returnships,'" *Career Wisdom Institute*, http://www.careerwisdominstitute.com/2013/02/returnships (accessed July 11, 2016).

21. Maggie Jackson, "Part-Timers Find Room at Law Firm: High Turnover Is Leading Law Firms to Rethink Flexibility: High Turnover Helps Change Attitudes on Work-Life Flexibility," *Boston Globe*, November 5, 2006, p. G1.

22. Ibid.

23. Pat Broderick, "More Firms Starting to Offer Flexible Work Arrangements: Business Model Changing as Attorneys Demand Between Home and Office," *San Diego Business Journal*, August 6, 2007, p. 29.

24. Ibid.

25. Jacob Goldstein, "As Doctors Get a Life, Strains Show: Quest for Free Time Reshapes Medicine; A Team Approach," *Wall Street Journal*, April 29, 2008, p. A14.

26. Ibid.

27. Victoria Fraza Kickham, "Filling the Ranks," *Industrial Distribution*, September 1, 2007, p. 24.

28. Richard W. Judy and Carol D'Amico, *Workforce 2020: Work and Workers in the 21st Century* (Washington, DC: Hudson Institute, 1997): 133.

29. Karen Springen, "Cutting Back Your Hours," http://tentiltwo.com/wp -content/uploads/2011/11/Newsweek-May-12-2008-CT.pdf (accessed July 20, 2016).

30. Ibid.

31. *Flexible Work Arrangements III: A Ten-Year Retrospective of Part-Time Arrangements for Managers and Professionals* (New York: Catalyst, 2000), p. 4.

32. Lin Grensing-Pophal, "Committing to Part-Timers: A Credit Union's Special Focus on Part-Time Employees Offers a Case Study on How to Make Such Workers Productive Members of the Team," *HR Magazine* (April 2007): p. 84.

33. Ibid.

CHAPTER 1: WHY WORK PART-TIME?

1. Wendy Wang, "Mothers and Work: What's Ideal?" *PEW Research Center*, August 19, 2013, http://www.pewresearch.org/fact-tank/2013/08/19/mothers-and-work-whats-ideal/ (accessed July 20, 2016).

2. Sylvia Ann Hewlett, *Off-Ramps and On-Ramps: Keeping Talented Women on the Road to Success* (Boston: Harvard Business School Press, 2007), p. 36.

3. Jane Swigart, *The Myth of the Bad Mother: The Emotional Realities of Mothering* (New York: Doubleday, 1991), p. 100.

4. Michele Kremen Bolton, *The Third Shift: Managing Hard Choices in Our Careers, Homes, and Lives as Women* (San Francisco: Jossey-Bass, 2000), pp. 286–287.

5. Judith Warner, "The Full-Time Blues," *New York Times*, July 24, 2007, p. A23.

6. Hewlett, *Off-Ramps and On-Ramps*, p. 30.

CHAPTER 2: MAKING THE LEAP

1. Bradley G. Richardson, *Career Comeback: Eight Steps to Get Back on Your Feet When You're Fired, Laid Off, or Your Business Venture has Failed—and Finding More Job Satisfaction Than Ever Before* (New York: Broadway Books, 2004), p. 222.

2. "Part-Time Employee Benefits," *City of Boise Idaho*, http://hr.cityofboise

.org/benefits/part-time-benefits/ (accessed July 14, 2016); "City of Los Angeles Flex Benefits," https://per.lacity.org/bens/assets/flex---overview.pdf (accessed July 14, 2016).

3. William Baldwin, "Paying for College: Discounts for Academics," *Forbes*, February 28, 2013, http://www.forbes.com/sites/baldwin/2013/02/28/discounts-on-tuition-for-university-employees/#5c9f9fbc671c (accessed July 14, 2016).

4. Wendy Kaufman, "A Successful Job Search: It's All about Networking," *NPR*, February 3, 2011, http://www.npr.org/2011/02/08/133474431/a-successful-job-search-its-all-about-networking (accessed April 30, 2014).

5. Ibid.

6. Ibid.

7. Katharine Hansen, interview by Randall S. Hansen, "Quintessential Careers: Frequently Asked Questions (FAQs) about Career Networking," https://www.livecareer.com/quintessential/career-networking-faq (accessed on July 20, 2016).

8. Ibid.

9. Joann S. Lublin, "One Household, Two Pink Slips," *Wall Street Journal*, May 12, 2009, p. D1.

10. Peter Morgan Kash, *Make Your Own Luck: Success Tactics You Won't Learn in B-School* (Paramus, NJ: Prentice Hall, 2002), p. 86.

CHAPTER 3: SCALING BACK: MOVING FROM FULL-TIME TO PART-TIME

1. Barbara B. Reinhold, *Free to Succeed: Designing the Life You Want in the New Free Agent Economy* (New York: Penguin Group, 2001), p. 23.

2. Karen Springen, "Cutting Back Your Hours," http://tentiltwo.com/wp-content/uploads/2011/11/Newsweek-May-12-2008-CT.pdf (accessed July 20, 2016).

CHAPTER 4: NO NETWORKS? NO PROFESSIONAL CONTACTS? AM I HOPELESS?

1. Sue Shellenbarger, "How Stay-at-Home Moms Are Filling an Executive Niche," *Wall Street Journal*, April 30, 2008, p. D1.

2. Penelope Trunk, *Brazen Careerist: The New Rules for Success* (New York: Warner Business Books, 2007), p. 26.

3. Jeremy Caplan, "The Six-Figure-Job Hunt," *Time*, December 2, 2008, p. 64.

4. Richard W. Judy and Carol D'Amico, *Workforce 2020: Work and Workers in the 21st Century* (Washington, DC: Hudson Institute, 1997): p. 57.

5. Betty Friedan, *The Feminine Mystique* (New York: W. W. Norton, 1963), p. 323.

6. Judy and D'Amico, *Workforce 2020*, p. 5.

CHAPTER 5: STARTING YOUR OWN BUSINESS

1. *Flexible Work Arrangements III: A Ten-Year Retrospective of Part-Time Arrangements for Managers and Professionals* (New York: Catalyst, 2000), p. 4.

2. Ibid.

3. "Multi-Level Marketing," *Wikipedia*, http://en.wikipedia.org/wiki/Multi-level_marketing (accessed September 10, 2008).

4. Scott Allen, "Too Good to Be True?: 6 Questions to Check Out an MLM/ Network Marketing Opportunity," *About.com*, http://entrepreneurs.about.com/cs/multilevelmktg/a/toogoodtobetrue.htm (accessed June 13, 2008).

5. Scott Allen, "The Real Problem with Network Marketing and Multi-Level Marketing (MLM): HINT: It's Not the Business Model Itself," *About.com*, http://entrepreneurs.about.com/cs/multilevelmktg/a/problemwithmlm.htm?p=1 (accessed September 10, 2008).

6. Scott Allen, "Business Ideas on a Budget: 10 Legitimate Businesses You Can Start for Under $20," *About.com*, http://entrepreneurs.about.com/cs/businessideas/a/10startupideas.htm?p=1 (accessed June 13, 2008).

7. "Can the Sharing Economy Provide Good Jobs?" *Wall Street Journal*, May 11, 2015, p. R6.

8. Ibid.

9. Rachel Botsman, "Yes, Different Kinds of Workers Derive Different Benefits," *Wall Street Journal*, May 11, 2015, p. R6.

CHAPTER 7: WORKING FROM HOME: GOOD OR BAD IDEA?

1. Elizabeth Garone, "How to Make Working at Home Work for You," *Wall Street Journal*, April 29, 2008, p. D4.

CHAPTER 10: EVOLVING OVER TIME

1. Sylvia Ann Hewlett, *Off-Ramps and On-Ramps: Keeping Talented Women on the Road to Success* (Boston: Harvard Business School Press, 2007), p. 1.

2. Ibid., p. 2.

SELECTED BIBLIOGRAPHY

BOOKS

Aburdene, Patricia, and John Naisbitt. *Megatrends for Women*. New York: Villard Books, 1992.

Bolton, Michele Kremen. *The Third Shift: Managing Hard Choices in Our Careers, Homes, and Lives as Women*. San Francisco: Jossey-Bass, 2000.

Brykman, Beth. *The Wall Between Women: The Conflict Between Stay-at-Home and Employed Mothers*. Amherst, New York: Prometheus Books, 2006.

Burrus, Daniel, with Roger Gittines. *Technotrends: How to Use Technology to Go Beyond Your Competition*. New York: Harper Business, 1993.

Davis, Kenneth C. *Don't Know Much About History: Everything You Need to Know About American History But Never Learned*. New York: Perennial, 2003.

Dowd, Maureen. *Are Men Necessary?: When Sexes Collide*. New York: G. P. Putnam's Sons, 2005.

Ephron, Nora. *I Feel Bad about My Neck and Other Thoughts on Being a Woman*. New York: Alfred A. Knopf, 2006.

Foley, Jacqueline. *Flextime: A Working Mother's Guide to Balancing Career and Family*. New York: Marlowe, 2003.

Friedan, Betty. *The Feminine Mystique*. New York: W. W. Norton, 1963.

Hewlett, Sylvia Ann. *Off-Ramps and On-Ramps: Keeping Talented Women on the Road to Success*. Boston: Harvard Business School Press, 2007.

Johnson, Tory, and Robyn Freedman Spizman. *Take This Book to Work: How to Ask for (and Get) Money, Fulfillment, and Advancement*. New York: St. Martin's, 2006.

Judy, Richard W., and Carol D'Amico. *Workforce 2020: Work and Workers in the 21st Century*. Indianapolis, Indiana: Hudson Institute, 1997.

Kash, Peter Morgan, with Tom Monte. *Make Your Own Luck: Success Tactics You Won't Learn in B-School*. Paramus, New Jersey: Prentice Hall, 2002.

Kelley, Tom, with Jonathan Littman. *The Art of Innovation*. New York: Currency Books, 2001.

Lobenstine, Margaret. *The Renaissance Soul: Life Design for People with too Many Passions to Pick Just One*. New York: Broadway Books, 2006.

Reinhold, Barbara B. *Free to Succeed: Designing the Life You Want in the New Free Agent Economy*. New York: Penguin Group, 2001.

Richardson, Bradley. *Career Comeback: Eight Steps to Getting Back on Your Feet When You're Fired, Laid Off, or Your Business Venture Has Failed—and Finding More Job Satisfaction than Ever Before*. New York: Broadway Books, 2004.

Ringer, Robert J. *Looking Out for Number One*. New York: Funk & Wagnalls, 1977.

Shepard, Molly Dickinson, with Jane K. Stimmler. *Stop Whining & Start Winning: 8 Surefire Ways for Women to Thrive in Business*. New York: Penguin Group, 2005.

Swigart, Jane. *The Myth of the Bad Mother: The Emotional Realities of Mothering*. New York: Doubleday, 1991.

Trunk, Penelope. *Brazen Careerist: The New Rules for Success*. New York: Warner Business Books, 2007.

Warner, Judith. *Perfect Madness: Motherhood in the Age of Anxiety*. New York: Riverhead Books, 2005.

MAGAZINES

Broderick, Pat. "More Firms Starting to Offer Flexible Work Arrangements: Business Model Changing as Attorneys Demand Between Home and Office." *San Diego Business Journal* (August 6, 2007): 29.

Caplan, Jeremy. "The Six-Figure-Job Hunt." *Time* (December 22, 2008): 63.

Grensing-Pophal, Lin. "Committing to Part-Timers: A Credit Union's Special Focus on Part-Time Employees Offers a Case Study on

How to Make Such Workers Productive Members of the Team." *HR Magazine* (April 2007): 84.

Kickham, Victoria Fraza. "Filling the Ranks." *Industrial Distribution* (September 1, 2007): 24.

Perriello, Brad. "Boomer Bust." *Industrial Distribution* (September 1, 2007): 25.

Rochman, Bonnie. "Economoms. Many Who Opted Out of the Rat Race Are Scrambling to Get Back In." *Time* (March 23, 2009): 69.

NEWSPAPER ARTICLES

Badat, Jaclyne. "To Retain Valued Employees, Companies Pitch Flextime as Macho." *Wall Street Journal* (December 11, 2006): B1.

Blumenthal, Karen. "Take This Dream and Crunch It." *Wall Street Journal* (May 6, 2009): D1.

Botsman, Rachel. "Yes, Different Kinds of Workers Derive Different Benefits." *Wall Street Journal* (May 11, 2015): R6.

"Can the Sharing Economy Provide Good Jobs?" *Wall Street Journal* (May 11, 2015): R6.

Garone, Elizabeth. "How to Make Working at Home Work for You." *Wall Street Journal* (April 29, 2008): D4.

Goldstein, Jacob. "As Doctors Get a Life, Strains Show: Quest for Free Time Reshapes Medicine; A Team Approach." *Wall Street Journal* (April 29, 2008): A1, A14.

Jackson, Maggie. "Part-Timers Find Room at Law Firm: High Turnover Is Leading Law Firms to Rethink Flexibility: High Turnover Helps Change Attitudes on Work-Life Flexibility." *Boston Globe* (November 5, 2006): G1.

Lublin, Joann S. "Bulletproofing Your References in the Hunt for a New Job." *Wall Street Journal* (April 7, 2009): D1.

———. "One Household, Two Pink Slips." *Wall Street Journal* (May 12, 2009): D1.

Needleman, Sarah E. "Explaining Your Layoff to a Job Recruiter." *Wall Street Journal* (December 9, 2008): D4.

———. "Negotiating the Freelance Economy." *Wall Street Journal* (May 6, 2009): D4.

Shellenbarger, Sue. "Extreme Child-Care Maneuvers." *Wall Street Journal* (May 20, 2009): D1.

———. "How Stay-at-Home Moms Are Filing an Executive Niche." *Wall Street Journal* (April 30, 2008): D1.

Tam, Pui-Wing. "For the Jobless, Web Sites Offer More Options." *Wall Street Journal* (November 25, 2008): D1, D4.

Warner, Judith. "The Full-Time Blues." *New York Times* (July 24, 2007): A23.

STUDIES

Bond, James T., with Ellen Galinsky, David Protlas, and Cindy Thompson. *Highlights of the National Study of the Changing Workforce*. New York: Families and Work Institute, November 3, 2002.

Flexible Work Arrangements III: A Ten-Year Retrospective of Part-Time Arrangements for Managers and Professionals. New York: Catalyst, 2000.

Harrington, Brad. *The Work-Life Evolution Study*. Boston College Center for Work & Family, 2007.

WEBSITES

Allen, Scott. "Business Ideas on a Budget: 10 Legitimate Businesses You Can Start for Under $20." *About.com*. http://entrepreneurs.about.com/cs/businessideas/a/10startupideas.htm?p=1 (accessed June 13, 2008).

———. "The Real Problem with Network Marketing and Multi-Level Marketing (MLM): HINT: It's Not the Business Model Itself." *About.com*. http://entrepreneurs.about.com/cs/multilevelmktg/a/problemwithmlm.htm?p=1 (accessed September 10, 2008).

———. "Too Good to Be True?: 6 Questions to Check Out an MLM/

Network Marketing Opportunity." *About.com*. http://entrepreneurs. about.com/cs/multilevelmktg/a/toogoodtobetrue.htm (accessed June 13, 2008).

"Direct Selling." *Wikipedia*. http://en.wikipedia.org/wiki/Direct_selling (accessed September 10, 2008).

Echevarria, Joe. "The True Economic Value of Women." *Fast Company*. May 11, 2012. http://www.fastcompany.com/1836989/true-economic -value-women (accessed April 25, 2014).

Erbe, Bonnie. "Moms' Preference for Part-Time Work." *CBS News*. July 16, 2007. http://www.cbsnews.com/news/moms-preference-for-part -time-work/(accessed September 23, 2008).

Holbrook, Karen A. "Statistics Mask the Real Story of Women in Higher Education." *New York Times*. http://www.nytimes.com/ref/college/ faculty/coll_pres_holbrook.html (accessed October 15, 2008).

Kaufman, Wendy. "A Successful Job Search: It's All About Networking." *NPR*. February 2, 2011. http://www.npr.org/2011/02/08/133474431/a -successful-job-search-its-all-about-networking (accessed April 30, 2014).

Kwoh, Leslie. "McKinsey Tries to Recruit Mothers Who Left the Fold." *Wall Street Journal*. February 19, 2013. http://www.wsj.com/articles/SB1 00014241278873237648045783144500063914388 (accessed April 25, 2014).

"Multi-Level Marketing." *Wikipedia*. http://en.wikipedia.org/wiki/Multi-level_marketing(accessed September 10, 2008).

Schaeffer, Sabrina. "Business Must Stop Coddling Women in the Work-place." *Forbes*. December 4, 2013. http://www.forbes.com/sites/ sabrinaschaeffer/2013/12/04/business-must-stop-coddling-women-in -the-workplace/#5a94c7ea552f (accessed April 25, 2014).

Springen, Karen. "Cutting Back Your Hours." *Newsweek*. http://tentiltwo .com/wp-content/uploads/2011/11/Newsweek-May-12-2008-CT.pdf (ac-cessed July 20, 2016).

Turner, Joe. "Quintessential Careers: Fast Track Your Job Search by Networking Through a Professional Association." https://www.live career.com/quintessential/professional-association-networking (ac-cessed July 20, 2016).

Wang, Wendy. "Mothers and Work. What's Ideal?" *PEW Research Center.* August 19, 2013. http://www.pewresearch.org/fact-tank/2013/08/19/mothers-and-work-whats-ideal/ (accessed July 20, 2016).

"Women Entrepreneurs: Why Companies Lose Female Talent and What They Can Do About It." http://www.catalyst.org/knowledge/women -entrepreneurs-why-companies-lose-female-talent-and-what-they -can-do-about-it (accessed September, 19, 2007).

OTHER

Deloitte. *The Initiative for the Retention and Advancement of Women.* 2006 Annual Report.

Donovan, Roxanne A., Andrew L. Pieper, and Allison N. Ponce. "Walking the Maternal Tightrope: Work and Family in America." *New England Journal of Public Policy: Special Issue: Women* (University of Massachusetts Boston, John W. McCormack Graduate School of Policy Studies, Spring 2007): 197–206.

Minehan, Cathy E. "Do What You Love." *New England Journal of Public Policy: Special Issue: Women* (University of Massachusetts Boston, John W. McCormack Graduate School of Policy Studies, Spring 2007): 223–225.

INDEX